JOHN F. PYLE
Rt. 2, Box 730, Calaveras Road
San Jose, California

50

JOHN F. PYLE
Rt. 2, Box 730, Calaveras Road
San Jose, California

PLACES TO FLY

A collection of travel articles from The AOPA PILOT, selected with a view toward informing general aviation flyers about spots that offer the best in fly-in facilities, accommodations and enjoyable vacations.

PUBLISHED BY THE
Aircraft Owners & Pilots Association

Second Printing November 1965
Aircraft Owners and Pilots Association
Washington, D.C. 20014

©Aircraft Owners and Pilots Association 1965
All rights reserved

"Places to Fly" was prepared for publication by the Art and Editorial Departments of The AOPA PILOT. Design by Hyman Speigel, Art Director; Jane Mahon, Editorial Supervisor.

PREFACE

One of the most frequent requests received by The AOPA PILOT is for reprints and tearsheets of articles previously published about places to fly for pleasure. Much like today's automobile, the average general aviation airplane is used for all-around transportation purposes —for business, weekend recreation, one-day flights for special occasions, vacations, etc. The only difference is that the aircraft owner and pilot can go farther in a short time without battling surface traffic every mile of the way. This increased mobility gives the user of a personal airplane greater opportunity to see more of the United States and plan trips abroad. For this reason he is constantly searching for interesting places to fly.

Travel features have been a part of The PILOT since its first issue. This volume contains some of the more interesting ones published in the magazine. It is by no means a collection of all such articles published in the magazine nor is it a flyer's guide to the United States. Keep this in mind and we believe you will enjoy the travel potpourri contained in this book.

A word of caution: An effort has been made to update the articles where important aeronautical information is involved, but the articles have not been rewritten. If you plan a flight to one of the places mentioned in "Places To Fly" it would be wise to check it out first. Either write the appropriate establishments or individuals mentioned in the articles, or check other sources, such as charts, airport directories, etc. AOPA's Flight and Travel Department will be glad to assist members in obtaining late information if it is needed.

The editors of The PILOT hope that "Places To Fly" will inspire you to get more pleasure from your plane and assist you in finding a place to fly.

CONTENTS

Photos on front cover by: Thurston Hatcher
      for the Jekyll Island Authority, Tom
      Root, and Robert Wenkam.
Photos on back cover by: Don Downie,
      Robert Wenkam, and Shell Oil Company.
Photo on page 7 by: Don Downie.
Photo on page 23 by: Dorado Beach Hotel.
Photo on page 51 by: Don Downie.

Flying a lightplane to Alaska from "the lower 48" puts a pilot over the longest flight strip in the world, the 1,523-mile Alcan highway. Navigating this trip is the easiest chore in the world, provided you don't follow the wrong road in a couple of spots.

We made this trip in the unsophisticated, efficient Piper *Tri-Pacer*, with just four days' notice. We flew over much rougher country between Las Vegas, Nev., and Salt Lake City, Utah (where the temperature was 110°F), than we did anywhere along the Alcan Highway. We came closer to getting lost between Idaho Falls and Butte, Mont., than we did anywhere in Canada or Alaska (we started to turn up the wrong canyon). There's nothing about an Alaskan trip that should cause any trouble for a proficient private pilot—*except* the weather, and this qualification applies to all flying everywhere.

The summer "tourist" season in Alaska is considered to be from June 1 to Sept. 1. June is normally the best flying month, but some of the dirt strips are marginal at this time because of the spring thaw.

It was late on a Friday afternoon in mid-July when N3665Z shook the dust of Lock Haven's Piper factory airport from her wheels. One week later, including a detour to Los Angeles to pick up the remainder of the family, the *Tri-Pacer* was in Fairbanks, Alaska, only 130 miles south of the Arctic Circle. The following day, N3665Z was delivered to Anchorage.

This same trip, without the California detour, was made in January a year ago by Charles M. Hallock (AOPA 86662), one of the two partners of Safeway Airways. He spent 22 days on the road because of weather—two weeks of this time at picturesque, lonesome Watson Lake in the Yukon. So it's basically a summertime trip.

The flight to Alaska is an ideal first-time-out-of-the-country trip for newer pilots. The "paper work" crossing the border into Canada and back into the United States is simple. There are no language or money exchange problems, no inoculations, no "payola" to border inspectors. Food, water and rest rooms are just as good as anywhere in the United States, though food is somewhat more expensive in the back country. Lodgings are clean and usually plentiful.

About the only thing that could cause a visiting pilot a headache on this trip is weather. It's quite a distance between reporting stations. For instance, the 190-mile airway hop between Fort St. John and Fort Nelson has a reporting point midway at Beatton River. However, the distance via the highway is 252 miles and you're as much as 47 miles away from the airway. On the next hop, the 154-mile airline leg to Smith river, you will total 235 miles along the highway. Thus, the pilot report of good weather from a multi-engine plane along the airway does not necessarily assure that you can make it up the highway—as we found out!

But enough of the preliminaries. Why not come along on one family's summer trip to Alaska? Next summer this same route might well be yours.

Our last stop in the "lower 48" was Cutbank, Mont., where we made an unnecessary landing to check out with U. S. Customs. This is not required and the approved procedure is to merely request that Canadian Customs be notified on your first landing in Canada at any one of the designated airports

When you fly to Alaska you pass over some of North America's most rugged terrain, but it shouldn't bother you if you watch out for the weather

The author followed canyons to the Watson Lake (Yukon Territory) Airport. He considers this airport—with its two hard-surfaced, 5,500-foot runways and log-fort style of architecture—one of the most picturesque he has ever seen

PHOTOS BY DON DOWNIE

By RUTH & DON DOWNIE

*Pilot of Tri-Pacer, who followed 1,523-mile highway on
flight north, recommends that you include air
trip to 49th State in your 'hot-stove league' planning*

FLYING THE ALCAN
ROAD TO ALASKA

of entry.

This Cutbank landing, however, gave us a chance to check out the procedures required when returning to the United States. The two operators of the Cutbank Flying Service, Bob Lehof and Ray Wilson (AOPA 93862), are designated Customs inspectors. There is no charge for clearing Customs from 7 a.m. to 5 p.m., daily except Sunday and the following holidays: New Year's, Washington's Birthday, Memorial Day, 4th of July, Labor Day, Veterans Day, Thanksgiving and Christmas. Overtime rates are figured according to the pay scale and seniority of the regular full-time Customs men. Lehof and Wilson advised that rates may be slightly higher in larger towns where men with longer service might be stationed.

After topping our tanks at Cutbank, we filed a flight plan for the short 74-mile hop to Lethbridge, Alberta. Lehof cautioned that it was advisable to keep a stamped carbon copy of the outgoing flight plan and on incoming border flights. Thus, if transmission is garbled or a line is out of service, the pilot has proof that he filed a flight plan.

The spacious Lethbridge Kenyon Field is typical of the World War II airports throughout Canada and Alaska. Taxiway borders are trimmed with white paint, hangars are spacious and the government-aided flying club was very active.

When you call the tower in Canada, you're "cleared into the circuit," not the pattern. When you check weather, you talk to the "climatologist."

After a very brief wait, the Canadian Customs man appeared, took a quick look at the registration papers on N3665Z and filled out a simple one-page flight permit for the number of days we expected to be in Canada. Almost apologetically, he said that he would have to charge $1.32 for mileage since his regular office was in town.

"If you had gone on to Calgary, there would have been no charge," he said, "be-

cause the Customs office is right on the airport."

We were the first visitors from the United States to land in Lethbridge in four days.

An overtime charge is made by Canadian Customs for private aircraft—the fee is $3.50 per hour or portion thereof with a $7 minimum.

From Lethbridge, we decided to visit the Canadian Pacific railroad's famed resort at Banff. The maps showed a 3,100 by 200-foot turf strip located deep in the canyon of the Cascade River. The air traffic control man of the Department of Transport took our flight plan over the phone and advised us that we could close with Edmonton radio on a toll-free phone located at the Banff Airport.

We took off into a brisk wind—18 knots with gusts to 25—and headed northwest along the railroad tracks. Dense smoke from nearby forest fires cut visibility to a minimum and part of the trip was almost like flying IFR. Under these smoky conditions, the full gyro panel of the *Tri-Pacer* was a distinct help and the AutoFlite autopilot took all the strain out of flying.

When we were close enough to Calgary to pick up their newly commissioned omni station, we found that their winds had increased to 35 knots with higher gusts. Since the airport at Banff showed up on the map as being deep in a canyon, we discussed the problem only briefly before notifying Calgary radio that we were diverting and would land there.

Each town in Canada and Alaska has its own myriad points of interest. However, because of space limitations, we'll restrict this narrative to the airport-by-airport story. Thus, we departed from Calgary late the next morning, facing a much more moderate breeze for the hop under broken clouds to Edmonton. On-airway VFR flights in Canada are at the even thousands of feet on the north and west headings toward Alaska and the odd thousands on return.

Only at Edmonton does the visitor begin

to feel that he's about to "leap off" away from civilization. Signs at the various refueling depots advertised survival kits and advised purchase of emergency rations there. One such kit, prepared by Northwest Industries, Ltd., weighs 17 pounds and sells for $27. In addition to sufficient food for two people for 10 days, the kit includes a compass, two 15-minute flares, fish line and a fishing net, a hunting knife, mosquito head nets, a first aid kit, water sterilizing tablets, a candle, signal mirror, matches and several other items of survival gear. Later in the trip, several Alaska-based pilots told us that they purchased at least one kit on each ferry flight of a new aircraft and sold the package later in Alaska.

We fueled at Taylor's Esso Service where 91/98 octane was 41.9 cents per imperial gallon plus one-cent airport license fee and a two-cent service charge. When we mentioned that our destination was Anchorage, they gave us a card published by Safeway Airways listing the tricky traffic patterns at Merrill Field in Anchorage, together with approach procedures and up-to-date radio frequencies. Even though our destination was still nearly 20 lonely flying hours distant, this casual bit of information made the trip seem much less adventuresome.

Once you leave the big beautiful airline terminal in Edmonton, you've left the last big town until Whitehorse on the Yukon river. There are a number of roads and railroads using Edmonton as a hub so some care must be taken in picking up the correct "iron compass." However, the highway, railroad and low frequency range leg all get together near the village of Gunn, 35 miles northwest of Edmonton and, from there on out, you drive the highway. You may as well turn off your omni receiver except for 122.2 communications and go back to the old days when there were no navigational aids except low frequency ranges. The next omni signals we heard were at Anchorage and Fairbanks, the only two omni stations in Alaska at that time.

For flight in this area, the Canadian Surveys and Mapping Branch (Department of Mines and Technical Surveys, Ottawa, Canada), has put out two strip maps, ARC 11 and 12, that seemed to us to be much easier to handle than the four WAC charts (184, 185, 139 and 116) covering the area. The Canadian strip maps (25 cents each) outline the few roads in bright red and do away with the cockpit confusion so common when just the corners of two or three maps are used for reference.

Our next fuel stop was Grand Prairie, a two-hour 25-minute hop. Here the Canadian Pacific Airways pump added 17 imperial gallons at 57 cents each. A written arrival notice as well as a new flight plan to the next stop are required on all the Alcan highway airports. It takes only a moment and is a double-check on the whereabouts of each aircraft.

We logged a final hour for the day with a hop to Fort St. John. En route we passed over the busy town of Dawson Creek, official start of the Alcan highway. All distances are measured along the highway northwest of Dawson Creek. It is here that the highway from Seattle via the Frazer river connects with the Alcan highway.

A very complete booklet titled "Alaskan Highway, Road to Yukon Adventure" may be obtained from the Canadian Government Travel Bureau, Ottawa, Canada, without charge. While this 24-page booklet is prepared for the automotive adventurer, the single-engine pilot will probably know this gravel highway almost as well as the motorist. If you're planning this trip, write for one of these booklets when you order your maps.

Our 12-year-old daughter saw her first real Canadian "Mountie" at Fort St. John. They patrol the highway, not by horse or dog sled as she had been led to believe by TV, but by modern automobile. This "Mountie" advised us that there was no law against landing on the highway in an emergency. However, to be completely legal, you're supposed to notify the Royal Canadian Mounted Police after you have landed.

Adequate overnight accommodations at the Blue Bell Motel were only $7 and the proprietor is considering free pickup and delivery to the airport for transient pilots. The field is four miles out of town.

Since thunderstorms build up during the middle of the summer days along the Alcan highway just as they do over Texas, we took off shortly before 6:30 a.m. for Fort Nelson. While driving out to the edge of the airport, we saw a Luscombe tied down with a pup tent slung beneath one wing strut.

No single-engine night flying is authorized in Canada for planes carrying revenue-paying passengers, but private flights are allowed. Summer days are longer than most pilots want to fly anyway. It was daylight long before 4:30 a.m. in Fort St. John—and it gets lighter earlier the farther north you go.

It was a lonesome hour and 40 minutes over solid forests—but with that ever-lovin' highway within easy gliding distance, it felt better. Dust from occasional fast-moving trucks makes the highway clearly visible for miles ahead in the clear early-morning air. The long dirt strip at Prophet River looks amply big from 5,000 feet. There's a wind sock and what appears to be a gas pump.

Far off to the left, stark snowcapped peaks begin to appear on the horizon, foretelling the Rocky Mountain range that comes up on the

Big, lighted, hard-surfaced airport at Fort Nelson still bears grim signs of its wartime use: burned-out hulls of World War II are visible within traffic pattern

next leg of the trip.

We landed on the big, lighted, hard-surfaced airport at Fort Nelson after circling the area. The burned-out hulls of several World War II transports are visible within the traffic pattern of the airport—grim reminders of the year-around military operations in this wilderness.

Cost of 91/98 octane gas was 68 cents per imperial gallon and our total bill was $9.84.

"You're lucky," said the gas man, "If you'd come up the highway, you'd have taken at least $15 in automobile gas at 57 cents per gallon and there's a good chance that you would have blown a tire."

We had taken time for only a quick cup of coffee before takeoff, so we checked about the possibility of breakfast at Fort Nelson. There is neither food nor lodging available on the field for transients. Cab fare to town is $3 each way, so we filled out a 2½ hour flight plan to Watson Lake and went on.

The country is flat and heavily wooded for the first 50 miles out of Fort Nelson until you cross the Muskwa river and then it goes straight up and down. The highest spot in the area, Churchill Peak, is actually only 10,500 feet high, but everywhere there are bare mountains studded with snow patches as far as the eye can see. It's really quite a sight —and that highway looks better all the time.

There is no need to go above 8,000 feet on this leg of the trip because the highway follows down a series of river valleys. However, the canyons are deep and this portion of the trip should definitely not be flown when heavy winds are reported in the area; not if the

pilot has any respect for his dentures. Normally an early morning departure would make this hop more comfortable.

This rocky pass area stretches for about 90 miles before you reach the Laird river valley and a broad emergency strip. You can contact Smith River radio at this point and report your position. Smith River is some 20 miles north of the highway along the airway. It's an easy run up the river valley from here to Watson Lake.

Each pilot who has traveled afar has his own list of the most picturesque airports he's ever seen. High on this list should go Watson Lake in the Yukon. The airport has two hard-surfaced runways, 5,500 feet long and lighted. Administration building architecture copies the old log forts. There is a huge hangar, a seaplane base off the east end of the airport and the most beautiful blue-green lake you've ever seen.

We landed, taxied in and closed our flight plan. By now it was definitely time to eat, but here again neither food nor lodging was available on the field. Cab fare to town was $4 each way, and we nearly took it. However, it was only another two hours and 20 minutes to Whitehorse where we planned to stop for the night, so we tossed a coin, ate a couple of candy mints and climbed back into the airplane.

Had we known ahead of time, it would have been a simple matter to order a box lunch from the all-night restaurant in Fort St. John. Until this route becomes more heavily traveled and hot-dog stands begin to mar the exquisite beauty of the wilderness, by all

Fort St. John's 6,700-foot airport was a welcome sight to the author after his flight from Grande Prairie, in Canada's Peace River area

means carry some sort of a lunch for each of your passengers along this portion of the flight.

Fuel at Watson Lake was understandably 75 cents per imperial gallon. After all, it's 628 road miles from Dawson Creek and the end of the railroad, and 287 road miles back from Whitehorse. Here, you're really a long way from the bright lights of a big town.

We checked with the climatologist, who foresaw no problems, filed for Whitehorse and took off. Locally the weather was scattered clouds at 4,000 feet and no reported weather en route. It's 176 road miles to Teslin radio, the next reporting point, so we headed up the road into the canyon of the Rancheria river. The weather deteriorated gradually and we dropped down closer to keep the highway in view. There was moderate rain by the time we passed over the 6,000-foot Pine Lake emergency strip.

As we crossed over into the Swift River valley, the tempo of the rain increased. Lowering clouds put us down closer to the waving treetops. To add to the enjoyment, the storm window on the left side of the cockpit chose this particular moment to pop open. We had neglected to close it tightly before takeoff. When we had been forced down to about legal minimums, we discussed the possibility of putting the *Tri-Pacer* down on the Alcan highway and waiting for the weather to blow by. This could have been accomplished without any problem. However, the weather didn't get any worse as we floated along in the driving rain so we continued to "drive" down the highway. Soon the rain turned to mist,

then to sunshine and the three of us took a deep breath as we tuned in Teslin radio for a position report.

Teslin advised us that the climatologist at Whitehorse had expressed some doubt about our being able to continue to Whitehorse under VFR conditions. Along the Northwest Staging Route of Canada, between Fort St. John, B. C., and Snag, Yukon Territory, VFR minimums are 2,000 feet and five miles. (Elsewhere in Canada, except in controlled airspace and certain areas of British Columbia west of the ridge of the Coast mountains and adjacent waters, minimums are 2,000 and one mile; they are 2,000 and two miles in the special B. C. areas.)

The Department of Transport will not authorize your flight plan unless ceiling and visibility minimums are met at your takeoff point and there is reasonable expectation that visibility and ceiling requirements will be met at your destination.

The weather ahead looked good—particularly after what we'd just come through, so we asked the Teslin controller for permission to proceed up Teslin Lake to Johnson's Crossing and take a look. The controller approved, we looked and then continued on through a few mild rain showers, a little turbulence and a 4,000-foot ceiling.

Soon we were over Marsh Lake, picked up the Yukon river and circled Whitehorse with its 7,200-foot paved runway and two shorter runways, 6,600 and 3,400 feet. Whitehorse—and lunch; well almost. Our watches said 2:15 p.m. when we landed, but we had been going westward all day and it was 12:15 p.m.

local time. From our brief experience, don't plan on fuel, transport or other service during the lunch hour. There was a cafe on the field —we found out later—but it was substantially after 1 p.m. local time before we were able to get a rental car, fuel the aircraft and go into town for food. However, it should be remembered that there are only a few transient aircraft now using this picturesque route (N3665Z was the only visiting plane in the big storage hangar). To keep a two-man fueling team on duty would not be economically justified at this time.

The next morning our call to the climatologist gave us time for a leisurely breakfast before a low deck of stratus clouds would burn out in the Pon Lake area. Overnight hangar fee was $1.35 and fuel was down to 58.1 cents per imperial gallon.

Before departing from Whitehorse, we telephoned across the airport to Canadian Customs. They merely asked if we had a single-page Canadian flight authorization or a more complicated form. When we advised that it was the simple, one-page form, they didn't even ask to look at the paper work, at us or at the plane.

"Just turn that paper in when you land at Northway," Customs advised.

In our flight plan to Northway, Alaska, we added the required, "Please advise Customs."

We took off under a broken overcast and headed west along the highway. True to the climatologist's forecast, the low clouds at Pon Lake and Haines Junction were breaking up by the time we arrived. FAA safety directors report that a number of experienced pilots, on flights south to the "lower 48," have made the wrong turn at Haines Junction and followed the 135-mile highway toward Skagway rather than the road to Whitehorse.

It's a more difficult mistake to make heading north, so we continued our tour over the Alcan route past Kloo and Kluane Lakes. The first of many glaciers in the area, the Kaskawulsh, was visible far off our left wing.

Canadian weather reports are made at 12 and 42 minutes after the hour so that station operators can maintain a listening watch on the 500 kc emergency frequency at 15 and 45 minutes after the hour.

It's a two-hour 45 minute hop by *Tri-Pacer* to Northway on the Alaskan side of the border. Cross-country pilots, particularly those with families aboard, should remember to carry a supply of ice cream cartons and lids on the ledge back of the rear seat or within easy reach. They're fine for *mal d'air* and will double for a nonexistent powder room in dire emergency.

First stop and airport of entry on the Alaskan side is the broad, paved airport at Northway. When you taxi up here, the young man that operates the gas pit also picks up the single sheet of paper that Canadian Customs gave you, and that's all there is to clearing the border.

For the past three years, Floyd Miller (AOPA 81061) and his family have operated the transient facilities at Northway. They have meals and fuel service available 24 hours a day. They can sleep 29 people in four single rooms and seven doubles. A new motel with six units and private baths is now under construction and should be completed early in 1961. We were the 60th transient aircraft to land at Northway in 23 days and over 400 planes cleared in and out of the airport in 1959.

The Millers also operate a general store for the 11 FAA families on the airport and the nearby village of Athabascan Indians.

Fuel sells here for 70 cents per U. S. gallon. We carried three fuel credit cards on this trip: Standard of California, Shell and Texaco. A review of our gas receipts showed that the Standard (Esso) card was used on all our stops except Fairbanks where the Texaco card covered. Shell service also was available on many of the airports and we didn't pay cash for gas or oil on the entire trip.

The pilot has a choice of two routes out of Northway. He can turn left at Tok Junction and follow the Glenn highway to Gulkana and the Matanuska valley into Anchorage—or he can continue northwest to Fairbanks. There are two mountain passes to cross on the Gulkana route and only one on the railroad route from Fairbanks back south to Anchorage.

Aerial view of the Northway (Alaska) Airport, where the author re-entered the United States. Clearing Customs and other U.S. services proved to be simple after preparation had been made at Whitehorse

Since both partners of Safeway Airways, Charlie Hallock (AOPA 86662) and Ed Swartz, were to be in Fairbanks this particular evening on their first annual Mukluk Caravan, we elected to meet them there. After the rugged country farther down the line, the trip to Fairbanks is almost anticlimactic just as long as the weather is good. It was, and we "drove" down the highway for another two hours and 20 minutes.

The airway from Northway to Big Delta is marked 270° magnetic on the charts, yet it angles up off the page at a 30° angle. That's because this area lies on the 30° easterly magnetic variation line. Your true heading will be some 30° greater than your magnetic (compass) heading. East Coast pilots should double-check that they *subtract* their

25° to 30° easterly variation. However, these compass gymnastics should never be a problem since the radio range legs are marked on the maps in magnetic headings—and who's going to get that far from the highway, anyhow?

As we started up the sprawling Delta river north of the Big Delta radio range station, little evidences of impending civilization began to appear. First it was a picturesque, isolated lake—just like thousands of others we had flown over—but this one had a lone boat in it, and a fisherman in the boat. Then there were two float planes parked along the banks of the Tanana river, long before the big Eielson AFB came into view.

At Northway Mrs. Miller had advised that we could keep out of the way of most of the traffic around Fairbanks by entering the area low over the river. We did. Almost as an afterthought, we turned on the omni and watched the needle zero in on Eielson radio. It wasn't really necessary because we had a highway and a river pointing directly toward our destination.

We circled town and landed on the gravel at Phillips Field where the Mukluk Caravan had stopped. This was the first time that N3665Z had been landed off pavement since it left the factory a week earlier. The big, hard-surfaced Fairbanks International Airport lies just outside the traffic patterns of Phillips for those whose planes are prone to propeller scuffing. However, Phillips has 1,500 feet paved at the west end of the airport; 1,500 feet is a complete airport in itself for most Alaskan pilots.

Fairbanks is the terminus of the Alcan highway, 1,523 miles from Dawson Creek. Some Alaskans consider Fairbanks a "frontier town" while Anchorage is "modern." It took us only slightly over 10 hours by *Tri-Pacer* to cover this highway distance because we were able to cut across so many of the curves in the road. A twin-engine plane going airways would fly an appreciably shorter distance.

The following morning we checked with Fairbanks weather to find out which of the succeeding days would be the best for the flight through Windy Pass to Anchorage. He advised "the sooner the better," so we cut short our stay in Fairbanks and "cranked up" N3665Z.

The following distance comparison might give some indication why almost everyone flies in Alaska. It's 445 miles by highway from Fairbanks to Anchorage.

It's 356 miles via the Alaskan railway, whose bright blue and yellow trains are sometimes called the "Moose goosers"; by airline, it's only 270 miles.

We took the most traveled air route via the railroad. After takeoff, you fly over the broad valley of the Tanana river and the radio range station at Nenana. Then it's almost due south to the Alaskan range. Towering Mt. McKinley was visible some 60 miles off our right wing.

Peaks of the Alaskan range were covered with clouds and Anchorage was giving a solid overcast at 6,000 feet with 15-mile visibility. However, we first had to go through Windy Pass.

Approaching this pint-sized slot in the towering mountain range reminded us vividly of the old Jean Arthur movie, recently rerun on television, titled "Only Angels Have Wings." The film spent nearly two hours showing the trials and tribulations of pilots battling a

hypothetical pass and its violent weather in old Ford tri-motors.

This was the same kind of a pass; not so high and not so treacherous, but rugged enough for a flat-land pilot. Actually, one can fly through Windy Pass, as we did under a cloud deck, and never get above 5,500 feet. The pass itself scales out on the map at only seven miles. You're able to talk with the FAA radio range station at Summit on VHF soon after you enter the pass.

So Windy Pass is recommended for VFR weather and light winds. Then it's merely another piece of spectacular Alaskan scenery.

There are a number of tiny railroad maintenance villages along this route. Some have the picturesque names of "Colorado," "Honolulu," "Hurricane" and "Gold Creek."

Once out of the mountains, the railroad passes over Talkeetna where the FAA has a broad 5,000-foot airport. When we passed over the field, there wasn't an airplane on it. However, just a mile away there is a 1,600-foot strip operated by famed Bush Pilot Don Sheldon where we counted 10 land planes and three float jobs tied up at the end of the strip in the Susitna river.

Then you "drive" the last 85 miles down the railroad and tune in Anchorage omni. Anchorage is a very busy place with four airports and four control towers within seven miles of each other: Elmendorf AFB, Anchorage International, Merrill Field and Lake Hood. Ten percent of all the float planes in the 50 United States are based at Lake Hood.

Since the ILS approach leg to Elmendorf AFB extends out over Cook Inlet, pilots approaching from the north are required to stay above 2,750 feet or below 500 feet within 10 miles of town because of jet traffic. We dropped down to 500 feet over Big Lake and closed out our flight plan with Anchorage radio. There were a number of float planes far beneath us.

When we were over the mud flats of Cook Inlet (there's a 36-foot tide) we called busy Merrill tower and were cleared to land on Runway 33. We came in south of town and saw a big 30 painted on the end of a runway. A little study convinced us that this was the busy International Airport and we headed farther downtown in search of Merrill Field —which has no painted runway numbers. After a tight circle in the crowded traffic pattern, we landed and taxied up to the Safeway Airways office. The ferry flight was completed.

We spent four rainy days in Anchorage before returning to Seattle on a plushy Northwest Airlines DC-7C aircoach.

So many books and pamphlets have been written about Alaskan flying and bush operations that it would be most presumptive for a casual visitor to give any helpful hints. However, FAA personnel repeatedly stress that flight plans are required. Families in the "lower 48" should be advised of a pilot's whereabouts by regular telephone or telegraph so that they will not harass the FAA to find a pilot and plane that are already safe. If off course and lost, pilots are urged to pick up the nearest river and fly downstream— since rivers eventually flow past habitation and airports.

A lightplane junket to Alaska can be a pleasureful, memorable trip. All it takes is a little good sense, good weather and a good look at the Alcan highway—the longest flight strip in the world. ◆

By GUNNAR BRUNE | AOPA 21661

FLYING VACATION
IN CANADA'S
MARITIMES

Last year the U. S. Soil Conservation Service in Fort Worth, Tex., told me they could get along very well without me for three weeks. So my wife, Lena, and I began preparing for a flight to the Canadian "Maritimes," which we had long wanted to visit.

The Maritimes are the extreme eastern provinces of Canada. This hayfever-free area includes eastern Quebec, New Brunswick, Nova Scotia, Prince Edward Island, Newfoundland (including Labrador), and many smaller islands. Also in this area lie the small islands of St. Pierre and Miquelon, the last remaining remnant of the once vast French empire in North America.

From AOPA we obtained the necessary Coast and Geodetic Survey World Aeronautical Charts (WAC's) for 25 cents each and Operational Navigation Charts (ONC's) for 50 cents each. The charts covering the Maritimes area are WAC's 311, 263, 262 and 261 and ONC's E-18 and E-19. These charts proved to be accurate in their portrayal of coast lines, but not so accurate in showing inland lakes, roads, towns, or airports. Nevertheless, they were indispensable when used along with the Canada Air Pilot and Radio Navigation Charts.

These last two items were obtained from the Surveys and Mapping Branch, Department of Mines and Technical Surveys, 615 Booth Street, Ottawa, Ontario. The Canada Air Pilot is a handbook containing instrument and visual approach charts and information on gasoline and services for all of the important airports. A year's subscription to the Air Pilot for Eastern Canada (there is one for East and one for West) was $7.50. This is a very helpful handbook even if you plan to do only VFR flying.

We bought an annual subscription to the one Low Altitude Radio Navigation Chart for the Maritimes, LE-9, for $1.50. This chart proved to be very useful in navigation. The omni compass roses are not shown on the WAC charts. Since compass variation is as much as 32 degrees in this area, serious mistakes in navigation can be made by using only the WAC charts.

AOPA furnished two Flight Reports, "Flying to Canada" and "U. S. Customs Facilities for Private Aircraft." Both of these were a great help. They list airports of entry and outline Customs and flight regulations for Canada and the U. S.

Since our *Bonanza* is the single-engine type and the trip would take us over wild areas and as much as 40 nautical miles (46 statute miles) of water, we decided to take some survival equipment along. We bought a two-man rubber raft and aluminum oars for $35, two kapok life vests for $3 each, and a survival

EDITOR'S NOTE: AOPA members in growing numbers are discovering Canada as a place to fly for an ideal vacation. High up on the list of attractions are the "Maritimes," although few lightplanes now visit some of the more remote areas. The Maritimes include the extreme eastern provinces of Canada — eastern Quebec, New Brunswick, Nova Scotia, Prince Edward Island, Newfoundland and their many smaller islands. In 1962 Gunnar and Lena Brune spent three weeks flying the Maritimes. In this article, Gunnar describes what they found in this intriguing part of North America, the preparations necessary for such a flight and details of the flight itself. It is an article you will want to read if you are thinking about making a flight to eastern Canada some day. According to the author, if you are not thinking about such a flight, you should. "You will have the time of your life in the Maritimes," he says.

Texas geologist and wife spend three weeks flying in eastern provinces in a Bonanza. Lightplanes get flying tourists to out-of-way places not easily accessible to more prosaic means of transportation

kit for $34.50. The survival kit included a first-aid pack, a dehydrated food pack, compass, knife, flares, flashlight, cooking equipment, fishing kit, signaling mirror, burning glass, and innumerable other items.

We took along a French phrase-book and dictionary. This proved to be a necessity not only on French St. Pierre but also on the French-speaking Gaspé peninsula and Magdalen Island.

We carried our birth certificates, but found that nothing but a driver's license was needed for identification, even on St. Pierre. Immunization certificates for smallpox also proved unnecessary.

So, the last of August, we finally got everything loaded into 97 Delta and pointed her northeast, leaving sunny, but hot, Texas behind us, and our adventure in the Maritimes began. We filed a VFR flight plan to Moncton, New Brunswick, being sure to include "advise customs." After landing, we found that although Moncton is an airport of entry, there is a $2 charge for the Customs officer to come out from town.

The Moncton Flying Club, a very friendly place on the other side of the field, sells gas. Here, as at every airport we visited, there were no tiedowns for transients. We "borrowed" the tiedowns of one of the flying club members who was away on a trip. We also discovered that in Canada, No. 40 oil is called "80" and No. 50 is called "100."

We rented a Valiant from Avis for $7.50 a day plus nine cents per mile. We also received a 20% discount for being AOPA members. We obtained similar rates throughout the Maritimes, but in some localities where there was no car rental agency, we had to make arrangements with a private individual. That evening, we drove out to Magnetic Hill near Moncton, an interesting spot where our car appeared to coast uphill because of an optical illusion. From a comfortable motel in town near the park we could watch the world famed, 40-foot "tidal bore." This is the home of the highest tides in the world. Twice a day the 40-foot tide surges up the Bay of Fundy and into the Petitcodiac River through Moncton. The bore is a three-foot-high wave at the head of the tidal advance.

We visited the bank here to exchange United States currency for Canadian money. Under the prevailing exchange rate, we were given 7¼ cent premium for each dollar exchanged, since U. S. money was worth more than Canadian at the time. We later found that in the United States the bank exchange rate was 10 cents. Hence, travelers will fare better by exchanging U. S. for Canadian money in the United States before entering Canada, and by exchanging Canadian for U. S. money before leaving Canada. Also, we always received a better rate of exchange at banks than at stores or restaurants.

Later we drove to Fundy National Park, about 50 miles southwest of Moncton. It was a very scenic drive past numerous covered bridges and intriguing rock formations at Hopewell Cape. At the park we stayed in one of the charming little Alpine chalets. We swam in the warmed salt-water pool and tried our hand at a fascinating game called "lawn bowling." Sea food in this area is excellent. We bypassed Halifax and went on to the fine airport at Sydney. Here and at Gander we were able to buy 100 octane gas for only 29 cents (U. S.) per U. S. gallon. (The imperial gallon used in Canada equals 1.20 U. S. gal-

lons.) Near Sydney on the Cabot Trail, at Baddeck, is the Alexander Graham Bell Museum. Flyers especially should be interested in Bell's early experiments with kites and aircraft which are preserved here. Baddeck was also the site of the first flight in Canada, by J. A. D. McCurdy in 1909.

Before filing for St. Pierre, we took the opportunity of checking over our survival equipment and making sure it was all there. From here on we would be over much water and barren uninhabited wastelands. We found flight plans to be very desirable although they are not usually required. Our flight plan to St. Pierre had to be sent by telegram because there is no aeronautical radio there. Twins can go direct from Sydney to St. Pierre. With only one engine, we found it is much safer to go by way of St. Paul Island and the southern coast of Newfoundland, although this route is about twice as long. We flew at 10,000 feet and kept in touch with St. Andrews Radio during much of the trip. Southern Newfoundland is mostly bare rock, with no trees and only an occasional fishing village. Being a geologist by trade, I could tell from the U-shaped valleys that glaciers had covered this coast in the not-too-distant past. The radio beacon simplified finding St. Pierre.

St. Pierre is a small island, just about four miles across. The other two islands in the group, Miquelon and Langlade, have only small fishing villages. The 3,200-foot gravel strip is on the south side of the island. Maritime Central DC-3's make a daily stop here.

We landed on Labor Day, but knew in advance that this was not a holiday on St. Pierre. The French island has its own holidays, however, especially Bastille Day, July 14. Flyers should not arrive on a holiday, as Customs and Immigration charges are likely to be very high. We were charged $6.50 for Customs and $1 apiece by the Immigration officer for a tourist card. General declaration forms, furnished by AOPA, were necessary in clearing into and out of St. Pierre.

Canada does not permit single-engine planes to depart from Gander en route to Europe. Hence St. Pierre has now become the major refueling and jumping-off point for these foolhardy souls. Gasoline prices have been raised to take advantage of this situation. We paid 67 cents per gallon here, the highest anywhere in the Maritimes.

George Dubet, the airport director, told us that the airport will be paved and will have two-way radio in 1963. He offered to send an airport map free to anyone requesting it.

Everything is very close together. We were able to walk easily to most points of interest. The town is quaint, with brightly colored houses. Narrow streets and blind corners necessitate a constant blowing of horns. A taxi trip around the island cost $5.

St. Pierre has not been advertised much in the U. S., because there is a shortage of accommodations. Still, the tourists increase each year. There is only one hotel, the Ile de France, worthy of the name, and it is not elaborate. It is American plan, with wine included in the meals. The Weather Bureau is next door to the hotel. This is primarily a night-life island, with much merriment and good times. The University of Toronto runs a summer school, with classes conducted in French, here from about July 15 to Aug. 30. This is the best time to visit the island. Nearly everyone speaks French.

Prices on many imported French articles

PHOTOS BY THE AUTHOR

—perfume, glassware, sweaters, and Scotch whiskey—are considerably below U. S. prices.

Shortly after leaving St. Pierre, we called the U. S. Naval Air Station at Argentia and asked them to file a flight plan to Torbay Airport, St. John's, for us, and advise Customs. There are many military bases in the Maritimes, both Canadian and U. S. Because they require 24 hours' advance notice for

ABOVE *The fishing village of Alma, New Brunswick, was on the Brune itinerary. Note the covered bridge at the left*

BELOW *St. Pierre was one of the picturesque islands visited by the author. Here, a St. Pierre fisherman is photographed repairing a net. The St. Pierre business district is in the background*

of Newfoundland. We visited the free Newfoundland Museum in St. John's. It contains very interesting information on Leif Ericson's landing in 1002, John Cabot's arrival in 1497, the now extinct Boethuck Indians who inhabited this area, and mementos of Alcock and Brown's first transatlantic flight in 1919. From Signal Hill, we got a beautiful view of the city.

Near Harbour Grace we found that a construction company paving highways nearby had only the week before reconditioned and put into use the Harbour Grace airstrip. This world-famed airstrip was used from 1927 to 1937 by such distinguished pioneers in aviation as Brock and Schlee, Schiller and Wood, Eddie Rickenbacker, Amelia Earhart, and Kingsford Smith. It was the takeoff point for many early transatlantic flights. Its reactivation, after lying idle and unusable for 25 years, is of vital interest to all who love flying.

When we were ready to leave Torbay, the ceiling was only 500 feet, so we filed IFR for the short flight to Gander. On this and other instrument flights we were amazed at the personal treatment and the ease of IFR flying in the Maritimes. The difference, of course, is that there is very little air traffic in the Maritimes as compared with the United States. After waiting many a time in the States for over an hour for an instrument clearance, it was really an experience to receive ours in five minutes, with exactly the route and altitude we had requested. As usual, we were cleared by ground control down the active runway *into position*. After a short flight on top, Gander radar took us in tow, brought us down, and put us on final approach. Although the Maritimes have many VOR's, there are no VOR instrument approaches. They are all range, ADF or ILS approaches. Gander tower, as always, told us to "check gear down and locked" before landing. With such individual attention, flying IFR or VFR is "no sweat" in the Maritimes.

The great air base at Gander was built in 1936-1940 with a view to establishing regular transatlantic flights. In 1959, the beautiful new terminal building, with its large and efficient weather office, was completed. A fine hotel and motel were opened in 1961. Transients formerly had to be housed in an old barracks building. Now that Gander finally has all of the modern conveniences, however, business is dropping off. Ninety percent of the jet airliners go direct from North America to Europe with no need for an intermediate stop. Most of the planes stopping here now are piston-engine planes of nonscheduled airlines such as Riddle and Capitol. A Cubana Airlines DC-3 stopped while we were there.

Except for the excellent Trans-Canada Highway, which passes through Gander, most of the roads in this area are gravel and in process of being improved. Newfoundland is as yet unspoiled. Very few tourists could be seen. Perhaps one reason is that the ferry round trip between Nova Scotia and Newfoundland, for a car and four persons, costs over $100.

Attractive sealskin slippers, bags, bracelets, earclips, lighters, and other articles were offered for sale here, and we bought several. We were urged to stay until Sept. 17, when the moose season opened, but regretfully had to push on. Moose, introduced to Newfoundland in 1904, have become the leading big-game animal.

Leaving Gander and flying across New-

landing, except in emergencies, we did not land at any of them. However, they proved useful at times for filing or closing flight plans. They could usually be contacted on either 126.2 or 121.5 mc.

All of the Maritimes, except Newfoundland, use Atlantic Time, which is one hour ahead of Eastern Time. Newfoundland has its own time, Newfoundland Time, which is 1½

hours ahead of Eastern.

At St. John's and Gander we were threatened with landing and parking fees. However, when we explained that ours was strictly a private tourist flight, fees were not assessed. St. John's, the oldest city in North America, has several excellent hotels and motels. We soon discovered that, to make a hit with the residents, we should accent the *last* syllable

Lawn bowling is one of the recreational activities the Brunes found in eastern Canada. The author snapped this shot of a lawn-bowling match at Fundy National Park, New Brunswick

The sign advises motorists to turn off engines and release brakes at a certain point. When this is done, the automobile appears to be coasting up Magnetic Hill

foundland, we were astounded at the number of lakes, large and small. Almost one-third of the province is water. It is no wonder that Newfoundland is unsurpassed for fishing, especially for salmon and square-tailed trout.

Our next destination was Magdalen Island. In crossing Newfoundland we stayed near the roads and civilization as much as possible, so as to have an emergency strip beneath us if necessary. Much of the province is very wild, with only lakes, forests and swamps. Buchans Radio advised us that the Buchans strip was abandoned and no longer usable. Deer Lake, with its 5,000-foot paved strip, is now the best airport for Corner Brook and western Newfoundland. We were also informed that a strip is being built in northern Newfoundland at St. Anthony, to replace the present seaplane base.

We homed in on the Grindstone radio beacon to Magdalen. House Harbour turned out to be a fine airport with two paved runways, 3,725 and 3,600 feet. Maritime Central Airlines, which operates the field, collected a 50-cent landing fee.

Magdalen Island, which belongs to Quebec, is really a chain of islands about 60 miles long, connected by sandbars and roads, mostly paved. It had three hotels but two recently burned. Consequently, accommodations are rather short and frequently the surplus has to be put up in private homes.

We went swimming and tried out our life raft. The water was not cold, even in September. Magdalen and Prince Edward Islands claim to have the warmest water north of Florida. It is probably caused by an arm of the Gulf Stream curving in toward these islands. One afternoon some commercial fishermen took us hook-and-line fishing for mackerel, using large fish scales for bait. We hauled in 10- and 15-pounders as fast as we could bait our hook. Incidentally, you can go out with commercial fishermen at nearly any seaport in the Maritimes. No license is necessary. We visited the very clean fish-processing plant. The leftovers are fed to mink.

This is a genuinely unspoiled group of islands. There was no tourist bureau until two years ago. The Customs officer with whom we became acquainted said we were only the second U. S. tourists to visit Magdalen that summer. Most visitors are businessmen from Montreal and Quebec.

However, the residents want tourists and talk about advertising and building motels. So there is no doubt that the tourist invasion is coming. But for another five years at least, Magdalen will remain a wonderful, restful place to get away from it all.

The Maritime Central agent in Gander had told us that we could buy gasoline from the airline on Magdalen, but there was no gas at House Harbour Airport. We decided we could make Charlottetown, Prince Edward Island, on our remaining gas. Since we knew that there were numerous fine beaches on the north shore of Prince Edward Island which could be used for an emergency landing if necessary, we elected to go ahead.

Prince Edward is highly developed for tourists, and we had no trouble finding excellent accommodations. We drove out to the beautiful beaches and golf course in the national park on the north shore. Paved roads are plentiful but they were so poorly marked that we got lost several times. It reminded us of the situation in the States back in the

Mrs. Brune checks survival gear before over-water flight to St. Pierre Island. The Brune Bonanza, in which they made the flight to Canada's Maritimes, is parked at the Sydney, Nova Scotia, Airport. Note control tower and Canadian Department of Transport building in the background

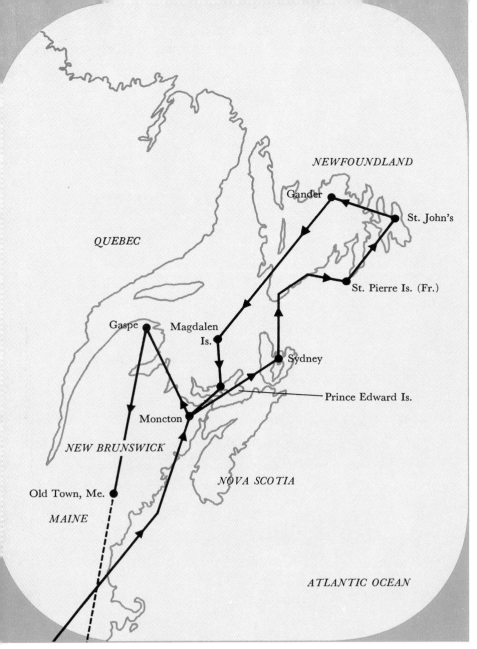

BRUNE'S ROUTE THROUGH THE MARITIMES

The author's plane lands at Gander, Newfoundland. Mrs. Brune is leaving the Bonanza. Gander's new terminal is very much in evidence in the background. Transatlantic jet traffic seldom stops at Gander, which used to be the takeoff point for most of the flights to Europe

20's. The island is largely agricultural, with bright red soils. Red pottery souvenirs made of this red clay attracted us. We also stopped to see the ancient Provincial Building in Charlottetown, where Canada was born in 1864.

The next day the weather was poor. We wanted to get started for the Gaspé Peninsula. Since there is no instrument approach at Gaspé, VFR weather was necessary. The following day, ceilings were high enough so that we could reach Gaspé by following the coastline. Tops of the mountains in the interior of the peninsula, over 4,000 feet high, were in the clouds.

The 4,000-foot sand strip at Haldimand Airport, Gaspé, is operated by Trans-Gaspesian Airlines, which uses DC-3's. There was a $1 landing fee, but TGA tied our plane down to some large pieces of steel at no charge.

Quebec is the only province in the Maritimes in which flyers can get a gasoline tax refund. We later obtained a refund of the 13-cent provincial tax. It was necessary, however, to submit the original invoices, showing the tax as a separate item.

The coast around Percé, south of Gaspé, is an area of breathtaking beauty. The sea is working furiously here to erode the mountains. The results are towering jagged cliffs and Percé Rock. This is a favorite spot for painters and many paintings are for sale. However, the painters are somewhat limited in points from which they can sketch the scene. By plane you can see "the rock" and the coastline from better angles than the painter ever dreamed of.

We had planned to return to the United States by way of Quebec City, but bad weather forced us to take a more easterly route. We entered the States at Old Town Airport, Maine. The Customs officer charged $3 for his trip out from Bangor, as this is not a regular airport of entry. We had visited Quebec before, and would certainly recommend that pilots include this beautiful city on their Maritimes itinerary.

This was a trip that we will long remember. The flying clubs and everyone we met did everything in their power to make our visit enjoyable. One thing was very conspicuous. That was the nearly complete absence of private planes except for the few belonging to flying clubs. This situation is bound to change, because the Maritimes are so ideally suited to a flying vacation.

In talking with many weathermen, especially at Gander, we formed a picture of the climate in this area. The winds are normally westerly and stronger at higher altitudes. However, in April and May, low pressure areas are likely to stall off the east coast over the Gulf Stream. This brings in moist, warm east winds. When these winds strike the cooler land, fog and poor flying weather result. June, July, and August generally offer the best flying weather. Fall and winter are fair to middling. Winter temperatures are not extreme because the Maritimes are surrounded by the relatively warm Gulf of St. Lawrence and Gulf Stream. Hotel and motel rates are much lower outside of the June through September season.

Warm clothes, including sweaters and jackets, are recommended even in the summer, as the nights can be cool. Properly prepared, you will have the time of your life in the Maritimes! ◆

Lightplane makes even a spur-of-the-moment weekend in Canada's famous park practical and rewarding

TO BANFF
-ON IMPULSE

Holiday in Banff National Park—weekend style! We wouldn't have thought it possible in our pre-airplane days when it was 800 miles by automobile or two days by rail from our home on the northwest tip of Washington State. By a fully-loaded *Tri-Pacer*, it was only six hours away and, with an early start and a late return, it was possible to make a two-day trip practical.

From Port Angeles, Wash., our route was airways across the Cascade mountains to Spokane for refueling, then north through Idaho and across the border to Cranbrook, Alberta, for customs, then via the highway through the Rockies to Banff. This route is reasonably safe and practical what with airways in the states and the excellent highways in Canada constantly below you. This route also does away with the necessity of topping any real high mountain ranges which could be encountered over other routes.

We sleepily departed from Port Angeles at 5 a.m., into a star-studded sky with weather reported CAVU all along the way. The sun rose in a blaze of glory right in our eyes while we passed massive Mt. Rainier in the Cascade range, and we spent the next half hour, until a jog in airways took the sun off our nose, silently reprimanding Mr. Piper for not installing sun visors on his *Tri-Pacers*. After landing at Felts Field in Spokane, we had a belated breakfast and inquired about border-crossing procedures at Cranbrook, Alberta, the Canadian airport of entry. We found to

our chagrin that on weekends there is no personnel on duty at Cranbrook to perform the ritual of formalities one is obligated to attend to when flying from one country to another. This arrangement seemed rather strange, naturally, since the weekend is the most logical time to expect the ordinary fellow to pack up and head north—including us. On top of this bit of disheartening news, we were also informed that every other Sunday there is a $50 customs charge if you enter the United States through Spokane, which we would be compelled to do the following day. [To avoid similar situations, it's best to check with AOPA's Flight Department for border-crossing information before the trip.—Ed.]

By an ingenious system of search and communications plus $5 long-distance phone calls, we nabbed our unhappy Customs officer at his home in Cranbrook preparing to depart for a weekend of fishing with his family. He reluctantly submitted to my pleading and agreed to clear us at the Cranbrook airport if we would take off immediately from Spokane and arrive in an hour and a half. Also, on the other count, we discovered that this was the "other" Sunday coming up and that Immigration would clear us through Spokane the next day—no charge.

With all the immediate problems seemingly overcome, we left Spokane, crossed into Idaho, then turned north roughly following highways over Pend Oreille Lake, Bonners Ferry and across the border to Cranbrook. We were

gradually working our way into the foothills of the Rockies as we approached Cranbrook, and some of the higher snow-covered peaks of the main range were visible to the northwest.

Cranbrook seemed to be primarily a lumber town and has a beautiful 5,000-foot paved runway with facilities maintained by Canadian Pacific Airlines. Our frustrated fisherman was anxiously awaiting our arrival and, after donning his uniform cap over his fishing attire to make it all look official, proceeded to establish a new record for clearing U.S. citizens into Canada. We sincerely hoped that the poor fellow caught some unusually large fish to partially compensate for the hour and a half he so unselfishly donated to the cause.

After departing Cranbrook, we passed over Kimberly radio and got the latest weather to the north while filing our flight plan for Banff. We were informed here that we should use caution while landing at Banff since a pilot report indicated that there was a large hole at one end of the runway. (It turned out that the hole had been patched, or at least we never did see it, and we gave Kimberly the word while passing over the following day.) Heading north from Cranbrook takes you up the beautiful Kootenay River Valley which skirts the western slopes of the main Rocky upthrust. Eighty miles north, the highway to Banff turns east directly into the mountains at Radium Hot Springs and then climbs through two 5,000-foot passes into Banff National Park. We had climbed to 8,000 feet as we

Banff grass strip is located in wide valley between towering peaks of Canadian Rockies. Despite 4,540 foot elevation, author Owens reports he had no trouble landing, even with fully loaded Tri-Pacer. He is shown here with his family

Lake Louise, northwest of Banff area, looks like a reflecting glass at base of high snow-capped Mt. Victoria

PHOTOS BY THE AUTHOR

entered the area of towering granite peaks and suddenly were completely surrounded by walls of ice, snow and rock. The fall colors of the turning aspen trees below (it was October) and higher alpine vegetation against the brilliant blue sky and always the ice and snow of the peaks above were a photographer's paradise, and our cameras were busy at all the windows.

After passing over the Continental Divide at Vermillion Pass we broke out into the beautiful, peaceful Bow River Valley between Banff and Lake Louise. Never trusting the weather, we decided to go out of our way and fly over Lake Louise before touching down at Banff, just in case the weather moved in during the night and deprived us of the opportunity of seeing it from the air. The view from the air presented an entirely different panorama from the usual postcard scenes of the lake and Mt. Victoria with which we were all so familiar. It is quite spectacular with the turquoise lake nestled below the glacier of towering Mt. Victoria. After a good look at the country from the air we turned back and headed down the valley for a landing at Banff.

The new Trans-Canada highway follows this valley and, since most of it appears to be four lanes, would make an excellent forced landing strip.

Banff is located between towering peaks in a narrow portion of the valley and the airport is located within walking distance (a long walk) of downtown on the main highway to Calgary. The Banff strip is 4,540 feet in elevation and 3,000 feet long, which presented no problem for the *Tri-Pacer*, even fully loaded. It is a beautiful strip, apparently well taken care of with the grass mowed short, and has good approaches from both ends. After circling over looking for our hole as reported, which we couldn't find, we settled down on the grass and stepped out into the fresh, invigorating mountain air. There appeared to be no tiedowns available but we didn't look hard or inquire. A *Comanche* was departing for Calgary and we utilized its ground transportation for a ride into town. They say there is a telephone adjacent to the field on the highway if transportation is desired into town. Also, we later found out that gas is available in town if desired. We were told in Spokane that it would be impossible to refuel here and we had planned accordingly. There is also gas available at Jasper, 150 miles north, if one would wish to continue north to see the entire park.

In Banff we rented a car with the idea in mind of driving the 40 miles to Lake Louise and spending the night. The larger hotels and many facilities are open only from May to Oct. 15 in the Banff area and from June 1 to Sept. 15 or 30 in outlying areas, but there are still adequate accommodations available either at Banff or Lake Louise throughout the year. One certainly obtains a completely different perspective driving through such country after having just flown over it. There are advantages to both, of course, and we especially enjoyed watching the antics of the elk herds which the first October snows had driven down where they could be seen from the highway. Also, the brilliant yellow aspen trees were much more spectacular close up along the roads. A full moon rose over the peaks that evening to make it a perfect day.

The next day, we leisurely drove back to Banff, stopping occasionally to observe the elk which were everywhere. The remainder of the morning was spent sightseeing around Banff and we departed shortly before noon for the flight back.

This was one of the most interesting short trips we had ever taken, and we recommend it to any flyer with an available weekend and nothing to do. ◆

By RICHARD OWENS, Jr. | *AOPA 46578*

19

If you have the yen to do some bush flying to a spot where the fish grow big and bite often, then follow our course to Reindeer Lake in northern Saskatchewan.

Well within the range of most lightplanes, the 200-mile lake lies deep in the Canadian bush, halfway to the Arctic Circle. Arctic Lodge, the lake's pioneer fishing camp, has its own 5,000-foot strip, located on a nearby island, which allows pilot-guests to fly all the way to the lake without having to transfer to float planes. Thanks also to the strip, when you depart you can take off with your maximum gross weight in trout filets.

All you'll need to bring with you are warm clothes and fishing tackle; the rest of your needs will be provided by the lodge, which can handle up to 80 guests in its individual cabins and main building. There are also accommodations for about 12 to 20 fishermen at the lodge's outpost camp, moved each year to assure unexcelled fishing and accessible only by chartered float plane or cabin boat.

Our trip was organized last year by Art Heck (AOPA 68833), operator of the Willard, O., airport. The other seats in his *Bonanza* were quickly filled by Charlie Wyandt, a farmer from nearby New Haven, O.; Harold Mack, supermarket owner from my home town of Plymouth; and myself. Although all of us had fished just over the border in Canada, none of us had ever penetrated the far north. This trip promised something new.

We wrote to Arctic Lodges, Ltd., 3402 University Ave., S.E., Minneapolis 14, Minn., asking for reservations at the camp starting July 1. At our request, they sent us the general information sheet on the lodge's airstrip, which contains complete instructions on the route from Winnipeg, radio frequencies, etc. WAC charts 218 (Lake Manitoba), 183 (Saskatchewan River), and 141 (Reindeer Lake) cover the route from Winnipeg.

Since the last omni station is about 100 miles out of Winnipeg, planes should be equipped with ADF to work the low frequency homing beacons north of Winnipeg. Pilots can follow a railroad all the way to Lynn Lake, and from there a tractor road runs all the way to the edge of Reindeer Lake, a point about 15 miles from the airstrip.

For communications with the low frequency stations, you should be able to transmit on 126.7 and 122.2 mc. Flight plans can be closed or filed with the Arctic Lodge radio, which operates on 1681 kc. The return flight involves penetrating a MIDIZ and this report can be made to Cranberry Portage radio on 122.2. Fuel is obtainable at The Pas, 250 miles from the airstrip, or at Lynn Lake, 50 miles away from the camp. The airstrip at Arctic Lodge carries limited gas for those who don't want to stop at Lynn Lake.

Our preflight planning included writing ahead to the Gasoline Tax Division, Revenue Building, Winnipeg 1, Manitoba, for application forms to buy tax-free gasoline while in their province. This saved us 11 cents per gallon.

We left the Willard at 1 p.m. on June 30. A front lay across Michigan but we were able to circumnavigate all buildups VFR. A "lake-watch" was filed with Muskegon radio for the Lake Michigan crossing and closed with Green Bay.

Our first stop was Clintonville, Wis., to pick up Harold Mack, who had driven out there a few days earlier with his family for a

Arctic Lodge's 5,000-foot airstrip, on a sand island four miles from the camp by boat. The mist in center of the strip is dust stirred up by plane's takeoff on exceptionally calm morning

ABOVE *Located right on Reindeer Lake, Arctic Lodge's main fishing camp accommodates 80 in its cabins and main lodge building. The lake is on about the 57th parallel, stays unfrozen only from mid-June to fall*

RIGHT *A cluster of fishing rods being unloaded from the Norseman, a vintage seaplane that carried the fishermen to the outpost camp*

By TOM ROOT | *AOPA 6929*

SASKATCHEWAN

If your favorite waters are usually crowded, there's a lake in the remote Canadian bush country where the fishing is well worth the half-day's flight from the border. Accessible only by plane, Reindeer Lake has a 5,000-foot strip and plenty of peace, quiet and trout

FISHING FLIGHT

vacation. Our next stop was Winnipeg, where we cleared Canadian customs and spent the night. We were now about 600 miles from the airstrip at Arctic Lodge; an early morning departure from Winnipeg would mean we could spend most of the afternoon fishing.

The next morning we followed airway "Amber 9" to the last omni range at Langruth. Then we switched to the ADF to Dauphin and The Pas, where we set down for gas and coffee. We had another 250 miles to Reindeer Lake. Since The Pas was to be our last refueling stop, the mains and aux tanks were nursed to capacity.

Weather north of The Pas (pronounced "the paw") has to be VFR for flying; fortunately, it usually is, as it was this morning, with a mild front in between. We took off with a spanking tailwind directly out of the south and settled down with a reduced power setting to follow the railroad 200 miles to Lynn Lake. We used gas from each tank so there would be no overflow.

From Lynn Lake, we followed the instructions we had been sent by Arctic Lodge. The tractor trail, now upgraded into a passable road, ran about 40 miles to a settlement on the edge of Reindeer Lake called Kinoosao. From this point, we followed a course of 240° for 15 miles to the Arctic Lodge airstrip, which is visible almost all the way from Kinoosao. Before landing we circled the camp, per their instructions, to announce our arrival.

It was 1:45 p.m. when we landed on the 5,000-foot compacted sand and clay runway. There were half a dozen other planes parked at the north end of the strip, where a lineboy directed us to a parking spot. We found out the lineboy was stationed at the field that particular day because several planes were expected. After the *Bonanza* was securely tied down, the engine compartment was sealed with tape and cardboard to protect it from blowing sand. Be sure to take along a tiedown kit and some tape for this purpose if you plan to make this trip.

The camp had sent two boats over to meet us and bring us the last four miles of our trip. On hand to meet us at the dock and show us to our cabin was Mrs. Fred Lockhart, whose husband runs Arctic Lodge. Things are keyed to relaxation at the lodge; there are no fixed hours to eat and the dining room is open all the time. There are hot showers, indoor plumbing, and a bar in the main lodge. Actually, we found more of the comforts of home there on the 57th parallel than we had been accustomed to on previous fishing trips in more southerly climes.

Two guides were assigned to us and we were out on the lake within an hour after landing. Unfortunately, our fishing got off to a slow start. The fish weren't hitting, a general condition most unusual for Reindeer Lake. Things weren't much improved the next day, although we did catch our shore lunch of lake trout and a few northerns. We were somewhat encouraged when another guest brought in a 22-pound trout that day.

To solve just such a problem, Fred Lockhart came up with the idea for his outpost camps, which are moved each year to new locations. He promised to get us to the northern outpost camp as soon as he could arrange it.

Reindeer Lake is extremely cold, even in the summer. The ice doesn't go out until mid-June, and the water temperature stays in the thirties all summer long until freezeup in the fall. Consequently, the air around the lake is always quite cool, especially if it has swept across the water for any distance.

Because the water is so cold, lake trout, great northerns, and the wily little Arctic graylings are caught at the surface.

On our second day there, we struck out a greater distance from the main camp with some success but still without finding any trophy fish. Under mounting pressure from the guests, Lockhart chartered a seaplane for the following day to start a mass movement of fishermen and supplies to and from the northern outpost camp. The boat that Arctic Lodge normally uses for this purpose was laid up with mechanical problems.

We left on the second flight the next day, nine of us, with our overnight gear, some supplies and our pilot. The first item that had been loaded on the seaplane, an old *Norseman*, was a 55-gallon drum of gasoline, which would take us the 70 miles to the outpost and back. An interesting feature of the *Norseman* is that the ailerons extend out along with the flaps, utilizing the entire trailing edge of each wing.

It took us 45 minutes to reach the outpost camp, located on an inlet near the northern end of the lake, almost on the 58th parallel. It was a collection of two-man tents surrounding a large tent-building which served as the mess hall and kitchen.

From the first cast, the fishing at the outpost camp was nothing short of fantastic. We tried almost every lure in our tackle boxes with success. We soon filled the boats with fish and lost count of the total number we caught. The sun was still high in the sky when it was time to return to the outpost for dinner.

After dinner we headed up a nearby river to a waterfall where the customers were great northerns and what must be the world's most voracious mosquitoes. Repellent and clouds of pipe smoke kept all but the most daring of the mosquitoes away while we caught and released a few dozen "jacks." Toward midnight, with the sun low on the horizon, we returned to camp and called it quite a day.

We fished most of the next day, again filling the boats with trout. Late in the afternoon we departed on the big boat for the five-hour trip back to the main lodge.

We left Arctic Lodge early Friday morning, with the extra baggage of a 40-pound box of iced trout. We could have brought home four times that much fish if we had been able to carry it. On our return trip there was a MIDIZ to penetrate, but the larger lakes are easy to identify and we had no trouble advising Cranberry Portage radio of our exact position and time of penetration. We arrived home in Willard that same night at 10 p.m.

We hadn't caught any trophy fish at Reindeer Lake, but we sure caught a "mess of trout." We were gone just seven days and fished four and a half of them. If we hadn't flown, we would have used the entire week just getting to Reindeer Lake and back.

We made the entire trip VFR and this included penetrating three cold fronts. Facilities and airports up through that part of Canada were generally excellent and, even without an ADF, the trip to Reindeer Lake would be a perfectly safe one for the pilot who wants to see some far north country. ◆

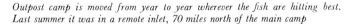
Outpost camp is moved from year to year wherever the fish are hitting best.
Last summer it was in a remote inlet, 70 miles north of the main camp

LATIN AMERICA &
THE CARIBBEAN

AZTEC TO BARBADOS

If you have a little faith in your Lycoming —or Continental—and a good supply of General Declarations (gladly supplied by AOPA's Flight and Travel Department) plus a few ONC charts that cover the area, you can take yourself on the nicest trip ever created for a private airplane—the Bahamas, Puerto Rico, the Virgin Islands, and places even· farther down the Caribbean—Antigua, Guadeloupe, Barbados, to name just a few.

A few embellishments help, but aren't necessary. Such as two Lycomings, which we had in Piper *Aztec* N 4807 P, an ADF, an automatic pilot, and Jeppesen radio charts, both for the area and the individual airports. A Shell International Credit Card helps, too. It wasn't until a month or so later that we found out other nice things about Shell Service. When the bills finally came home to roost, only then did we realize what Shell 100/130 gasoline costs per U.S. gallon—25 to 26 cents!

Add to that another genial couple—in our case Shelton and Louise Fisher, also from our hometown of Darien, Conn. — and you have the ingredients of a really wonderful flight.

For us, the trip started as a germ of an idea last fall, and sprouted into a 2½ week trip that covered nearly 6,000 miles from Westchester County Airport near New York City, about 32 hours of automatic flight in a straight line from omni to omni or beacon to beacon by ADF. Past Florida, this latter method of navigation took on added aspects of ease and simplicity since everything down there, with the exception of a few omnis, is ADF. The beacons are strong and powerful and reception is generally better. It's true of VHF communications, too. You seem to be able to talk a lot farther. For instance, we made reservations with the Rock Sound Club on their airport's Unicom while more than 100 miles out and while at 3,000 feet, but that's near the end of the story. We're getting ahead of ourselves.

Our route covered, after Florida, Eleuthera in the Bahamas; South Caicos, half-way to San Juan for fuel; St. Croix in the American Virgin Islands; Guadeloupe, the French West Indies; Barbados; Antigua; St. Thomas, Virgin Islands; South Caicos and Eleuthera on the way back.

In between, we had nothing but routine flights—10 of them international from one country to another—and anything but routine scenery.

While we enjoyed the serenity of two purring 250 h.p. Lycomings out either side, it proved to be a trip I wouldn't hesitate to make single engine. If you've ever flown to West End on Grand Bahama or to Nassau, you've flown water stretches about as long as the legs required anywhere else down the line. In other words, no hop between islands is much more than 25 minutes in a *Comanche* or *Bonanza*—or about 80 miles. There are a fair number of boats and you usually have something always in sight. In most situations too, you're within VHF range of some ground station or within shouting distance of another airplane aloft. For instance, a friend of mine who flies with Pan American heard us working Grand Turk Air Force Base while he was southbound over Guantanamo in a 707—on 126.2 mc. Incidentally, this and 118.1—plus

Detailed and entertaining account of flight from New York to enchanting islands of Caribbean is given by one who enjoyed every minute of it. He describes trip as 'nicest ever created for private plane'

121.5, the emergency frequency—will get you anywhere in the Caribbean. And 118.1 is the universal tower frequency.

Getting back to single-engine considerations, the only variation from "Yankee Route" which is the direct line from Florida to San Juan would be more southerly routing with a fueling stop at Great Inagua rather than South Caicos. Then after Inagua, you can head southeasterly and pick up the shore of Haiti just 60 miles across. From there you skirt the Haitian and Dominican coasts, hop the 60-mile Mona Passage to the west tip of Puerto Rico. Flight over Haiti requires 48 hours' advance notice to be sent by the pilot before landing, and the Dominican Republic requires 24-hour notice. Nonetheless, it is dry land and would provide a suitable refuge for a limping single-engine airplane.

Emergency equipment, of course, is a must, single or twin engine. This should consist of inflatable life rafts, a Mae West for each person, a little food and water for sustenance. It's wise, too, to have die marker which makes a big yellow spot on the water, some shark repellent, flares and a flashlight. I also took along a Narco VT-4 battery-powered VHF transmitter for good measure.

So much for some basic considerations. Now for some specific details. The trip of Zero Seven Papa started fittingly in five-above-zero weather the last day of January from Westchester Airport. As we left home, the Opel station wagon was not only overloaded inside but had four suitcases on the luggage rack above. Someone should have said "tilt" right then and there, because too much baggage proved to be the only drawback on the whole trip. We later found we could just comfortably get everything and ourselves into a standard size Chevy station wagon. We once had to use two taxis to get everything from airport to hotel. Moral: don't let the baggage load of an *Aztec* lure you into using it all. Keep your "going ashore" require-

By W. D. STROHMEIER | *AOPA 52032*

ments to one suitcase per person plus the usual camera case, etc.

While I took an extra long time (purposely) to recheck weather and file IFR to Raleigh-Durham, the crew finally found a place for everything—and everyone was mumbling that it was too bad we didn't have an *Aztec B* with those big baggage compartments. We were airborne at 8:30 a.m. with the clear crisp sun sparkling on the winter snow.

We cleared Customs at Palm Beach—just a simple case of having a copy of your General Declaration stamped for presentation to Bahamas Customs. This serves the purpose of proving to the Bahamas where you came from —and not from Cuba. Our first "overseas" destination was Rock Sound on Eleuthera, 260 miles out the 115° radial of the West Palm Beach VOR. We'd be getting there an hour after dark, hoped they'd still be holding our reservations and hoped, especially, that their field lights would be on. If not, we'd go back to Nassau, 80 miles west of Rock Sound.

Right off Palm Beach we tuned the ADF to Rock Sound's own private homer and it came in loud and clear. Soon after total dark, the moon made its presence known straight above us, by reflections off the nacelles, and we could even see bright and clear the white sand in the shallow Bahamian waters. The lights of Nassau passed quickly by our right wing tip and we soon left them astern. Now a few lights on Eleuthera showed and to our great relief we saw the single 6,000-foot runway beautifully outlined with lights. We buzzed the little village of Rock Sound to alert Customs and then the Rock Sound Club to alert the chef. Customs was a simple formality, cost a pound sterling or $2.80. The landing fee is also one pound.

The Rock Sound Club, a favorite of mine for years, was never a prettier sight—its Olympic-size swimming pool bordered by beautifully illuminated Royal Palms. Franz Gross, the manager, who learned the hotel business in his native Vienna, was on hand with his handsome goatee. Rose Maire, the dining room hostess with her wonderful French accent and figure to match, was still there. Also David, and Harold and Sam, waiters who had served us on our last visit two years ago. It is a wonderful place and one that is becoming increasingly popular with "island hoppers". In fact, people travelling in their own private planes are representing a considerable share of the business at Rock Sound and other resorts in the Bahamas.

To leave Rock Sound after breakfast, as if it were just a motel stop along the road, seemed a crime but we had a fair bit of travelling to do this day, 900 miles, and would lose an hour since St. Croix, our destination, is on Atlantic Standard Time.

By now our system of assigned crew duties was working beautifully. I had appointed Shelton Fisher our "chief of protocol" which put him in charge of all Customs formalities and other similar details. This left me free to handle fueling, parking, airport fees, and flight plan filing. It left my good wife, Bea, and Louise with the job of packing. Couldn't have worked out better—for either Shelton or me.

Assigning one person, other than the "captain," to Customs duties is a very practical idea. If you do it yourself, as I've always done previously, you're pretty busy at every landing. Filling out forms, waiting for Customs to appear, then fueling, then parking. With our system Shelton had all the papers in order before landing. He saw to it that the baggage

Barbados-bound and eager to leave 5°-above-0° weather at Westchester County Airport are (left to right) Louise Fisher, Bea Strohmeier and Shelton Fisher. Bill Strohmeier, in background, is preparing to enter the Aztec

Aztec delivers vacationers to Barbados, 2,925 miles from Westchester County, N.Y., Airport, starting point for the Caribbean flight. Standing beside the plane at the Barbados Airport are (left to right) Shelton and Louise Fisher, Bea and W. D. (Bill) Strohmeier. Fisher was designated "chief of protocol," whose duties were to handle Customs and immigration with local officials along the route. Strohmeier was chief pilot and master of the plane

was taken to Customs, the papers cleared and a taxi secured. This took about the same amount of time as refueling (service was exceptional, I might add, except in the U.S. Virgin Islands) and parking. Thus our group was headed for the hotel in about half the time it would take if you as the captain handled everything alone.

This seems to give the impression that there's a lot of paper work. To the contrary, there is only one form you need—the General Declaration. You prepare about five of these prior to each flight, using carbon paper, of course. This document merely details basic data on the airplane, owner, date, flight route, crew and passenger list. I had typed up about 50 forms with basic data prior to the trip, so that simplified things even further. Customs everywhere (except in the Virgin Islands) was businesslike and efficient. A smile and patience seem to solve all problems, but watch your holidays. We went to Nassau once on Boxing Day, the day after Christmas, and it cost $20 overtime. I cleared out of Mexico on Good Friday last year for a $28 overtime charge.

There is usually no charge for customs during regular hours. At some places, such as the Bahamas, however, there is a departure tax or airport tax on passengers—around $2. For this reason, always sign on one of your group as copilot since crew members aren't taxed. Used to be you could name everyone aboard as a crew member from navigator down to stewardess, but they've caught on to this and I believe the rule now allows only two crew members for the average four to six passenger aircraft.

We've had a lot of delays getting this story off the ground out of Eleuthera. It took us an extra, unexpected stop to get the flight on to the day's destination, St. Croix. The unexpected stop was on Cat Island, 70 miles down the Bahamas from Rock Sound. Cause: Fr. Murillo Bonaby, an Angelican priest, who showed up at the airport just as our lovely lady baggage handlers had finished their job, miraculously leaving the four seats uncluttered with baggage. Brion Leary, the handy man at the airport, introduced the Father and explained his plight. It seems the Father had missed the Bahamas Airways flight the day before to Cat Island and there wouldn't be another trip for three days. The good Father had a church service to conduct that night on Cat Island at one of 13 churches he served. Could we take him? We pondered the Lord's work vs. FAA and decided Mr. Halaby wouldn't mind three people occupying the two middle *Aztec* seats for a cause such as this, so Shelton, Bea, and Louise took up a position aft and Father Bonaby sat up with me. And a very interesting man he proved to be. Born in the islands, educated for the ministry first in Barbados and then in England. While we couldn't bring any of the Father's baggage, he did carry on his lap a tape recorder which was one of the Lord's most potent tools as used by Father Bonaby. It seems he had trouble getting his parishioners to choir practice until he got the tape recorder. Now attendance is no problem at all, he said. "We record the singing on the tape recorder, then I promise the people that I'll have the tape developed in time for them to hear themselves sing at next week's choir practice."

The Cat Island strip was typical of the many new ones cropping up all over the Bahamas. About 4,000 feet long, paved, period.

Nothing else. We dropped the Father off, engines still running, paused until we were sure he could get his Land Rover started, then took off—and for me this was the real beginning of the trip because I'd never been southeast of the Bahamas before.

You're supposed to fly by flight plan down these areas, so I filed with San Salvador which soon was abeam of us to the left. There is a U.S. missile tracking site on the island, where Columbus made his initial discovery in 1492. The U.S. Air Force has other bases, with landing strips, at Grand Turk, Eleuthera (north of Rock Sound) and at Grand Bahama. They can be contacted on 126.2 mc and you address them as "San Salvador Radio" rather than "San Salvador Tower." San Salvador "rogered" the flight plan info, and after a five minute pause while apparently contacting San Juan direct, came up with San Juan weather and winds aloft. Apparently these way stations don't have teletype weather at hand but can, under most circumstances, get the weather for you.

The South Caicos beacon came in loud and clear with a distinctive high-pitched tone for

Aztec's "chief of protocol," Shelton Fisher, poses with Customs officers at South Caicos "terminal," where cold Cokes and snacks are available. Putting one crew member in charge of Customs details is highly recommended by Author Strohmeier for foreign flights

its "CM" identifying code. The beacon, incidentally, is owned and operated by Pan American World Airways. On this route, you're seldom out of sight of an island of some sort, although with the typical scattered cumulus it's hard to distinguish between an island and a cloud shadow. That's why it's always important to make an estimate for your next landfall and to believe your watch. Don't get lured to one side or the other by what appears to be your destination only to find it's a cloud shadow which your watch would have told you was appearing much too soon.

South Caicos, 320 miles out of Cat Island, was one hour 40 minutes, our 170 m.p.h. ground speed bearing out the almost automatic 20-25 m.p.h. winds aloft which prevail out of the southeast. South Caicos is really an "Out Out Island"—isolated, remote. It

has a 6,500-foot strip left over from World War II and a salt industry of sorts. It has now come to life under the aegis of Caicos Holdings Ltd., who are expanding their salt production, planning eventual home building and tourism. In the meantime, they've set out to make the airport the best, most efficient fueling spot between Florida and San Juan, a monopoly previously enjoyed by Great Inagua. A live-wire Englishman by the name of Ian MaGuire runs everything and it's a pleasure to see him operate. Max Karant of AOPA and Gil Quinby (AOPA 37841) of Narco had spent a night there in South Caicos in November, and this heightened my curiosity as we circled town to get someone to come to the airport.

This was not necessary. The airport was agog with a dozen people and a new *Baron* in Brazilian markings at the fuel pump. Our "reception committee" consisted of the missionary, his wife, several children, the doctor's wife and a nattily attired policeman who doubled as customs officer and quickly expedited our papers. Apparently the arrival of any airplane draws a number of the locals, who are anxious to come talk with people from the outside world. This day, too, the airline was due in from Nassau and points in between.

The service at South Caicos is really excellent. We were on the ground just 35 minutes and could have made it sooner except for chatting with the local people. Customs is the simplest formality but does exist even if you come from the Bahamas, because South Caicos is so far from Nassau that they have elected to be independent and do business directly with London. We had understood earlier that they were under Jamaican jurisdiction, but this has changed too. Oddly, the whole British Islands in the Caribbean are currently in a state of confusion as to which direction they will head in their efforts to get out from under colonial rule. Most of them are in a Federation whose seat of government is at Trinidad, but even so they require Customs inspection even on inter-island hops.

Fuel at South Caicos is on a cash or cheque (pardon our British influence!) basis, since they apparently don't have a bank through which to handle credit cards. Fuel was 59 cents a gallon and there was a $4 Customs charge. No landing fee. They have a very clean restroom and a little canteen where cold Cokes and snacks are available. Since we had brought box lunches from Rock Sound we enjoyed lunch aloft with cold South Caicos Coke en route to San Juan.

We filed our flight plan, after takeoff, with Grand Turk, the USAF missile tracking base about 20 miles east, and the last bit of island until you reach San Juan, unless you veer to the south and pick up Haiti.

It's 410 miles from Caicos to the powerful San Juan homing beacon — SJU — which is west of San Juan International, but we picked it up loud and clear. The winds, as nearly as we could determine, were straight on the nose. So much so that the compass agreed precisely

so very blue below and with good reason because as you approach Puerto Rico you pass near the Brownson Deep, over 30,000 feet down. The first checkpoint is Y-3, or Yankee Three, about an hour from South Caicos and just a spot on the map. It comes just before penetrating and you determine it roughly by taking an ADF bearing on Caucedo, a powerful beacon on the south side of the Dominican Republic. Not that it does much more than give you something to do. You're too far out to report to anyone. Half an hour later comes Idaho intersection and this gets a little more positive since it's a bearing on the omni at Ramey Air Force Base on the northwest tip of Puerto Rico. All the other checkpoints around the island are named for states also— Ohio, Vermont, Alabama, Iowa, etc. The airways are all "routes"—Yankee Route, which we were following, Route X-Ray, Route Two and so forth.

As we passed abeam of Ramey, we were getting into rain and had an upper deck of broken cloud. In fact it looked pretty thick ahead of VFR at 7,500 feet so we started a slow descent and finally wound up at 1,000

We broke out of the clouds just east of Puerto Rico and the islands to the northeast were beautiful — Vieques, St. Thomas, St. John and others. Just before we could see St. Croix we had to go through another rain cloud and this produced a beautiful setting for our first glimpse of the island. Suddenly we popped out of the overcast and there below us and ahead was St. Croix, very green and very beautiful.

We cancelled IFR, swung wide to let a Caribar *Convair* at 3,000 feet land first and came in behind, landing east as always anywhere in the Caribbean. It was 6 p.m. local time and a very flustered Customs man could only speak of "complications." He talked so much about the "complications" of his job that there was little wonder he was overloaded. He wouldn't start processing us or our baggage until the health officer came eight miles from Christenstad. Finally a phone call settled things and we were on our way. It is important to remember, however, that, especially in the Virgin Islands, the U. S. Department of Health has to be notified well in advance so they can send a man out from

Control tower at airport on the island of Antigua, with the Aztec in the left foreground. There's a 7,500-foot jet strip there. From Puerto Rico south, the islands are so close together that you can get all your traveling done in an hour or so after breakfast

Under the division of work on the Strohmeier-Fisher expedition to Barbados the ladies, Bea Strohmeier (left) and Louise Fisher, were elected to handle the baggage. It is reported that they did not have to carry all this baggage themselves—merely see to it that someone did that chore

with the prescribed course. It showed 129° magnetic on the chart for Route Yankee, and with the ADF pointing dead ahead, the *Aztec's* compass read precisely 129° and stayed that way for the entire two hours. It's when you're on a long overwater haul aiming at an ADF that you really appreciate an automatic pilot with heading lock, because it holds a course so much better than you can do manually and gives you much better indication if there's any drift at work.

For two hours it was hard to stay awake. So little possibility of traffic at 7,500 feet that you didn't feel very alert. The others took naps and I let the seat back in maximum recline position and just watched the clock. Cloud condition was typical and beautiful, just scattered, harmless baby cumulus with tops around 6,500 feet or so. The water was

feet going through a series of solid lines of rain which lasted two or three minutes. This, we understand, is typical midafternoon weather.

In the meantime, I had pondered the necessity of landing at San Juan at all. Why not proceed direct to St. Croix? A call to San Juan FAA produced assurance that St. Croix had Customs. Because of the rain and cloud formation at all levels it looked as if Puerto Rico could best be traversed IFR. San Juan ATC came back with a clearance, routing us at 3,000 feet from the SJU beacon to the San Juan VOR on the airport. We just broke out in time to catch a beautiful rainbow with our color camera. From there it was climb to 5,000, turn south on Route Seven to Point Tuna, on the south side of the island, then east on Route Yankee to St. Croix, 75 miles out.

town to look at you and your International Health Certificate. We had similar delays in St. Thomas. Be sure, therefore, to get in a request for Public Health to meet you in your original flight plan or at your earliest radio contact.

St. Croix for four days was wonderful. The Fishers had been there before so knew places and people. We had good fun, got too much sun, of course, and did much of our shopping, thinking, for instance, that Beefeaters would never be cheaper anywhere else—$1.50 a fifth instead of $2.25 at Nassau which I always thought was a real bargain. Scotch, good standard brands like Black and White and Dewars, is $2.75—same price whether you use it locally or take it with you, in contrast to Barbados, for instance, where you can only get the tax-free price if it's delivered to your airplane out of bond. Cigarettes were $1.20 a carton!

We loaded down therefore with our legal gallon per passenger and took it with us for the rest of the trip.

St. Croix retains much of its charm when it was a Danish Island. It is mountainous to the west and north, quite flat along the southern shore and very dry, like Arizona, on the eastern or windy end, which also is the easternmost part of the United States.

There's a smattering of private flying evident, but most of the flying is charter. Bill Bohlke (AOPA 67416), well-known former operator of the Spring Valley, N. Y., Airport, operates several *Apaches* and *Commanders*. There's a *Tri-Pacer* and *Cherokee* there, too. Fuel was 45 cents a gallon—100 octane—landing fee was $1 (collected before I even had a chance to get off the wing walk) and tiedown was a buck a night, too. Typical of the inexpensive prices we paid everywhere, much to my surprise.

There's a wide variety of places to stay at St. Croix, from new luxury hotels to small guest houses. Standard rates everywhere in the Caribbean seem to be $20-$25 per person, with meals. One could probably do much better at guest houses, and the rates after April 15 and until around mid-December are considerably lower.

Our next leg out of St. Croix proved to be perhaps the most interesting. It took us over Saba — an immensely awe-inspiring island that juts up from the ocean 90 miles east of St. Croix. From a distance it looks almost like a perfect volcano, stretching up some 2,800 feet. As you get closer you see the sides of the island go straight down into the ocean. There's no harbor, only a few very rocky beaches—yet three villages exist high up the slopes. Friends who had cruised these parts had told us to be certain to fly around it. They had gone ashore on native whale boats through the surf onto the rocky shore. The islanders' main livelihood comes from fishing and building boats. One town is called Bottom, yet it's high up the mountain in what was once a volcanic crater. The very top was obscured by cloud, as was the case in all volcanic mountains on the whole trip. We circled, taking pictures, and were suddenly surprised as we rounded the eastern edge to see a landing strip carved out of a shoulder on the northeast side.

We went down a little lower to take a closer look and saw that construction was apparently still in progress. We made a note that on some future trip we'd land and visit Saba. Upon my return, I ran into Bob Gift, a Piper service technical representative who had recently landed on that strip from nearby Dutch St. Maartin with a *Cherokee* 180. He said the strip is 1,200 feet long and that's all they'll ever be able to stretch it. Both ends are sheer cliffs down to the water.

From Saba you head more southerly and start down the chain of islands which eventually take you all the way to Trinidad. First come St. Eustatius (called Statia), then St. Christopher (St. Kitts), Nevis, then Montserrat. Each has its DC-3-size strip and is served by BWIA or Leeward Islands Air Transport using anything from *Apaches* to four-engine *Herons*. These islands are very similar. Each has a left-over volcano, perennially shrouded in cloud. The mountain sides slope off gradually to the shore, and all land that's anywhere near level is planted with

La Caravelle Hotel on Guadeloupe has a modernistic lobby under a flowing concrete roof. Miss Guadeloupe, 1962, poses in foreground

Fast service is given aircraft on South Caicos. The Brazilian-bound plane prepares to depart for San Juan as the local service crew turns its attention to the visiting Aztec

sugar cane. Many of the islands even have narrow gauge railroads to haul the cane to the sugar mills.

South of Nevis looms the French island of Guadeloupe. It's really two islands barely connected at the midriff. Grand Terre, the eastern island, is shaped roughly in a triangle about 25 miles on each side and is relatively flat. The west island, Basse Terre, runs about 30 miles from north to south. It is most inappropriately named, since Basse in French means "low" and the island is anything but, with one peak going up to 4,800 feet. Pointe au Pitre, the main city, bustling with some 40,000 black French people, and the nearby airport, are centrally located at the narrow waist which connects the two islands.

Guadeloupe has two homing beacons and an omni, the only one south of St. Croix. It was probably installed after an Air France 707 several years ago strayed during an ADF approach in a violent thunderstorm and drilled a hole in one of the mountains.

You wonder what kind of a French reply you'll get when you call the tower, but the English instructions with a strong French accent came back clearly to land, as always, to the east "cleared straight in." We had no trouble landing—the runway is 10,184 feet long. As we parked in front of the *Douane* (French for Customs), a Shell service crew was there pronto to take care of our fueling.

In two small French taxis we were off to La Caravelle, 16 miles away, through Pointe au Pitre which is certainly every bit what you'd expect to see in Central America . . . thousands of natives, many carrying bundles on their heads, milling through the narrow streets . . . open gutters, and a smell that didn't quite border on a stench. The main roads were good but narrow and full of curves. And the driving was 100% French. Never use the brakes, just blow the horn. Ultimately, we turned off onto a fine new road which curved round a low hill and revealed La Caravelle—an $8,000,000 monu-

Town of Castries on mountainous St. Lucia Island, its land-locked harbor and airport are all close together. Beach alongside airport is reported to be one of the best in the Caribbean

Louise Fisher and Bea Strohmeier enjoy the first touch of sun on Pelican Cove beach at St. Croix

ment in cast concrete to some way-out French architect. It would be best not to try to describe it, and only hope there's room to publish a picture of the big, completely open main lobby area with flowing concrete roof. The place had been open only two weeks and was really just getting started.

But not the chefs—they were in good form. Five of them were brought straight

THE AUTHOR

William D. Strohmeier (AOPA 52032), author of "Aztec To Barbados," is executive vice president of Davis, Parsons and Strohmeier, Inc., New York City advertising and public relations agency. He resides in Darien, Conn.

from Paris by the Parisian owners who are determined to make La Caravelle's reputation on its French cuisine. They have not failed. The food was superb and our only complaint was its abundance and richness. The rooms were super modern, each with a balcony overlooking the excellent beach and beautiful surroundings.

We were there three nights and the weather was "standard." Ideal temperature, beautiful scattered cumulus that has a special softness to it from the Bahamas south. You look up at them, especially near sunset, and have a tremendous urge to go fly through them and over them.

While most of the clientele was straight out of Paris, we ran into another fellow American air tourist — albeit with a French name, Jacques Istel (AOPA 74361)—the parachute impresario who had made it single-engine. It was he who pointed out to me the observations mentioned earlier about the relative ease of doing the trip on one engine if you

skirt the Dominican coast to Puerto Rico.

Jacques suggested we try snorkeling at a nearby spot where there are some cannon from an old galleon. Next morning with Alex Sabattier, our breakfast waiter and former French Navy frogman, we set forth in an outboard several miles down the coast, couldn't find the cannon but saw some lovely underwater scenes. That afternoon we had a real adventure. We took a bus into Pointe au Pitre and this wasn't just an ordinary kind of a bus ride. As on many Caribbean islands, the buses are owned by individual drivers—small buses that carry around 20 people. As a result there's a bus about every five minutes, and what a ride! Like the cab drivers, they rely on their horn instead of their brakes. On the way back to the hotel, Shelton said, "We're sure knocking them off." I asked what he meant and he said, "Knocking off the things we don't have to do again."

Incidentally, Hertz cars are available at Guadeloupe and are highly recommended. The mountainous part of Guadeloupe is very picturesque and would most certainly make an interesting all-day drive.

All currency on Guadeloupe is, of course, French—filthy French paper money—worse than you see even in Italy. While France has gone to New Francs (worth 20 cents each), Guadeloupe still operates mainly on old Francs. It takes 500 to equal a dollar. That meant our landing fee and parking for three nights came to 29,120 francs or just over $5.90.

The flight plan you must file at all these spots is the world standard ICAO form which looks especially formidable in French. However, the lady in the airdrome office gladly put in the numbers as I explained in my fractured French that we were going to Barbados next, 260 miles away. With a little sightseeing we'd take 1:30 hours. I might add that a little French is almost essential on Guadeloupe, at least to avoid delay of trying to find an interpreter. Virtually no one speaks English with the exception of the hotel clerk and the tower people.

The flight plan also brought out another curious fact. Nowhere in the ICAO flight-plan form is there any place whatsoever where your home address, whereabouts, or "next of kin" can be entered. Typical ICAO thinking that assumes all aircraft are airline-type and the owners readily known, should a search and rescue operation be required. If you have any concern on this score on such a trip, you'll have to write your name and home address down on a piece of paper and give it to the clerk.

South out of Guadeloupe, you pass over flat sugar-planted Marie Galante, then shortly pick up big, black, forbidding Dominica, heavily forested with wild jungle-like vegetation, high water falls, primitive villages, narrow tortuous roads and rain and no sugar cane at all, quite in contrast to the sister British islands just north. These may be harsh words for an interesting and intriguing island. No doubt it would be a fascinating place to roam and explore. On a future trip I would most certainly want to do just this.

Thirty miles south of Dominica you're back over French territory—over the island of Martinique, guarded at the northern tip by 4,800-foot Mount Pele which in 1902 erupted, wiping out the city of Saint Pierre with a loss of 40,000 lives—one of the worst disasters in world history. Curiously, none of the travel books we took with us mention a thing about this.

We skirted the eastern shore of Martinique admiring its coast line which looks quite like Maine. The booming surf appeared extra white as it foamed onto the shore in the bright tropical sun. Already, of course, we had our ADF locked on our destination which lay 30° to the left—some 100 miles across "on the diagonal." Barbados, if you look at the chart, stands aloof from the other islands, farther to the east, alone, well out in the Atlantic Ocean. It has not, however, been bypassed. On the contrary, it is perhaps the most developed, the most British, the most established of all the islands in the Caribbean. It prospered long ago on the slave trade and rum. It is today the most thickly populated of all the islands. Its main city of Bridgetown is almost a "metropolis." Newly marrieds from other islands come to Barbados for their honeymoon. It is a favorite vacation spot for people from Venezuela. Its south shore between the airport and Bridgetown boasts dozens of hotels and guest houses of all sizes, shoulder to shoulder facing on the excellent beach.

We were, all in all, amazed at the number and excellence of the places to stay in Barbados. Our reservation was at the Colony Club on St. James Beach on the western side of the island. If you like surf, this is not the side to stay on, as the water is very placid and quite a few boats are permanently moored off shore even though there are 100 miles of open ocean to the west. Another example of the fact that the trade winds blow steadily and forever from the east or southeast.

We took a drive through the countryside and everywhere you went the roads were walled in on either side with sugar cane which reaches up, something like corn, well over 10 feet high. While we were there the harvesting got underway, and the whole island turns out to do the job. Some of the cane is converted into a marvelous liquid known as Mount Gay Rum which sells for 80 cents a bottle, in bond delivered to your plane, and is really good. Other prices were considerably lower than in the Virgin Islands, too.

It was tempting to continue southward to other islands with exotic names—Grenada, Tobago, Trinidad—but we were now out 10 days and the inevitable northbound trek had to start. We were glad we saved Antigua for the end because this proved to be another gem. It's located just 30 miles north of Guadeloupe so we were retracing our steps. However, we altered our route slightly, heading from Barbados more to the west to take a look at St. Lucia. The main town of Castries on the north end of the island is on a beautiful harbor and there's a fine looking airport on the north side. We didn't land, but circled several times, making a mental note that here, too, would be a place not to miss "the next time."

Our guide book said one of the Caribbean's finest beaches is located right alongside the runway and it looked just so from the air. South we could see really spectacular mountain scenery with two twin peaks which led to a discussion on board about the origin of the Spanish word "Teton."

Northbound out of St. Lucia we chose to pass by the western side of Martinique and confirmed what I suspected, that the air is much rougher on this, the leeward side. If you have no reason to the contrary, there-

fore, plan to go by these islands on the east or windward side for a smoother ride. We did that, very close and low, going by Dominica and further confirmed the impression of primitiveness and raw nature which sets Dominica apart. The beaches were black, the foliage on the hillsides had a genuine jungle look. Everywhere except right along the shore, it was overcast and raining.

We climbed on top and passed over Guadeloupe at 9,500 feet enjoying a tailwind for the first time in over 3,000 miles. Through the always beautiful scattered cu we picked up Antigua ahead and as we passed the south shore were impressed more than ever with the amazing variety of topography which you see from one island to the next. Antigua has many inlets and harbors and a very irregular shore line. This explains why Lord Nelson chose English Harbor as his base of operations from which the British Fleet sailed to win the famous battle of Trafalgar. The dockyards, as they existed during Nelson's time, have been restored and now constitute one of Antigua's main attractions. The well-protected harbor is a haven for private and charter yachts.

A new 7,500-foot jet strip makes the old original USAF WW II runway look like a taxiway, and we were cleared to make a right turn in—working the tower, as always, on 118.1. One of the nice things about planning your trip, from Puerto Rico south, is that the islands are so close together that you can get all your travelling done in an hour or so after a leisurely breakfast and be all checked in at the next place before lunch. This, of

course, is one of the big advantages of operating with your own airplane. It's trouble enough getting hotel accommodations without having to worry about airline schedules, too. Generally, we were airborne around 10 a.m. and were on the ground before noon.

Antigua surprised me with its very dry, Arizona-like landscape. Lots of sugar cane, of course, and lots of cactus, too. Our taxi driver was an affable West Indian by the name of George. He took us in his slightly tired Chevrolet to the Caribbean Beach Hotel and wouldn't accept our money. We could pay him when he took us back to the airport, thus assuring himself of a fare two days hence. The CBC—as the Beach Club is known—has a unique setup. The rooms are in motel type arrangement on the very bottom of the beach. The dining terrace and office are on a bluff several hundred feet above the beach, affording a magnificent view of the approaches to the harbor at St. John's, two miles away, and the higher hilly part of the island farther south. To get up and down, they have a little funicular cab which runs up and down on tracks and is self-operated like an automatic elevator.

Here, as at Barbados, the Club maintains reciprocal dining privileges with other establishments and this permits you to eat meals at a variety of places all for the same standard $25 a day, approximately, per person.

St. John's, the main town on Antigua, isn't any great tourist attraction and nothing to waste any film on. It did have, however, the finest shop we saw on the whole trip with a wide variety of fine dresses at ridiculously low

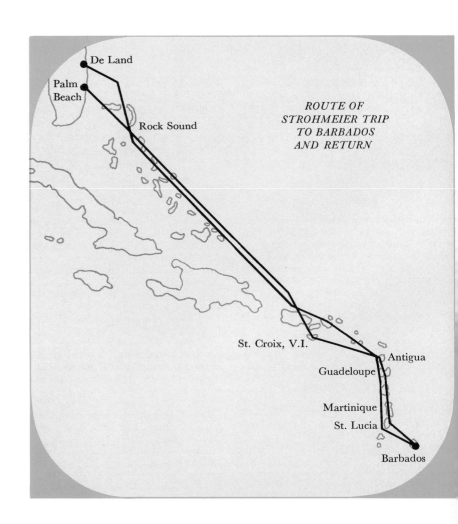

ROUTE OF STROHMEIER TRIP TO BARBADOS AND RETURN

De Land

Palm Beach

Rock Sound

St. Croix, V.I.

Antigua

Guadeloupe

Martinique

St. Lucia

Barbados

prices and other excellent items. It was called the Coco Shop. Bea bought several dresses, muu-muus and other items for presents. I felt I had lost my shirt in the process.

We were at Antigua just two days and two nights when we decided that, much as we liked it, we'd be better off making the long haul back to the environs of Florida on Thursday, have Friday as a final day in the sun, then make the long haul back to Connecticut on Saturday thus avoiding two 1,000-mile days back to back.

George was there on the dot to take us to the airport and collect his money which was $6 "Beewee" each way. "Beewee" money is what you use in all the British West Indies, from which the name was derived. A "Beewee" dollar is worth about 60 American cents and they have 100 cents to the dollar, the same as we.

George, and we found this true of all our cab drivers, served as a great source of information on local facts and customs. In fact, you should be sure to spend a lot of time in cabs just to talk to the drivers and find out about the islands. Their native lingo and manner of speech are fascinating. George, for instance, explained that a Pan-Am DC-8 on the ramp that morning "sleeps here."

We left Antigua with the intention of getting to Rock Sound on the off chance they might have a couple of rooms still available. If not, we'd try Grand Bahama or go on to Florida. To "collect" one more island we landed at St. Thomas, 225 miles from Antigua, passing Saba again to settle a bet Shelton and I had, as to the location of the airstrip. He said it was southeast. The dollar bill you might have seen hanging from the ceiling of the *Aztec* on our approach to St. Thomas, was won by me. The strip's on the northeast tip!

Public Health was late coming out to the airport and we had an irritating delay of 20 minutes until the man arrived, looked at our International Health Cards, said okay. Why it takes a special person to inspect four yellow pieces of paper beats me.

We had to be airborne by 1300 local time to make Grand Bahama before dark if necessary. I elected to stay at the airport and refuel while the crew went in town on a quick one-hour sightseeing/shopping excursion. It took nearly an hour to gas the airplane—from five-gallon buckets through a chamois yet! Such primitive facilities, in comparison with such modern ones at such far-out places as Rock Sound and South Caicos, are beyond my comprehension. And on this airport at St. Thomas were the first signs of big private flying activity, too: 15 or 20 airplanes from an *Ercoupe* to a *Twin Beech* parked there.

I had a quick sandwich with Jack Chapman (AOPA 97614), a refugee from Teterboro who now operates a couple of *Apaches* in charter service, and heard awesome tales about the slow-motion Customs people on just a simple flight from St. Thomas to San Juan.

The take-off from St. Thomas into the prevailing wind is interesting and I understood why the Caribair *Convairs* are Jato-equipped. There's a ridge a couple of hundred feet high right at the east end of the runway. With 4,700 feet of runway, of course, it's no real problem, but it just doesn't look right to stare at this obstruction as you wait for V2. Some pilots handle it differently. I saw a DC-3 and a *Cessna* 170 take off west, down wind. We were now headed back to South Caicos

and made it in two hours and a half, a distance of 486 miles. It was beautifully clear, so we had a good view of San Juan which is a really large city and built up along the shore line like Miami Beach. Going northwest on Yankee Route, we could clearly see the Dominican Republic and Haiti off to our left even though we were never closer than 55 miles. We got Nassau and Florida weather from Grand Turk Radio, pre-filed for our next leg, cancelled our existing flight plan out of St. Thomas just before letting down to South Caicos. We were barely out of the airplane when a pick-up truck arrived with the refueling crew and Mr. Liam MaGuire himself, a very pleasant, energetic type who was most charming. This time he had two officials — customs and health — and they quickly took care of our papers, then had a Coke. The poor health officer had a terrible headache so we turned tables and administered a little health to him in the form of a couple of aspirin. With a double crew we figured we'd be paying double the $4 for customs service we paid on the trip down. "No charge at all," explained MaGuire. The reason we paid $4 before was because it was during lunch hour! The more you ponder Customs customs the less you understand it.

MaGuire said business was picking up quite nicely, that they averaged three or four airplanes a day, and they'd rapidly gone from 200 gallons a week to over 2,000. "Great Inagua is not very happy about this," he chuckled.

We finished our Cokes, shook hands all around, including the missionary and his wife

who showed up, and charged on northwest bound up Yankee Route to Yankee land. We passed through what apparently was the leftover of a weak front, which involved steady rain for 30 minutes and in-and-out IFR at 1,000 feet. It was about this time we experienced the excellent range of VHF communications out here over the water. As mentioned in the beginning, we raised Rock Sound over 100 miles out at 3,000 feet. And the word was good. They had room for us.

Next day, our final one in the sun, was perfect and we didn't leave until late in the afternoon for Ft. Lauderdale, filing with Nassau Radio (126.9) as we passed Nassau. They really were busy with private aircraft arrivals and departures. As we tracked outbound from Nassau with one of our omnis, our second omni tuned to Bimini and the ADF on Bimini, too, for good measure, I couldn't help but think of the first trip eight years ago to Nassau by *Tri-Pacer* with no ADF, no omni on Bimini (no airport there then either) nor at Nassau. Only eight years ago, but a century of progress in between. Airports everywhere, radio facilities everywhere. Even the engines don't seem to go into "automatic rough" like they used to. If you can make Bimini you can make Barbados. You ought to try it sometime. ◆

[*Since this article was published, entry and cruising formalities for tourist flyers in the Bahama Islands have been reduced, and customs and immigration fees have been eliminated. These things should be checked before making a trip to the Bahamas.—Ed.*]

DISTANCE, TIME AND FUEL COST OF FLIGHT IN AZTEC N4807P FROM WHITE PLAINS, N.Y., TO BARBADOS AND RETURN

DATE 1963	LEG	STATUTE* MILES	TIME	FUEL COST
Jan. 31	White Plains, N.Y. to Rock Sound, Bahamas Stops at Greensboro, N.C., Vero Beach, W. Palm Beach, Fla.	1460	8:20	$ 93.81
Feb. 1	Rock Sound-St. Croix, V.I. Stop at South Caicos	890	5:20	77.33
Feb. 5	St. Croix-Guadeloupe FWI via Saba Is.	230	1:50	13.50**
Feb. 8	Guadeloupe-Barbados via Martinique	265	1:45	12.41**
Feb. 12	Barbados-Antigua via St. Lucia	320	1:50	15.85**
Feb. 14	Antigua-Rock Sound Stops at St. Thomas and South Caicos	1077	6:15	76.65
Feb. 15	Rock Sound-DeLand, Fla. Stop at Ft. Lauderdale	490	2:25	39.52
Feb. 16	DeLand-White Plains Stop at Raleigh-Durham	972	5:30	61.05
	Totals	5704	33:15	$390.12

*Distances are via shortest airways or direct island to island. Additional mileage actually flown sightseeing not calculated.

**Fuel in Guadeloupe, Barbados and Antigua is priced at approximately 25¢ per gallon. Fuel at Rock Sound and South Caicos was highest—48¢ per gallon.

Harry S. Truman Airport on St. Thomas, gateway to the Virgin Islands. The airport, which has a beacon, has a 4,700-foot, hard surfaced east-west runway with lights. 91 fuel is available

Lying deep within the Caribbean, but still in range of the light aircraft, the Virgin Islands offer the visitor the conveniences of modern times built around a historical setting. While sitting under the caressing touch of the Trade Winds, one may sunbathe on the very beaches where pirates of long ago fought bloody battles over their ill-gotten booty. Who knows, the sea may wash up an offering of Spanish doubloons for your inspection.

The Virgin Islands are a group of small, rocky islands which are located in the northeastern West Indies, 60 miles east of Puerto Rico. Volcanic in origin, they rise from a submarine bank which extends westward from Puerto Rico.

The islands are divided politically between the United States and Great Britain. The United States Virgin Islands are made up of three main islands, St. Thomas, St. Croix, and St. John, with about 50 other small islets. The British Virgin Islands include Tortola, Virgin Gorda, Peter, Norman (Treasure Island), Anegada and Jost Van Dyke, along with numerous other small islands and cays.

The pilot arriving over St. Thomas will be greeted on 126.7 by St. Thomas FSS (no tower) and given the local traffic and landing conditions.

The airport on St. Thomas is Harry S. Truman, which has 91 fuel and can boast of a hard-surfaced runway which can handle anything up to and including the latest turboprop equipment. The airport has a rotating beacon and has runway lights on the 4,700-foot strip. The runway lies east and west and the pilot almost always lands to the east because of the prevailing easterly Trade Winds.

LEFT BELOW *The author's son Marc tries his hand at spearfishing. Because of the clear waters of the Caribbean, snorkling and spearfishing are popular with tourists. Hoffsommer cautions that novices should always be accompanied by someone with experience in case they run into barracuda, sharks or other underwater hazards*

RIGHT BELOW *Looking down Dronnigan's Gade (street), which has an Old-World appearance similar to New Orleans' French Quarter. The shops which line the narrow, winding street are renovated pirates' warehouses*

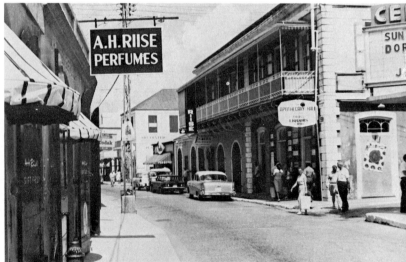

By ALAN HOFFSOMMER | AOPA 57445

VIRGIN ISLANDS' VACATION

Contrary to popular belief, there are no customs or immigration services to go through on entering the islands from the United States or Puerto Rico. However, when heading back home, the visitor must pass through both customs and immigration upon entering either Puerto Rico or the United States. No passports, birth certificates or immunization cards are required, unless the visitor plans on going "down island." This includes the British Virgin Islands.

After touchdown on the Harry S. Truman Airport, the visitor will be guided to the tie-down area by a jeep named "Follow Me." There is a landing fee of $2. After this painful necessity is taken care of, you're on your own. Rental cars may be obtained at the airport for less than $10 a day (including gas and oil), or for $65 a week (including gas and oil). This is almost a must for those wishing to get out and explore the mountain roads and secluded beaches on their own. The tourist must obtain a temporary Virgin Islands driving permit and this can be handled through the rental agency by showing your current U. S. driver's license. Remember—in the Virgin Islands, you drive on the left side of the street!

Some years back, the island government tried to change all driving to the right side of the street as most of the cars on the island are driven from the lefthand side, the same as they are here in the States. However, the donkeys which frequent the streets and roads refused to make the change, resulting in confusion and mayhem. Hence, back to driving on the left!

Those who don't care to try their hand at driving on the left may hire a taxi, of which there are an abundance, for the ride into town or for a tour of the island. The rates are reasonable and are fixed by the island government. If you think you are being charged too much (which does happen once in a while), you have only to request the taxi driver to take you to the Fort (police station) and the matter will be swiftly handled.

Now you are established in a hotel of your choice, which can run from a suite at the Virgin Isle Hilton to a one-room beach hut, and are ready to go out and see the sights. (If you are planning a trip to the islands between the 1st of December and the 1st of June, make sure you have reservations). A stroll through Emancipation Park and down Dronnigan's Gade (street) will acquaint the visitor with the old world charm of Charlotte Amalie, the principal and only city on St. Thomas. The women will especially enjoy this walk. Shop after shop line the streets in which you will find a wide array of goods to tempt the eye and the pocketbook. As there is no tax or duty in the islands, items such as cameras, watches, fine china, perfumes, etc., may be bought at a fraction of the cost one would pay here in the States. Be sure to check with customs as to how much duty-free merchandise you are allowed to take back to the States.

In addition to the merchandise, the shops themselves reek of adventurous atmosphere. These same shops were once the warehouses and storerooms in which pirates kept their plunder. The only change made to the buildings in these ancient, narrow, twisting lanes since the days of Bluebeard and his buccaneers has been the installation of electric lights and water.

In the afternoon, everyone heads for the beaches. (Or any other time, for that matter.) Be sure you heed the advice of those who are in the know and take precautions not to get too much sun all at once. Under a tropical sun, sunburn can be both painful and dangerous. Even sitting under a palm tree with a rum punch can produce a good tan from the reflection of the sun on the white sand beaches.

There is swimming, sunbathing, fishing, sail-boating, snorkling, horseback riding and golf to keep the visitor occupied. For those a little more adventurous in spirit, there is spearfishing and scuba diving. It would be well, however, for the novice to have an experienced diver along with him, even if snorkling in shallow water. The coral reefs surrounding the islands abound with moray eels, barracuda, shark and sea urchins. While these denizens of the deep rarely bother the diver, it would be wise to have someone along who knows what to expect, what to touch and what not to touch.

There are guided tours around the island of St. John, where most of the land has been turned into a national park. Buck Island, off the coast of St. Croix, offers an underwater trail for the snorkler over some of the most beautiful coral formations to be found in the world. A visit to the British Virgin Islands can be arranged by boat or seaplane service.

In the evening, cocktail and dinner parties take precedence over other activities. Dinners are both formal and informal, depending on the day of the week and where you go. During dinner, you may be serenaded by a steel band or a calypso singer, singing tales of romance in the islands. Night life flourishes with cocktail parties and dancing at night clubs lasting until four in the morning.

For clothes, the visitor should bring lightweight suits and dresses for daytime and evening wear, formal wear for night. Bermuda shorts are acceptable for both men and women, but the wearing of short shorts by women on downtown streets will bring a gentle rebuke by police. Swim suits can be bikinis for the women, but something a little more conservative for the men.

Don't be surprised if you keep postponing your day of departure after spending a few days in this land of enchantment. The boss back home can get along without you for a little while longer. And there's a little beach on the other side of the island where you haven't gone snorkling yet. Besides, the sun is shining, and the water is warm, and I met some people who invited me over to dinner tonight, and—

◆

SOUTH AMERICAN CHALLENGE

Cessna 140 pilot makes swing around continent without difficulty; finds people friendly and cooperative

I had looked down the coast of South America for years, longing for time and courage to make the big loop around it in my own plane. It may sound crazy, but sometimes the feeling was so strong that I could almost hear the mountains and deep jungle call out to me, "Hey there, fella, come on and take a chance."

On several previous flights, I had reached the fringes of Latin America. There was a short hop to Mexico in a Cessna 120 in 1947. Then I flew to Panama in 1949 and to Ecuador in a Mooney *Mite* in 1953. But it wasn't until January 1957 that, with a good friend signed on as copilot, I decided to fly around the continent.

I have a 1948 Cessna 140 with a 90 h.p. Continental engine which I bought used for $1,750. It's had some fixing up. In 1956, the wings were recovered with metal and an extra 15-gallon fuel tank was added to give me an eight-hour range. I confess that on foreign flights I would rather have this additional gasoline than all the navigational equipment money can buy. Nothing adds to your peace of mind more than the knowledge that you have fuel enough to reach an open airport beyond your intended stopover.

We were so loaded with extra gasoline and baggage that we could take only a minimum of emergency equipment, though much of the flight would be over dangerous country from which there would have been little chance of escape in case of a forced landing. In addition to two single-man life rafts which were to serve as seat cushions, we made up a kit consisting of a machete, spark plugs, one exhaust and one intake valve, piston rings, a set of gaskets, a set of brake blocks and retainer clips, a screw driver, pliers, a few wrenches, tiedown ropes and stakes. At the last minute I threw in an extra tube for the tires.

The big item was a 24-quart case of oil. This weighed 55 pounds but I considered it necessary. Many foreign airports carry only the heavier grades of oil used in airline engines, and we wanted dependable American oil in the engine at all times.

A few days before our departure we had an unexpected blow which lightened my load by 210 pounds and increased my cares by a ton. My friend announced that his leave had been cancelled. Our plans had gone so far, however, that I decided to carry on alone, following the route we'd charted on our WAC's.

Since you must enter and leave each country through the airports of entry, the location of these airports tends to determine the route to be followed. Still, I have found from experience that one can use almost any airport located at a seaport or point where some main highway or railroad crosses a border. Customs and immigration officials are stationed at these places and can usually be called out to the airport to clear planes. This was true of my first stop beyond Panama—Buenaventura, Colombia.

Bad weather in the Colombian central valley forced me to fly on to Buenaventura—not the usual airport of entry—and there, as was the case in several places, airport officials didn't seem to know what to do about me. When I arrived, the soldier at the airport talked things over with the airline station

By JAMES D. CHURCH | AOPA 38111

34

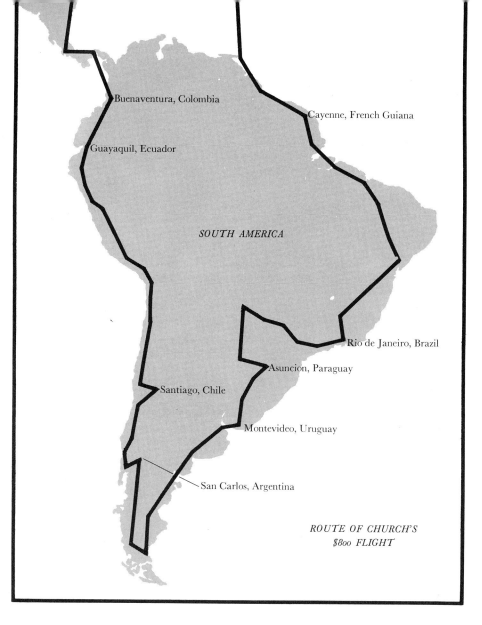

Buenaventura, Colombia

Cayenne, French Guiana

Guayaquil, Ecuador

SOUTH AMERICA

Rio de Janeiro, Brazil

Asuncion, Paraguay

Santiago, Chile

Montevideo, Uruguay

San Carlos, Argentina

ROUTE OF CHURCH'S
$800 FLIGHT

afternoon. I had known that my old WAC chart didn't show the airport, but I didn't dream I'd be in for the most uneasy 30 minutes of my trip. Shadows were spreading below me but the airport was nowhere to be seen. Worst was that there was no place, not even a short stretch of unobstructed road, where I could possibly make a landing without cracking up. The only alternative seemed to be to try to find a break in the clouds and make Cali, 50 miles away on the other side of a 7,000-foot mountain range.

Finally, I reasoned that since only one paved road led out of town, the airport must be somewhere along it. I would follow this road and continue on to Cali if the airport didn't show up. About 12 miles out it appeared, a strip surrounded by high jungle growth which hid it from view until you were almost directly overhead. I went dov 1 gratefully.

Solid jungle was below me most of the way to Guayaquil, Ecuador, but near the Peruvian border the land became a barren desert which extended almost to Santiago, Chile. For 2,000 miles I was over sand dunes and rugged, bare hills which sometimes plunged straight into the sea.

Approaching Santiago, I entered the famous Central Valley of Chile which I followed all the way to its southern extremity at Puerto Montt. Such hours as these made me glad I took up flying—not a cloud, and below lay green fields and vineyards. On my left were the Andes with Mt. Aconcagua rising 22,835 feet.

In Chile, I had my introduction to the Club Aero which I later found very common in Argentina, Uruguay, Paraguay and Brazil. The one at Osorno had 2,000 members, including the most influential men in town, though not more than 100 of them actually did any flying. In addition to owning several airplanes and a hangar, they maintained a luxurious clubhouse which also served as the airport terminal building. At many places such clubs sold me gas, offered mechanical service, hangared or tied down my airplane, furnished free transportation to town and found hotel accommodations for me.

Overnight accommodations, incidentally, were never much of a problem. Officials, control tower operators, pilots, taxi drivers and others readily volunteered information. Their idea of *muy cara* was usually something we would consider ridiculously cheap. Santos Dumont Airport in Rio de Janeiro has a booth in the lobby where hotels are spotted on a huge map of the city with symbols denoting rates. I stayed at the fine Hotel Aeroporto, only a short block away.

At Caravelas, where the town is some distance from the airport, a Brazilian army unit invites transient pilots to sleep in their airport barracks and share their excellent food for less than $1.

I crossed the Andes from Puerto Montt. In dead calm air I went easily across at 7,000 feet, passing the snow-covered cone of Osorno Volcano on one side and the 11,660-foot peak of El Tronador (The Thunderer) on the other. Beyond the mountains, I let down over a deep blue lake with resort hotels dotting its shore. It could have been our own Lake Tahoe without the hot dog stands and billboards.

The wind began to haunt me south of Bariloche, Argentina, where the country became dry and barren, broken only by an occasional

agent and decided that since I was remaining only overnight no formalities were necessary. Next morning I found six soldiers with fixed bayonets guarding my ship. When they bundled me into an army truck and drove the 12 miles back to town, I thought I was on my way to jail. Instead, we ended up at the port captain's office.

Two officials started to fill out a long form and argued over the number of lifeboats I was required to carry. I was frantic until the captain himself finally came in and discovered that they were using a form designed for ocean-going vessels. He merely stamped my tourist card and ordered the soldiers to drive me back to the airport.

Again in Guayaquil my arrival threw the airport staff into an uproar. A dozen officials buzzed around me and took turns examining my papers. From the way they acted, I suspected some of them couldn't read. Each was sure that he was supposed to do something, but didn't seem to have the slightest idea what. Don't get me wrong—these fellows weren't trying to give me trouble—they were just bewildered by the arrival of a foreign airplane as small as mine. It was a good-natured rhubarb.

While they were wrangling among them-

selves, the airport manager arrived and dispersed them. A quick look at my baggage and 10 minutes in his office completed formalities.

The only radio I carry is the General Electric low-frequency transceiver already in the plane when I bought it. The fact is, my flight turned out to be almost entirely without the use of radio. At first, I tried to contact control towers at some of the larger airports, but after a few attempts, I found it easier to watch for light signals. English is the international language for air traffic control and tower operators are supposed to speak it, but these fellows came back at me in incomprehensible accents. I gave up and started putting "no radio" on my flight plans. At no time did I ever need it. The need for precise navigation was eliminated to a great extent by planning flights that follow coast lines, rivers, railroads and other well-defined topographical features.

As far as Panama, it was routine flying in calm, clear weather. In Colombia, as I have said, the Andes were covered with clouds that prevented me from crossing to Medellin and Cali, but the weather down the coast was good. I was nearly singing with confidence when I approached Buenaventura late in the

Ruins of the Paraguassu Convent in Bahia, Brazil, dating from the colonial times

Machu Picchu, sacred city of the Incas, hangs on a crag high in the Peruvian Andes

sheep ranch or isolated village. It was a strong, southeast wind, and signs on the ground indicated that it blew continually and violently. There were no trees, but the shrubs and bushes were permanently inclined. Aeolian sands extended downwind from each small, dry lake bed. Landing at the tiny sheep ranching town of Lago Buenos Aires, I needed the help of all three radio operators to wrestle the plane to the leeward side of the building and tie it down. The wind howled all night.

Next morning, I was again crabbing at 45° over terrain that grew even more barren. The high wind the night before had dissuaded me from refueling, and, without a single landmark that could be identified, I began to worry. I knew that my destination, Canadon Leon, would be only a small spot on the desert, and that if I missed it I was in trouble. The chart did not show another airport for 120 miles. Canadon Leon appeared 19 minutes too soon, and without the painted runway markers, I would never have seen it. A river shown prominently on the map was nothing but a dry stream bed no different from others I had passed, and everything—houses, town, airport, even the streets—was

the same light brown as the surrounding terrain. To complete the dismal picture, I learned on landing that the only gasoline available was 130 octane which I could not use.

Strangely enough, this was the only place on the whole trip where 80 or 91 octane was not available, although at Port-of-Spain, Paramaribo and Pointe-a-Pitre, the proper octane was obtained by blending 73 with higher grades.

Almost everywhere the old "bucket and funnel" method of refueling is still in use, perhaps not as fast as our gas pumps, but you don't have to worry about it. Attendants are careful, and every drop is put through a strainer as it goes into your tanks. The only thing I had to watch was an occasional tendency to use heavy airline equipment that might damage my light metal wings. At Congonhas Airport in São Paulo, Brazil, I even had to forego refueling because there wasn't a gasoline truck on the field with a hose nozzle small enough to fit my tanks. Of course, we could have hunted up a funnel, but I didn't need the gas that badly.

Local prices ranged from 17 cents at

Buenos Aires Aeroparque to 75 cents at Asuncion, averaging 42 cents a gallon.

I ran into an odd situation at three airports in Brazil. Shell dealers at Belem, Bahia and Rio flatly refused to accept cash for gasoline and would not sell it except through use of a credit card. At the time of purchase they quoted me the local price of about 45 cents a gallon, but later I found myself billed for this gasoline at $1.34, $1.18 and 75 cents a gallon.

At Canadon Leon, however, the nearest 80 octane was at San Julian 125 miles away. Maybe I had enough fuel left to fly there, but without any reserve, I didn't dare try. I was stranded. Fortunately, while I wondered what to do, an Argentine CAA inspector landed his Piper *Supercruiser* carrying an emergency medical case from an outlying ranch. The pilot seemed unconcerned about the wind and remarked that it was usually much worse. Upon learning of my situation, he immediately drained five gallons of gas from his tanks and put it in mine, refusing any payment.

The wind finally beat me down. All the local people agreed that it would continue to increase in force as I went south, so I abandoned the idea of flying to the tip of the continent, grinding along at 50 or 60 miles an hour at the risk of having my plane destroyed by the gale. I flew on to San Julian and then started north for home.

The coastal area north to Bahia Blanca is pretty uniform. Cattle begin to replace the sheep, and vegetation like our western mesquite appears. I passed a large oil field at Commodoro Rivadavia where the country looked like West Texas. But the 350 miles across the pampas into Buenos Aires was something to remember—one solid checkerboard of wheat fields and pastures full of fat, black cattle. None of the ranches were poor, and many looked like country clubs with their own airports and racetracks. Railroads ran everywhere, but, in spite of the obvious wealth, there was a surprising lack of paved roads and automobiles.

Between Buenos Aires and Montevideo, you cross the 30-mile-wide Rio de la Plata. In Spanish the name means "River of Silver," but it is muddier than our own silvery Rio Grande. As you proceed north through Uruguay, cattle and sheep ranches gradually replace the small neat farms of the border. On the rolling grasslands ostriches graze along with the livestock. Wherever I saw sheep, there would usually be a flock of these huge birds nearby. As the airplane flew over, they would spread their wings and try to outrun it.

By this time I had a pretty good idea of what to expect in border clearances, and I must confess considerable surprise. The petty graft and attempts to extort bribes that I had been warned against were conspicuous by their absence. Instead, officials were courteous and honest. All along the line, I found myself dealing with men who were conscientiously trying to do their duty with a minimum of inconvenience and expense to me. Total cost of border clearances was $62.85 which includes visa and tourist card expenses before leaving home. At David, I paid $10 in overtime fees. Guayaquil had a $5 immigration fee, and the first airport in Peru assessed an airway fee of approximately one cent per mile for the total distance I was to travel through Peru. These were legitimate charges supported by receipts. Cab fares of $1.50 were paid for officials at Tapachula, Puerto Montt and Paramaribo. In Argentina I was charged a total of $2 for "protección de vuelo", which was flight plan service, but in Brazil I did not pay one cent anywhere.

I got taken once. At Chimbote, Peru, an impressive man in uniform came up and collected 10 soles (50 cents) parking fee. After he had mounted his bicycle and dashed away I found out that the uniform was that of a street sweeper instead of an airport official.

Cab charges, incidentally, can run high and sometimes turn out to be the result of a battle of wits between cab driver and foreigner with the driver trying by clever questioning to classify you financially. Whenever a driver extracted the information that I was an American and had arrived in my own airplane, the fare would skyrocket. Invariably he would go dashing into the hotel ahead of me shouting, "This man is an Americano. He is capitan of his own airplane."

How much this increased the hotel bill I do not know.

In Buenos Aires such a ride cost me 100 pesos; going back on a regular meter it was 11.30 pesos. But I didn't take a cab often. Nearly always someone would drive me to town. A few times, I put my shaving kit in my pocket and rode the bus in. Buses run everywhere in South America and you have only to know where they are going. I can vouch for the importance of knowing, for several times I had to ride to the end of the line, then come back and start over.

One of the most impressive scenic spots was Iguassu Falls up the Alto Parana River. There was no mistaking them. Mist from the falls rose straight up until it disappeared into the base of a lone cumulus cloud. I saw it miles away, and from a distance, it looked like an atomic bomb explosion.

At the falls there is an excellent sod airstrip near the Argentine hotel. Although you could easily walk to the hotel, a rickety bus comes out for you without charge. The rate at this attractive resort is only $1.50 per day for a room with bath and all your meals. There is only one catch—if you are alone you share a room with another guest. I drew a Buenos Aires architect who spoke excellent English and enjoyed his company.

There is one feature of Iguassu that will seem unbelievable to Americans. Not a single billboard, advertisement or commercial activity of any kind marred the scene, so that except for the hotel, this masterpiece of nature remains exactly as it was when discovered.

Brazil, which is reputed to be strict toward foreign airplanes, proved to be the easiest and most pleasant to fly through. Entering at Corumba, I was told that they had not re-

ceived any telegram of authorization and that my entry had been illegal. But instead of making trouble for me, the DAC (Brazilian CAA man) smilingly assured me that there would be "não problema"; he would send a wire to Rio explaining the situation and would soon have an answer allowing me to proceed. While he was doing this, an assistant found the missing telegram. It had been received 60 days before and had already been buried deep in the storage files. At other stops in Brazil, the pleasant DAC men often insisted upon buying me beer and sometimes even a meal after they had finished checking my papers.

I cut off the nose of Brazil, traveling from Bahia to São Luis by the inland route. Instead of the jungle which I anticipated, the area proved to be dry, much like the hill country of southwest Texas. Several times I saw groups of giant ant hills, like mud wasp nests seven or eight feet high. At Petrolina on the São Francisco River, people were unconcernedly swimming in water which they told me was full of piranhas, the little man-eating fish which are supposed to nibble one to pieces in a few minutes.

Without complete faith in your engine there are many flights over South America's swamplands and jungle which would be pretty harrowing. One such trip is the lap from São Luis to Trinidad. Except for sugar cane fields on the Guiana coast, you see swamp and jungle all the way, and I mean the real thing—dense forest with water standing between the trees and either rain or threatening skies to harry you. Across the Amazon River delta and up the west bank it was almost solid swamp, though once in a while the land would rise a few inches, allowing some hardy soul to try to raise cattle. I kept thinking of a remark made by an official in Asuncion: "If you have to land, the alligators will eat you very carefully."

Before each flight I would tell myself that since my little engine had run so many hours without missing a beat, it was bound to keep running as far as the next airport. Thus having convinced myself, I would settle back and enjoy the ride. On the final lap along the northern coast, however, the prevailing winds blew out of the East, provided a 25-mile tail wind which added to my peace of mind. It stayed with me all the way home and was very comforting during the time I was out of sight of land between the Caribbean Islands.

From Cayenne on, I began to hear English again. Perhaps I haven't mentioned it, but I understand no Portuguese and can remember only a little textbook Spanish from high school and university courses I took years ago. Traveling alone, I developed an intense feeling of loneliness from weeks of not being able to talk to people and not understanding what went on around me. You can imagine how I welcomed the English-speaking people of Paramaribo, and guess how good Her Majesty's colored officials sounded at Georgetown.

The linguistic ability found in Paramaribo was amazing. Everyone spoke English and Dutch, and many also used Spanish and French. Heavy rains forced me to lay over for a day and I stayed at a pension where all the guests ate at one large table. During the meals at least four languages flew back and forth and everybody seemed to be understanding everything that was said. Much of the conversation was about a curio shop owner from Virginia City, Nev., who had been there

BORDER CLEARANCE COSTS
A selected list of border clearance costs paid by Church in Latin America:

Entering:		Total (U. S. $)
MEXICO AT BROWNSVILLE, TEXAS Tourist permit $3.00; charge by City of Brownsville for use of international facilities, $3.00.		$ 6.00
ECUADOR AT GUAYAQUIL Immigration fee.		5.00
ARGENTINA AT SAN CARLOS DE BARILOCHE Overtime fee for customs, 16.50 pesos; "flight protection" 45 pesos.		1.85
URUGUAY AT MONTEVIDEO Customs, 10 pesos.		2.60
BRAZIL AT CORUMBA No fees.		—
SURINAM AT PARAMARIBO Immigration fee.		3.00
TOTAL FOR TRIP		$62.85

a few days earlier wearing a Hollywood-designed Wild West outfit and calling himself Buffalo Bill. They had liked this man very much and many of them seemed to think he was the real thing. Back home he sells ice cream cones to the tourists.

Three days after leaving Port of Spain I was back in the United States.

All in all, it was not a difficult trip. There were no real navigational or weather problems, and with the engine running perfectly there was no reason to get in trouble. Credit for this must go to Bill Westover, mechanic at Amador County Airport, Jackson, Calif., who overhauled the engine before the trip and did such a good job that it went 21,500 miles in 230 hours without being touched.

The entire trip cost under $800, of which $498 was for gasoline. Everywhere prices were lower than at home and in some countries food and hotels were unbelievably cheap. In Argentina, for example, a good steak cost only 15 cents — sometimes it came from a sheep, but it was always good. My hotel bills averaged $2.85, often including meals. Room with meals was less than $1 at three different places, Lago Buenos Aires, San Julian and Campo Grande. Admittedly, I was avoiding the swanky tourist traps, but I always stayed at a good first-class hotel. My highest bill was $6.55 at the Othon Palace Hotel in São Paulo. This was one of the best hotel rooms I've ever seen and the bill included breakfast in my room. By contrast with these items, a taxi driver in Buenos Aires told me his old 1942 car was worth $2,500.

Looking back on the trip, to me the outstanding thing was the way I was treated. All along the way people practically knocked themselves out trying to do things for me, and in some places it was difficult to spend my own money. Whenever I was faced with any kind of a problem somebody immediately came to help me.

Uncle Sam has a lot of friends in the countries to the south, and they are all worth getting acquainted with. ◆

THE AUTHOR

James D. Church, author of "South American Challenge," is a CAA airport engineer now on assignment with the International Cooperation Administration in Kandahar, Afghanistan. A commercial pilot with an instrument rating, Church has logged more than 5,000 hours in single and multi-engine aircraft. In 1953, Church took a similar trip alone to Ecuador in a Mooney Mite.

Shirley and Bob Forbes and their Skylane at typical Mexican airstrip on flight from Palo Alto, Calif., to Puerto Vallarta, Mexico. Trip down was over 1,500 miles, took the Forbes' a leisurely two days

One of the quaint streets in Yelapa, a two-hour excursion by boat from Puerto Vallarta

Chino Beach, near Puerto Vallarta. Fish are barbecued on sticks and served with corn roasted over open fires

Little did my husband [Dr. Robert Forbes (AOPA 218677)—Ed.] and I think when we started flying two years ago that we would own a plane, a Cessna *Skylane,* and that we would be taking off for Puerto Vallarta, Mexico, from Palo Alto, Calif. Our experience was so much fun that we decided to tell others about the joy of private plane flying in Mexico.

We wrote to AOPA and Esso motoring service for any help they could offer. They both replied with maps and tourist tips.

On the big day of our departure we drove to Palo Alto, parked the car for the next two weeks and then line-checked our plane. We had a survival kit of water, canned goods, dried meat, hard candy, medicine, band-aids, flashlights, knives, and a blanket. We filed our flight plan with the FAA for flight following as far as Mexicali.

We took off at 8 a.m. and climbed to 9,500 feet. By 11 a.m. we were in Mexicali. This airport has a 5,446-foot runway, 91 and 100 octane gas, mechanic, telephone, taxi, and a tiny restaurant. The homemade tacos were excellent.

Upon leaving Mexicali we changed from following an omni station to ADF radio for the rest of our flying in Mexico. Our next stop was to be Hermosillo and there we planned to spend the night. The airport there has two runways (5,775 feet long, and paved and lighted), has RAMSA facts, flight plan, weather, telephone, all octane gas, a tower, taxi, and a good restaurant on the field.

We tied down for the night at Hermosillo and took a taxi in to the Motel El Encanto. We enjoyed the old world atmosphere, charming rooms, and elegant dinner dancing. The swimming pool was one of the most beautiful we have seen. There was a waterfall over rocks, columns holding a roof to shade part of the pool, and grass and flowers in profusion surrounding the area.

In the evening we hired a taxi with an English-speaking driver to take us on a tour of the city. We enjoyed the 17th century cathedral, Madero Park, new government buildings, country clubs, golf course, and marketplace.

Arising early the next morning, we were on our way to Mazatlan. The airport has a 5,280-foot paved runway with lights, RAMSA facts, weather information, mechanic, telephone and transportation. We refueled our plane and taxied into this truly beautiful resort city. Mazatlan is famous for sailfish, swordfish, marlin and dolphin. One of the world's highest lighthouses is to be found here. A fabulous drive takes one to the top of a hill for a panoramic view of the city and harbor. This was a lunch stop for us and we enjoyed a spectacular shrimp lunch at the Hotel de Cima, located right on the beach.

The last leg of our flight was to be over mountains—as a matter of fact the only mountains on our way to Puerto Vallarta. These mountains hold much for the hunters; jaguar, wild turkey, dove, quail and some alligators are still to be found. Our trip to date had been mostly over desert and seashore, with truly magnificent scenery. One hour and a half later we were landing at Puerto Vallarta. The airport runway is 5,400 feet long, has paved runways, 80, 91 and 100 octane gas, no telephone, no tiedowns, and no hangar. There is a restaurant at the field, and taxis to take you into town. We carefully put rocks under the wheels and hoped a big wind did not arise during our visit.

VFR TO PUERTO VALLARTA

California couple take Cessna Skylane on

two-week vacation

to sleepy little Mexican village

There are many hotels in town; however, they are not luxurious. We stayed in the Posada de la Selva which we liked very much. The rooms there are separate cottages of adobe and lacy tile. The landscaping is delightful. This hotel is on the river and ocean, about three blocks from town. The walk to town is interesting, either over the large river rocks or the bridge. Every morning the señoras and señoritas are on the banks of the river doing their daily wash! You may see them doing your laundry if you send it to the "laundry."

The streets in Puerto Vallarta are all cobblestone so it is wise to bring a pair of flat shoes for daily walking. There are no telephones, so transportation on a moment's notice is a problem. All the hotels have good-to-excellent food. The seafood is really outstanding, especially the jumbo fresh shrimp. The fresh fruit and fresh hot bread are indeed a treat. La Palapa restaurant at the beach has some "crepas" that defy description. One exciting restaurant, Los Comales, serves only tantalizing good Mexican food, and, in addition, has a remarkable Aztec-dancing floor show! The fresh, frozen lime pie is not to be missed in El Patio, an outdoor cafe.

There are two exciting tourist trips to take, one by boat and one by bus. The launch carries about 50 people to the town of Yelapa. This is a two-hour excursion on the water. Beer and soft drinks are furnished on the boat.

Yelapa is an Indian village on the ocean consisting of one hotel and many palm-thatched cottages. Many Americans have retired here. Lunch at the hotel was a pleasure: fresh turtle, fried chicken, and fresh fruit. After lunch there was time for a hike to the waterfall and a swim in the surf. As in much of Mexico, the pigs, chickens, donkeys, dogs and cats wander at will through village trails and houses alike.

The other trip all tourists take is to Chino Beach by open-air bus. This bus carries 50 people, five sitting on each one of the 10 wooden benches. This trip takes about an hour to travel 10 miles over dirt roads. This included a stop to pick fresh corn for our lunch. Upon our arrival at the beach, lunch preparation started right away. The tourists can surf, hunt for shells, watch luncheon prepared, or just sit in the sun. Corn tortillas are made on a metate and then cooked over an open fire. Corn is roasted over an open fire, and chicken stew, beef stew and fresh shrimp combined with fresh fish cooked on a stick make a most hearty and incredibly good lunch. This is followed by fresh coconut and bananas and coffee. The final touch is presented as a huge finger bowl of hot lime water! This is most appreciated by the napkinless tourists.

Shopping in Puerto Vallarta is limited mostly to baskets, beach wear and hats.

Clothes may be made to order in a few days. The charm of this town lies with the natives, scenery, skindiving, fishing, hunting, and boating. At present it is possible to reach Puerto Vallarta only by private boat, plane or commercial airliner. To date there is no good through highway. We thoroughly enjoyed our stay and count it one of our most relaxing vacations.

It was most helpful to us to obtain a RAMSA credit card which enabled us to use the radio facilities in Mexico without further charge. A tourist card was obtained from the Mexican Consulate on Market Street in San Francisco, Calif. It was also necessary to have a smallpox vaccination before leaving the United States. A chamois cloth is needed for straining the gasoline. We found it helpful to carry a good supply of peso notes (worth about eight cents) for tipping. Informal clothes, beach clothes, flat heels, sun hats, sweater, and a light coat are needed for a vacation in Puerto Vallarta.

Our first VFR trip in our own plane to Mexico far surpassed anything we had dreamed. The weather, the flying, music, scenery, people, food, fishing, swimming, and relaxation could not have been better. We intend to return and rent a house for a month and live the way the natives do. ◆

By SHIRLEY FORBES

Want to visit a spot where there is no need for locks on the doors, where labor is $1.25 to $2 per day, where you can sleep in a hammock or stay in a million-dollar resort? Want to lure a myriad of exotic fish or track bobcat, deer, lion or javelina? Or would you like to meet some of the friendliest people on the face of the earth in an area still unspoiled by the paved highway or the TV relay station?

Then let's fly to Baja California, Mexico. It's a year-round vacationland, located right next door to the United States. Small numbers of pilots have been flying their light-planes to this semitropical paradise for years. You either fly or you don't go unless you want to spend from one to three weeks in a four-wheeled-drive vehicle over a "road" that changes its course after any occasional rain storm.

When you fly to Baja (Baa-ha), you're strictly on your own. The entire 1,000-mile peninsula has just four fully-airline runways with radio facilities. Your best flight insurance—and the most fun, too—is a two-plane flight with another somewhat adventuresome friend.

Your next-best insurance is a detailed "round-robin" flight plan filed with the last FAA station where you land before entering Baja. Once you've filed this "round-robin" flight plan listing routes, stops, where you plan to spend each night, when and where you will return to the United States, stick with it religiously because if you turn up missing in this vast finger of sand, granite and sandstone, the search will be along your flight plan route and nowhere else.

Here's a flight that any airplane can make, but some of the smaller flight strips are definitely not for new private pilots. We deliberately arranged to use an "economy airplane" on this Baja survey and flew a brand new Cessna 172 (N2058Y) furnished by Larry Hunt of the Air Oasis Company in Long Beach, Calif. The tour took seven days and we logged an even 20 hours from Long Beach to the southern tip of Baja and return.

It takes surprisingly little pre-flight preparation for the international flight to Baja. Mexican tourist cards are required for everyone 16 years or older. Mexican tourist cards are issued free of charge to U. S. and Canadian citizens at all Mexican airports of entry.

Palm grove and dam across the river at Mulege, a lush oasis in the desert. The luxurious Club Aero at Mulege has its own 2,300-foot strip, just a half-mile from the club

The author's teenage daughter, Dana Downie, checks the family's gear at Bahia de Los Angeles. The Cessna 172 that Downie flew on the Baja survey was loaned to him by the Air Oasis Company in Long Beach, Calif.

First leg of the Downie flight down the east coast of Baja California

PHOTOS BY THE AUTHOR

Lightplane provides best means of reaching colorful resorts on rugged Mexican peninsula. Its surrounding waters offer some of the world's best fishing for sportsmen.

BAJA CALIFORNIA
Beckons Pilots

These cards are for tourist purposes only.

A U. S. Public Health Service card (PHS-731) is required, listing a smallpox vaccination within the past three years—or the visitor will be given a smallpox inoculation upon his return to the United States.

Visitors should carry some form of proof of citizenship: birth certificate, passport, voter's registration, notarized statement of U. S. citizenship or military discharge papers.

In addition, the regular papers required for flight in this country should be aboard the aircraft. These include the registration certificate, airworthiness certificate, aircraft operating limitations (flight manual), evidence of last periodic inspection, loading information, aircraft and engine maintenance records (log books), pilot certificate, medical certificate and radiotelephone permit.

You'll also regret it immensely if you don't take a good camera and plenty of color film on a trip to Baja. The blue and blue-greens of the Gulf are almost impossible to describe except on film.

We were cautioned that expensive cameras or other equipment not declared with U. S. Customs prior to leaving the country may require customs payment when returning. A

prior phone call to local customs officials disclosed that a photostatic copy of our camera insurance policy listing imported cameras and lenses by number would take care of this problem.

While it is not specified as a requirement, pilots operating rented or borrowed aircraft should carry a letter authorizing out-of-the-country flight since the name of the owner of the aircraft must be filled in on each Mexican flight plan. We carried such a letter from Air Oasis, but were never asked for it.

Under present regulations, you do not have to land on the U. S. side of the border before entering Mexico. However, you should call the Flight Service Station nearest your border crossing to transmit a record of your flight into Mexico, to obtain the latest Mexican flight and airport information and to file your "round-robin" flight plan. Flight Service Stations for flights to Baja are located in San Diego and El Centro/Imperial, Calif.; Yuma

and Douglas, Ariz.; Deming (Columbus), N. M.; and El Paso, Tex.

John J. Masiello, veteran chief of the San Diego FFS, says, "We would prefer that 'round-robin' flight plans be filed in person rather than by radio so we can pre-flight the pilots on all phases of border crossing, weather, flight plans, Mexican rules and regulations. This procedure will also prevent congesting radio frequencies. However, a flight plan can be filed via radio, telephone or by mail."

Masiello recommends a landing at the nearest Mexican airport of entry as the best procedure (in the case of Baja California either Tijuana or Mexicali). "There are very good reasons for this," he says, "especially in case of a forced landing in trying to reach an Airport of Entry that is inland, such as La Paz or Hermosillo. You could be declared in Mexico illegally — with long drawn-out delays, inconvenience and severe penalties. Should

By RUTH & DON DOWNIE | AOPA 188411

Bahia de Los Angeles is a favorite stop with flying fishermen. Inboard-outboard fishing boat is owned by Dr. John F. Schneider, Imperial Beach, Calif. Fish were all hauled in in less than an hour

The Flying Sportsmen Lodge in Loreto has its own domesticated "zoo"—a Thailand ape, ram, monkeys and Bambi, the pet deer, shown here with Murray Hillman and his wife

you plan an 'inland' first destination, contact Tijuana or Mexicali Tower (118.1 mc) and they will file a Mexican flight plan either to Hermosillo or La Paz, placing you in Mexico legally."

The main airports have a small landing fee; 8 pesos for the 172, and $1.36 as the highest landing fee for private aircraft.

The quickest way to get into trouble on a flight to Mexico is to try to shortcut regula-tions on a commercial charter flight. If your flight is purely for pleasure, or if you're doing your own flying on a business trip, there's no problem. However, if you hire a professional pilot on a charter trip, you're breaking the law when you fly into Mexico. This service is understandably reserved for licensed Mexi-can operators. Just as in the United States on a purely private flight, there is no objection to a share-expenses type of pleasure trip.

Some of the isolated areas of Baja indi-cate carrying a survival kit in the baggage compartment. What you take depends largely on the space and weight allowance available without interfering with the short-field capa-bilities of your aircraft. We carried two tires, one for the nose gear and one for the main gear. (Emergency takeoffs can be made, how-ever, by most aircraft with a flat nose tire.) We carried a full set of spark plugs and a few hand tools, fish hooks and line. Food con-sisted of dried fruits, a couple of cans of Spam and beans. For liquid, we carried two 3-gallon "Jerry cans" with water, an assort-ment of canned fruit juices and soda pop for the daughter that disappeared in flight. We also carried four quarts of oil for the powerplant and burned just four quarts in 20 hours.

The regular first-aid kit was strengthened with a number of pill bottles—none of which we used. Not that we're hypochondriacs, but it's mighty handy to have some anti-diarrhea pills and a prescription of broad-spectrum antibiotics that will suppress or cure any-thing from a cold to you-name-it. Talk this over with your own physician before any flight into isolated country. Both the U. S. Public Health Service and our own physician recommended typhoid shots—it takes three over a period of a month and they're mighty uncomfortable—but all that is required is the smallpox inoculation.

Resort owners report that Baja is the clean-est section of all Mexico. There is no stag-nant water and therefore no pollution. All resorts obtain their water from nearby springs and samples are checked frequently. None of the ten people who flew with us at various times in Baja had any sickness or the "turis-tas." Yet we even ate vegetables and salads and drank the water that was provided.

The trip to Baja takes WAC charts 590 and 591 and ONC (Operational Navigation Chart) H22, since there are no Sectional charts for Mexico.

The very best map for a flight to Baja—and don't laugh—is issued by the Automobile Club of Southern California. Almost every pilot we met in Baja had a copy aboard since the map lists almost all the airports in Baja and is revised every 3 years. It is accom-panied by an excellent 60-page "Log of Baja California" that is "must" reading for any-one planning a trip into the area. Copies of both the map and booklet can be obtained by writing to the Automobile Club of South-ern California, 2601 S. Figueroa Street, Los Angeles 54, Calif. The cost is 50 cents for the map and $1 for the booklet. Pilots con-templating any part of this trip are strongly advised to carry at least the map. [It is re-ported that the "Log of Baja California" is now available only to members of the Auto-mobile Club of Southern California.—Ed.]

As far as navigation goes, you may as well turn off your VHF radios when you're out of range of the U. S. border. However, there are a few L/F ADF stations that are a help, particularly on flights across the Gulf. These include Punta Penasco ("PPE," 318 kc), Hermosillo ("HMO," 415 kc)—with deflec-tions reported to the West, Ciudad Obregon ("CEN," 345 kc), Los Mochis ("LMM," 227 kc) and La Paz ("LAP," 373 kc) on re-quest. Mexican border stations are Mexicali ("MXL," 292 kc) and Tijuana ("TIJ," 393 kc).

However, there is a good use for VHF radios in Baja. 122.8 Unicom is a "party line" all the way down the peninsula. Planes flying in pairs keep up a regular chatter while planes out alone find a great comfort in having someone to talk with. Frequently, a series of planes will relay weather information (a-la-Pony-Express) from an aircraft in contact with an FAA border station on down the line through three or four contacts.

When we entered Baja through Mexicali, we were unable to contact their tower on either 118.1 or 122.5. However, Raymond E. Tucker, chief of the Imperial FFS, advised us that this is frequently the case and to go right on in and land without prior radio contact. Two-way radio is not required in Mexicali, but is needed at Tijuana. For flights into Mexicali, Imperial FFS will notify Mexican customs by telephone while inbound flights to Tijuana are given advance arrival information by direct interphone from the San Diego FFS.

So, with this much information in advance, N2058Y circled the fine paved 5,445-foot airport at Mexicali and landed. Accompanying us on the complete southbound portion of the Baja tour was N9897T, a Cessna 172 flown by Irv and Cathy Culver (AOPA 117226). Culver, a research scientist with Lockheed since 1939, began flying gliders in 1924 and has logged over 6,000 hours. His wife has a private license and some 600 hours. Fourteen-year-old Roxanne Werden occupied the back seat of their 172 and matched age, baggage and interests with our daughter Dana. However, our new 172 had considerably more baggage aboard than the Culver's plane, most of it in photographic equipment.

It took our two airplanes 40 minutes to clear into Baja and, in that length of time, two more planes had arrived. In addition to the tourist card, this procedure involved a General Declaration (aircraft permit) that is issued without charge and must be turned in at your airport of departure from Mexico. A Mexican Customs official makes a cursory inspection of your aircraft and sends you on your way.

The trip down the East Coast of Baja is the most popular airway because it seldom has any weather, while the Pacific side can be frequently "socked in"—as we found out on our return.

Let's get into this tour as we drop full flaps and slide down over a rocky hill sprinkled with Saguaro cactus and mesquite. Ahead lies a handful of adobe buildings and a bare spot adjoining the beach that is the "airport." Our first landing in Baja was at Bahia de Los Angeles (the Bay of Los Angeles); and the 3,000-foot landing strip looked a bit skimpy by State-side standards. On our return, it looked like Dulles International.

In Baja, as elsewhere in the "back country," always drag the airport at a fairly low altitude before turning in on your landing. During the course of this tour, we saw runways obstructed by cows, burros, taxicabs, children and airline passengers. This "low pass" will also give you a chance to check for soft spots, humps, ruts and "over-shoot" possibilities.

You taxi back up the runway, swing off toward the boat shed that houses the gas drums at the beckoning of a small, brown-skinned young man, and step out into a new land: a land where time may not exactly stand still, but it certainly slows down by 90%.

There are actually two airports at Bahia de Los Angeles, but fuel and accommodations

Seven fishing boats are available in Mulege from the Club Aero. Over 387 different species of fish are caught in the Mulege area alone

Mountainous terrain near Punta Mangles just north of Loreto, the quaint and historic first capital of Baja California. This shot was made from Downie's 172

are available only at the more northern strip. The secondary field is used only for extreme crosswinds. Here Antero Diaz has 20 cabins that rent for $6 or $7 per person per day on the American plan that includes meals. His wife supervises a fine, clean kitchen.

The new motel units at Bahia de Los Angeles are located right on the water's edge. They're clean and comfortable. You'll get the feeling that you're "roughing it" just a bit,

however; when you go in to take a morning shower, there's only one water tap — and that's cold.

Gasoline here costs 65 cents per gallon and oil 60 cents per quart. All grades of fuel are the same price and we found that the 172 operated very nicely on 100 octane. The fuel cost is dictated by the 12-day round trip by truck to Ensenada for fuel. Señor Diaz ships live turtles that are caught locally to Enseñada and brings back 20 drums of aviation fuel each trip.

Throughout Baja, all fuel comes from drums and is pumped into the aircraft through a chamois-skin filter. Each airport has its own filters and it isn't necessary to carry one with you. However, some of the airports had filters with rips in them and we cautioned the men gassing the plane to make sure that these holes were secured outside the funnel.

Despite the great distances—when figured by surface transport—you're really not in bad shape in case of an emergency. Most resorts, including L. A. Bay, have low-frequency radio transmitters and handle radio-telephone calls through KMI in Oakland, Calif. These stations are usually licensed to the largest boat that the resort operates, since a mobile license is less complicated to obtain than one for a fixed-base station.

Should you have mechanical trouble and need parts and a mechanic flown in, Señor Francisquito Muñoz of Baja Airlines, Tijuana, can obtain parts in San Diego and have them delivered with his *Twin Beech* or Cessna 190 on charter or as part of his regular twice-a-week schedule.

After lunch and refueling at Bahia de Los Angeles, we started up the two Cessna 172's and headed south to Mulege. There's no concrete run-up pad at L. A. Bay, so the magnetos were checked during the early part of the takeoff roll.

There's no habitation for the first 55 miles down the coast until you reach Punta San Francisquito and Rancho Barrill, each with a tiny flight strip. This route goes by the "Canal de Salsipuedes" which, translated literally, means "get out if you can." The islands that lie close to the peninsula have sheer cliffs and vivid colors.

As you approach the copper-mining town of Santa Rosalia, occasional ranches and fishing camps begin to dot the coastline. There's a large flight strip on a mesa just south of Santa Rosalia but the daily DC-3's of Aeronaves land 10 miles farther down the coastline at San Lucas (3,000 feet long, elevation 5 feet). There are conflicting reports about the availability of fuel at Santa Rosalia, but fuel is not available at San Lucas.

There is a "road" for the remaining 25 miles to Mulege and its swank Club Aero. Mulege is an oasis in the desert with fresh water springs and thriving date palms. There are three airports in the immediate vicinity of Mulege and the latest runway information is available on Unicom (122.8) where the transmitter is located in the bar.

Aircraft as large as Lockheed *Lodestars* have landed on the 3,200-foot strip located five miles inland on a heading of approximately 10° from the Club Aero. Then there's a 2,300-foot north-south strip just a half mile from the Club. This strip has a 5° slope to the north and is normally used as an up-hill landing. Fuel can be trucked to this strip from the pumps on the main airport at the Club Aero.

However, most visitors land adjoining the hangar right at the Club. There are two flight strips; one 1,650 feet and a diagonal 1,350-foot strip. Landings are normally made toward the shore with a long, slow final approach from over town. There are no obstructions across the east end of the airport and a "zero" approach can be made.

If this flight strip looks short to you, remember that Señor Muñoz puts his C-18 *Twin Beech* into this airport twice each week on schedule.

On our first landing at Mulege, we used the 1,650-foot strip; on our return, we used the shorter strip because of the wind. The excellent slow-speed characteristics of the Cessna *Skyhawk* make landing at Mulege strictly "no sweat." We carried an indicated 70 mph down final approach, chopped the power over the cement run-up pad and turned off with at least one-third of the runway to spare.

Downie's plane approaches the coastline of Baja California. This photo was taken by Murray Hillman (AOPA 135086) in a Cessna 170

Richard M. Stockton (AOPA 215244) of Southgate, Calif., has a major investment in the Club Aero. He flies his Beech *Baron* in and out of the area almost weekly.

"The fishing around Mulege is unlike anywhere else in the world," said Stockton. "I began fishing there in 1950 when we slept on the beach and no boats were available. We have recorded as many as 387 different species of fish caught in the Mulege area alone."

Club Aero has 20 identical rooms, all with large double beds. There is an excellent bar, fine food and a spotless kitchen. There are facilities for skindiving, swimming and horseback riding. Five inboard boats are available

with guides at $50 per day. Stockton estimates that 98% of the patrons arrive by air (2% by boat or jeep) with 30% to 35% in private planes and the remainder on the airlines.

Don't miss a tour of the town of Mulege. You can travel up the river at high tide in an outboard boat, by taxi at 20 pesos per hour (though the drivers do not speak English), on horseback from the stable at the Club Aero, or afoot since it's only 1¼ miles.

Here we had our first close-up look at "El Camino Real" (The King's Highway) that links Tijuana with La Paz. It's a single car wide, rutted and hazardous even within the city limits of Mulege; out of town it must be almost impossible.

Stockton reports that there are three basic weather seasons in Baja. Northwest winds are usually strong from the end of October to April; it's generally calm from April through July, while August and September have sultry, tropical air masses. He reports that 90% of all rain is during this latter two-month period with the occasional "Chubasco" (very strong, almost cyclonic storms) occurring during these two months. In 1959, the town of Mulege was nearly demolished by a "Chubasco" that put 15 feet of water in the downtown area, but the storm had been forecast far enough in advance so that residents evacuated "to the hills" and there were no fatalities.

It's only a 75-mile hop from Mulege to Loreto. Takeoff from Mulege isn't at all precarious, as you can establish full throttle power on the cement hard-stand without damage to the propeller and actually fly right off the end of either strip. There's a "road" all the way and Mulege's fine Unicom was still readable at midpoint from 5,500 feet.

The airport at Loreto is variously reported at 2,800 to 3,200 feet long. There is extensive construction work at the north end. On a normal day, the proper procedure is to buzz town and a taxicab will come out the one mile to the airport and pick you up.

There's just one place to stay in Loreto and that's at Ed Tabor's Flying Sportsmen Lodge. Over the past 12 years, Mr. Tabor has built up the Lodge to where it will handle 35 guests most comfortably. Rates are $12.50 per day per person on the American plan. However, the night that we spent in Loreto, the Lodge held many more than 35 people. Tabor is planning to have custom aircraft interior work and special paint jobs available with local labor while small airplane owners enjoy the fine fishing and loafing of the Flying Sportsmen Lodge.

There's a wealth of early history behind the sleepy buildings that front on dirt streets in Loreto. This town was the first capital of Baja California and remained so for 130 years. The recently restored Mission of Nuestra Señora de Loreto was founded in 1697. Seventy years after it was founded, Loreto was the starting point for the settlement of California.

Allow a little time for fueling in Loreto since the gas drums are stored at the Lodge one mile south of town and must be transported to the airport, usually in five-gallon "G.I." cans in a pick-up truck. Gas was 60 cents per gallon.

While we were waiting for fuel, Ed Tabor showed us all his spacious bungalow, complete with L/F radio transmitter and, as he proudly pointed out, "the only bathtub in Loreto."

There's a friendly, though intense, rivalry between the operators of the many flourishing resorts down the inland side of Baja. Each reports "the best fishing in the world," and they are probably all just about right. In speaking of Loreto, Tabor says, "Nowhere in the world can you find so many different species of fighting game fish. Marlin, sailfish, dolphin, record-size roosterfish, tuna and yellowtail are caught a few miles offshore."

From Loreto, it's only 150 miles to La Paz. We followed the broad beaches to Punta San Marcial and, at Mr. Tabor's suggestion, went inland of Pico Cupula Mountain before coming back to the water at Punta Coyote. There's a short stretch of 15 to 20 miles where a forced landing would be a bit rugged.

However, this forlorn area doesn't last long and soon an occasional ranch appeared below. We changed the radio from the 122.8 "party line" to 118.1 and called La Paz Tower.

A Mexican accent replied, "Cessna 58 Yankee, this is La Paz Tower. The wind is from the north at 10 knots. Use runway 'won' and call downwind."

We were back in "civilization" and it seemed a bit of a shame. ◆

Dr. John F. Schneider's Cessna 172 parked near the bungalows at Bahia de Palmas, one mile north of Rancho Buena Vista. Dr. Schneider is a pilot from Imperial Beach, Calif.

Downie made this shot of Fred Heim (AOPA 147617) in his Mooney Mark 20, shortly after takeoff northbound from Mulege. There are three airfields in the immediate vicinity of Mulege

"The wind, she is from the north, 10 knots. Use Runway One," said the tower operator at La Paz, the single large town South of the Border in Baja California.

We taxied N2058Y, a Cessna *Skyhawk*, gingerly through the unpaved parking area and made our run-up on the paved turn-off strip in front of the modern administration building. Since the broad, paved 5,500-foot landing strip at La Paz has no taxiway, we punched the "mike" button again on 118.1 mc and asked for taxi clearance down the active runway.

"Cessna 58 Yankee, the wind, she is from the north, 10 knots. Use Runway One," was the reply.

After careful scrutiny of the approach area for incoming traffic, we taxied rapidly down the edge of the runway and made a final mag check before turning into the wind.

"La Paz Tower, 58 Yankee ready for immediate takeoff," we chattered into the microphone. Somehow we anticipated the reply.

"The wind, she is from the north, 10 knots. Use Runway One."

So we used Runway One and headed south toward the tip of Baja—a most enjoyable, semitropical tour of both small and large flight strips, quiet fishing villages and pretentious million-dollar resorts.

A few minutes ahead of us were Mr. and Mrs. Irv Culver (AOPA 117226) and teenage passenger Roxanne Werden in their 172. Directly behind us in the pattern were Mr. and Mrs. Murray Hillman (AOPA 135086) with their two small daughters in their 170B. Our first destination was the tiny dirt flight strip at Bahia de Palmas, midway between La Paz and the tip of Baja.

Touring the tip of Baja was the second half of a week-long survey flight for The Pilot to ascertain what a flying family may anticipate these days on a thousand-mile flight South of the Border, a flight that virtually takes the "turista" back two centuries. N2058Y, a brand new Cessna *Skyhawk*, was deliberately chosen from Larry Hunt's stable of aircraft at the Air Oasis Company, Long Beach, Calif., since it represented the least expensive new four-placer available.

La Paz is seldom the destination of the tourist. It's more the "jumping-off point" to some out-of-the-way coastal resort with a flight strip in its own backyard. Aviation fuel in La Paz still comes out of 55-gallon drums, pumped through the ubiquitous chamois-skin filter. Gasoline sales are computed from a dip-stick and figured with a pencil on top of the drum; 80-87 octane fuel sells for 51.8 cents per gallon, with 100/130 octane at 56 cents. Credit cards are useless and a receipt is issued only on request.

Should you spend a night in La Paz—it's a bustling metropolis with a tropical flavor all its own—the first real adventure of your trip begins. Yes, it's that ride from the airport into town in a Mexican taxicab. The fare is 20 pesos ($1.60), but establish this fee before you climb aboard the cab. Then hang on tight! There's a Mexican traffic sign labeled "alto." This translates into "stop" or into "high." Our cabbie took it to mean "slow down to 30 m.p.h. and go right on through."

Both cabs we had in La Paz had out-of-balance tires and languid shock absorbers as standard equipment. The drive is quite an experience and makes flying seem absolutely serene.

The President of Mexico and his party were in La Paz during our visit and accommodations were hard to get. After extensive telephoning by one of the airport attendants, we were fortunate to pick up a room at Hotel Los Arcos, not one of the gaudy tourist hotels but very clean and with a fine dining room. Virtually all lodging in Baja is on the Ameri-

ROUND THE TIP OF BAJA

The second half of a 1,000-mile flight

down the east coast of Baja California

By RUTH AND DON DOWNIE | *AOPA 188441*

On the rock-studded beach at the tip of southern Baja California. The Downies' daughter Dana is at the right

The Cessna 172 flown by the Downies at the Bahia de Palmas parking area. Thatched-roofed buildings in the background are guest cottages

can plan, with meals included, and the total cost for three of us was $25.

As is typical throughout Baja, the first refreshment when you arrive is usually "on the house." Unknowingly, we ordered a beer after flight. This arrived in the room, accompanied by a Pepsi for daughter Dana plus two tequilla cocktails. What a combination!

La Paz is a modern city of some 25,000 people with considerable agriculture, mostly cotton, in nearby farms. The big tourist attraction, however, is the excellent fishing to be found in almost all the nearby waters.

But there's little new in "big towns" for the pilot and we compared notes with Cathy and Irv Culver who had been in Baja before. Their favorite hide-away resort was Bahia de Palmas which quickly became our next destination.

Thus, the next morning, we pointed N2058Y westward over the mountains that ring La Paz and over the beautifully appointed 3,100-foot flight strip of Rodriguez Ranch. This is a private club for members and guests only, and not being guests, we admired the view and turned southward along the coastline of Bahia la Ventana. There were a few clouds flirting with the 4,100-foot-high peaks, but we had no trouble in flying down

the beach to Bahia de Palmas.

Although it's been open for over four years, the Bahia de Palmas airport is on neither the latest WAC 591 or the Southern California Automobile Club map, which is the best navigational aid for all of Baja. However, the airport at Bahia de Palmas is easy to find.

"Just fly down the coastline 'til you get to the Buena Vista airport," said Irv Culver. "Then look north about a mile and a half and there's Bahia de Palmas. The flight strip was 1,700 feet long the last time we were there (it has since been lengthened to 2,000 feet). It is parallel to the beach but in back of the resort bungalows. You come in right along the beach and usually land to the north. There's a small hump at the south end of the strip, and it may be a little sandy in spots."

We "drove" down the coastline, circled the resort, and read the white-washed stone sign that spelled out "Bahia de Palmas." Culver's 172 was already on the ground and tied down. After one low pass to be sure that no burros were on the airport (recently a pilot hit one), we flew a mile down the beach and turned back in to land.

There's always a bit of a psychological battle in the cockpit when you're getting ready

to shoe-horn into what looks like a mighty short airport, but if you're going to fly into the interesting places of Baja, you're going to become extremely proficient in short-field landings.

Previous landings had indicated that our Cessna 172 would fly comfortably with full flaps indicating 70 m.p.h. Thus, we squared away down the beach, set up a slow, full-flap power approach, and came across the fence at 70 m.p.h. Once the throttle was chopped, the 172 squatted easily and we were stopped at the 1,500-foot turn-off spot with only a mild application of brakes.

Murray Hillman, much more familiar with his own 170B, had to use power to reach the turn-off point into the parking area. Heavy steel cables made a very adequate tiedown.

Each airplane was met by owner John H. Mitre in a station wagon, even though it's only 100 yards to the 14-unit thatched-roof motel. By the time our bags were in the rooms there was a complimentary "Marguerita" (tequilla, Cointreau, lime juice and crushed ice in a glass rimmed with salt) and we had a chance to admire the lush tropical surroundings.

Bahia de Palmas is typical of many medium-priced resorts to be found close to the tip of Baja. Rates are $10 per day per person, including excellent meals. Children under 13 are at half price. A breakdown on prices shows that boats with large Johnson outboard motors rent for $20 to $40 per day including a boatman. Tackle is $2.50 per day while 80/87 aircraft fuel is 50 cents per gallon and 91/100 costs 55 cents. Each of the 14 units contains three beds, lights, hot and cold water and all modern facilities. It takes a full-time staff of 21 people to operate the resort, according to Mr. Mitre.

Like most other resorts in Baja, Bahia de Palmas has a L/F radio where long distance telephone calls can be placed with KMI in Oakland, Calif. No charge is made for this service except for the toll charges from KMI.

A twice-a-day bus passes the door that costs $2.60 all the way from La Paz to the tip of Baja. For those who do not want to fly their own planes off the paved strip at La Paz, Senor Jose Castaneda, a jet transport pilot, operates a new Cessna 185 on charter as Servicios Aereos de La Paz. He will fly two people in from La Paz at $15 each, in less than 30 minutes. According to co-manager Jorge Escudero, some visitors prefer the six-hour, $25 cab trip from La Paz, just to get a closer look at the scenery. One of the fishing boats came in shortly after we landed and two men from Los Angeles proudly displayed a 132-pound striped marlin that had taken them nearly an hour to boat.

Don't budget much time when you tour the "town" of Bahia de Palmas. "Town" is directly back of the aircraft parking area and consists of a gas station, general store, a brick "factory" and a small number of native huts. Most of the buildings near the tip of Baja are constructed of locally made brick walls and partitions with thatched palm-leaf roofs tied together with bamboo stringers.

When we asked about the airport facilities and accommodations at nearby Rancho Buena Vista, Co-manager Escudero grinned. "It's a good place, too," he said in excellent English. "Of course, we call it 'no name,' but if you'd like to look around, come along and I'll drive you down."

Rancho Buena Vista is understandably

In marked contrast to the primitive quality of most of Baja is the lavishness of the resorts at the tip of the peninsula. Typical of these million-dollar resorts is Palmilla's Hotel Las Cruces, a portion of whose patio and pool are shown here

Dana Downie in one of the boats at Bahia de Palmas that rent from $20 to $40 per day, including boatman. "Please don't write this place up," a couple at the resort told the Downies. "We have been coming here for years and it's so nice just like it is"

quite similar to Bahia de Palmas, both in rates and accommodations. The greatest difference is in the flight strips where the one-way up-hill runway at Buena Vista is being extended and a new hard-stand being built at the up-hill end of the runway. Fuel is available at both airports.

Later that evening while we were eating a fine dinner at Bahia de Palmas, a couple at our table said, "Please don't write up this place. We've been coming here for years and it's so nice just like it is. If there were too many visitors, the whole atmosphere might change."

Owner John H. Mitre just grinned.

There's another big "plus" in flying to Baja that will appeal to the male members of the group, and perhaps make the gals a little bit unhappy. Baja is not a good place to purchase souvenirs. There is little local merchandise available except perhaps baskets that convert readily into lamp shades and hand-woven hammocks. La Paz and the larger resorts "on the tip" have standard novelty items and the usual import bargains in French perfume and native jewelry from the interior of Mexico. However, most of these items can be purchased just as reasonably at any of the Mexican border towns. Our crew collected sea shells, "sand dollars" and a few polished rocks.

Mexican flying regulations have many similarities to those in the United States. As Mitre explained it, "You don't move an airplane after an accident under Federal law unless you have to clear the runway to make it safe for other planes to land. The plane is supposed to stay right where it stopped until investigators from our FAA come out to inspect the accident. Then they will decide whether the airport was inadequate, the pilot in error, or whether a mechanical failure caused the mishap. Only in this way can we continue to improve our flight strips and flying regulations for the safety of all."

Nobody throws away any empty oil cans at Bahia de Palmas. They either become flare-pots filled with kerosene for the runway, or flower pots, filled with vines or succulents.

Whenever an aircraft is expected approaching dusk or a plane circles after sundown, these flare-pots are lighted. However, single-engine flight in Mexico is prohibited after dark.

Since they had already toured the tip of Baja, the Culvers elected to loaf in the rope hammocks at de Palmas the next day while the Hillmans accompanied us on a tour of the tip of Baja.

Ranches and farms of sugar cane, corn and garden vegetables slipped by with flight strips fairly close together and it was only 20 minutes before we let down to circle the old town of San Jose del Cabo.

We circled the town and took a rather cautious look at the sandy flight strip just west of town. Our 172 made a low pass over the strip and we radioed back to Murray Hillman, "It looks quite soft and we can't see any recent tracks. Let's go on to Palmilla and we can ask about it there. It's only another five miles down the coast."

The Hotel Las Cruces Palmilla is one of the two luxury resort hotels on the tip of Baja. It has an excellent one-way 4,500-foot flight strip, with a 30-foot drop between the seacoast end and the mountain end. Unicom is available and a jeep comes to the airport when you land.

Manager Joaquin Palacios explained that the resort is closed from July 1 through October 15, "when there are storms nearly every day." This topflight hotel was completed in 1957 and has 27 double rooms with 54 beds. Rates are $20 per day per person with a 20% discount for children 12 years old or under. The very complete resort has 10 inboard fishing boats available with guides, although none of the boatmen speak English. Rates for boats range from $20 per day for outboards to $60 per day for modern sportfishing cruisers with expert crews.

Senor Palacios explained that the Palmilla airport easily handles DC-3's and always has both 80/87 and 100 octane fuel. The hotel operates two Lockheed *Lodestars* to shuttle guests non-stop from San Diego on a 3½-hour flight. These aircraft can clear Customs directly at Palmilla.

"Seventy percent of our guests have been here before," said Manager Palacios, "and over half of our visitors come by their own airplanes."

If you don't want to explore the crystal-white beaches with their patches of surf-studded rocks, there's a full-sized swimming pool in front of the hotel.

Water is chlorinated; meats, vegetables and milk are flown in via *Lodestar*. But who wants to eat meat with the superb fishing that's available.

The resorts of Palmilla and adjoining Cabo San Lucas must be seen to be believed. Here is some of the bluest water, the whitest beaches, a tailor-made climate and luxury accommodations that defy description.

It's a bit difficult to write this survey report on Baja without sounding unduly enthusiastic. Everyone we talked with, and the two other groups who flew with us on parts of the trip, were fortunate not to have any trouble with food, water, fuel, maintenance or short airports. Had we run into a problem —and some visitors have—this report would have been less enthusiastic.

Just five miles farther southwest along the coastline is the million-dollar Hotel Cabo San Lucas. It, too, has a fine one-way flight strip, listed on both WAC 591 and the Auto Club charts as "El Tule." This change of airport name caused enough confusion so that both the Hillmans and our group flew the few extra miles to the fishing town of Cabo San Lucas and looked over the broad dirt flight strip at Ciruelo before returning to "El Tule" and talking with the Hotel Cabo San Lucas on Unicom before landing.

The "El Tule" strip, listed on the latest WAC chart as 2,500 feet, is actually 3,600 feet long and it had a DC-3 in the tiedown area when we landed. This flight strip has a noticeable hump about two-thirds of the way toward the north (inland) end, so that it looks mighty short on takeoff. However, when we rolled down over the hump on takeoff, our 172 was already in the air and the remaining strip fell away rapidly.

The bar stools at the multi-million-dollar hotel in Cabo San Lucas on the tip of Baja were hand-carved from a single piece of stone. Hotel has its own 3,600-foot strip known as "El Tule"

Here 80/87 and 91/100 octane fuel sell for 50 cents per gallon and the hotel brochure advises that "qualified aviation mechanics" are available.

The Hotel Cabo San Lucas is pretentious in an absolutely overpowering way. There's a 35-foot pool backed up by a masonry waterfall. At present there are 24 four-person suites with bathroom installations made of onyx imported from Oaxaca on the mainland of Mexico. Stained glass for the windows came from Belgium and the bar stools are hand-carved from a single chunk of stone. There's already a million dollar investment in this resort, with 15 new units scheduled for occupancy by now. The resort is open year-round. Rates at the hotel are $25 per day, American plan.

Dale Jeffries, a well-known boat builder formerly of Santa Monica, Calif., has moved to Cabo San Lucas and set up his own boat

works adjoining the hotel. He employs 18 local residents who build boats when they're not guiding tourists in quest of marlin or dolphin. All boats are equipped with Unicom, and 31-foot boats charter for $65 per day.

The visitor can't help but wonder what sort of economics existed in these isolated villages before the advent of the tourist resorts with their fishing boats and flight strips. An overall figure for Baja indicates that there are nearly as many natives employed full-time at the resorts as there are rooms for guests. If it's service you want, there's never a problem.

There's little or no language barrier in Baja. Most airport attendants know at least a few words of functional English; words like "fill-her-up," "flight plan" and "how much?" Judicious pointing, a rough sketch or question relayed to someone with a greater knowledge of the language takes care of most problems. Even if you don't know a word of

Spanish, make the trip anyhow and rely on your ingenuity.

If you don't fly your own airplane to the tip of Baja, and there's absolutely no reason why you shouldn't, you can fly in from La Paz by Servicios Aereos de La Paz at $20 per person. A taxi will cost $35 to $40 and take 6½ hours.

"There's also a bus that costs $2.60 and takes 11½ hours," said the hotel manager. "I hadn't been on it so I didn't know, but after one trip I can speak with authority. Don't go!"

If and when you fly to Baja, be sure and visit these two luxury spas of Palmilla and Cabo San Lucas. Land at their large airports, walk through the palm-lined driveways, gaze into the placid swimming pools and admire the decor of the dining rooms and cocktail lounges.

We inquired about the condition of the soft strip near the town of San Jose del Cabo and were advised that it was usable. So Murray Hillman and his family and our group fired up the two Cessnas to retrace our steps, still undecided about another landing.

After another low pass over the San Jose del Cabo airport with its adjoining cemetery, we concluded that the surface still looked soft and elected not to land.

So both aircraft returned to Bahia de Palmas where the 2,000-foot flight strip looked bigger than on our previous landing.

Holidays and jobs being what they are, the Hillmans loaded their venerable 170B and headed for La Paz for an overnight stop with a very early takeoff planned for the next morning.

Later Engineer Hillman explained what happened to him. The President and his party were still in La Paz and there wasn't a hotel room of any kind to be had. After topping their fuel tanks, they even took a cab ride through town to check at each of the many hotels. The cab driver had a brother who worked at the airport and the brother had a friend who was a mechanic for Aeronaves. The final result was that the Hillmans spent the night comfortably with their sleeping bags rolled out in the aisle of an Aeronaves DC-3.

They took off shortly after dawn (breakfast was candy bars and crackers) and were safely home near Los Angeles by midafternoon. Their flight times, in almost calm conditions from La Paz, were 3:30 to Bahia de Los Angeles, 2:45 to Mexicali and 1:40 to the Cable-Claremont Airport east of Los Angeles, Calif.

The Culvers and our group spent the night at Bahia de Palmas and they departed early the next morning for the border. We had a day to spare and made only the short hop to La Paz.

Our stateside FAA "round-robin" flight plan, filed the week before with Imperial Radio, had anticipated a two-plane return and we had planned to island-hop from Punta San Francisquito to land at Nogales. However, this junket didn't look too inviting on a solo flight and time was running short. We checked with the Mexican FAA in La Paz and found out that San Diego, Calif., was zero-zero, indicating marginal weather all the way up the Pacific Coast.

Therefore, we changed our flight plan to call for an overnight stop at Bahia de Los Angeles and a midafternoon arrival in San Diego after the morning fog had cleared. The

The Bahia de Palmas resort as seen from the Downies' Cessna 172. The 2,000-foot flight strip lies between the thatched-roofed buildings on the beach and the white stone sign. The "town," which can be seen in the upper center of the photograph, consists of a general store and a gas station

change in flight plan was filed with RAMSA in the La Paz tower, and marked "Please notify Imperial FAA FSS," the originating point of our stateside flight plan.

We checked later with Imperial Radio and were advised by FAA Facility Chief Raymond E. Tucker that "we did not receive your change in flight plan from La Paz. It appears that the only reliable source of communication from Mexico is by telegram. We received your closure satisfactorily on your return."

Pilots returning to the United States through Nogales, Ariz. (including an FAA Flight Safety official on his day off) report that they have been "chewed out" by U. S. Customs officials there for not filing a prior notice of arrival. Since Nogales International has no radio except Unicom, prior-arrival

Irv Culver (AOPA 117226) inspects the simple oil-can landing lights at the Bahia de Palmas flight strip. The cans are filled with kerosene and a wick is inserted

messages should be sent by telephone or telegram from Hermosillo or filed by telephone from Nogales, Mexico, should the pilot elect to land 10 miles South of the Border.

Saved for a future trip was the flight up the very isolated West Coast of Baja. Among the spots to be visited on this trip are the missions of San Miguel de Comondu and Purisima Concepcion, the isolated fishing villages of Punta Abreojos and Bahia Tortolo, the massive Bahia de Sebastian Vizcaino where whales spawn each year, and the world's largest salt mine at nearby Scammon Lagoon. Visitors to this area can pick up Japanese fish-net glass balls, carried by trans-Pacific currents from the Orient.

Heading northward, we retraced our steps over Loreto and Mulege to land at the airline airport at San Lucas just behind the daily DC-3. No fuel available. Rather than tackle the cross-wind strip at Santa Rosalia, with the wind already whipping up whitecaps and dust where fuel might or might not be available, we doubled back the 25 miles to Mulege.

"We had a full house yesterday," said Manager Louis Frederico, "and we're out of 80 octane, but we have plenty of 100."

We had a sandwich while our tanks were being topped and had to guess on the amount of fuel taken aboard because the counter on the pump had broken. However, the 145 h.p. powerplant of the *Skyhawk* digested the 100 octane with relish and we flew off the end of the shorter 1,350-foot strip, after waiting for the crosswind to hit a lull, with miles-per-hour to spare.

Don't be surprised when you check a sample of fuel from your gas strainers and find that it's a clear liquid. The majority of aviation fuel that we bought in Baja was not color-coded as it is in this country. When we returned N2058Y to Air Oasis, one of the line-boys asked, "What have you been running this thing on, water?"

Fred Heim (AOPA 147617), a sales representative from Beverly Hills, Calif., took off in his Mooney Mark 20 right behind us from Mulege. We chatted briefly on the 122.8 "party line" and he flew up alongside for a few air-to-air pictures.

Enough daylight remained when we reached Antero Diaz' Bahia de Los Angeles so that we could have continued to Mexicali or the prominent airport on the maps marked "El Marmol," some 100 miles closer to the border. We found out later that "El Marmol" is an abandoned onyx mine with one watchman as the town's only inhabitant.

Thus, we were glad to let down and spend the night with "Papa" Diaz. Over a very fine dinner of locally caught lobster, he explained that his airport had been put in by the Mexican Government during 1942 and eventually extended from 1,700 to 3,000 feet.

"There's another good strip three miles farther north for east-west crosswinds," he explained. "We use the 122.8 Unicom only when the weather isn't so good, and that isn't often around here."

We took off shortly before noon and headed up the coastline to Bahia San Luis Gonzaga before turning westward toward El Rosario. A few days later, we talked with George Gibson of VIP Airlines in Las Vegas, Nev., who has plans to enlarge the existing turtle camp at San Luis Gonzaga. He advised that 1,200 feet of the 2,000-foot flight strip are now usable and that the north end is soft. Skiffs with outboards are available. Mr. Gibson reports excellent year 'round tortuva fishing. He hopes to extend the flight strip to 6,800 feet and install both a small cafe and trailers that may be rented for lodging.

From the coastline at San Luis Gonzaga, it's about 90 miles over the "road" and lonely El Marmol to the Pacific Ocean at El Rosario and "civilization." From 8,500 feet, we could see a heavy layer of moisture along the beach and there was considerable discussion in the cockpit on whether we should double back to Mexicali or drop down under the skud and drive up the highway to Tijuana. We made a call "in the blind" on 122.8, hoping that some aircraft in contact with a border station could give us current San Diego weather, but no one answered.

We decided to take a cautious look-see and let down around the corner of the canyon at El Rosario into hazy sunshine and a 3-mile visibility underneath. Things became more civilized with each successive mile. The dirt highway became wider and wider and, finally, pavement appeared.

We passed over Ensenada and called the tower on 118.1 and 122.5. No one answered and, since both daylight and weather were going down, we continued the additional 50 miles to Tijuana where the tower answered our first call on 118.1 mc with a clearance to land.

We remembered the caution of San Diego FAA FSS Chief John J. Masiello that one of the frequent mistakes of a pilot returning from Baja is in "planning their return flights to arrive in San Diego in the late afternoons or evenings. In the fall of the year, 90% of the time, conditions are below VFR minimums. Pilots then attempt to land at other airports in the area, which are not airports of entry."

Other popular mistakes listed by the FAA official include "failing to give prior notice of their intended landing at Lindbergh Field (San Diego) to the U.S. Customs/Immigration/Health officials . . . failure to comply with the Mexican Government regulations that all pilots must land at an 'airport of departure' before leaving Mexico to clear with Mexican Customs / Immigration / Health officials. . . . Failure to close their Mexican flight plans and failure to 'turn in' their Mexican tourist permit before returning to the United States."

We called San Diego Radio and notified them of our intended landing at Tijuana and gave an estimate of our landing time in San Diego.

We had taken three hours and 20 minutes on a leisurely flight from Bahia de Los Angeles to Tijuana, a flight that followed the wandering "road" and had detoured patches of weather. It took less than 30 minutes to fuel, turn in our tourist cards and flight permit, close our two-day flight plan from La Paz, and get back into the air.

Perhaps it was because of the worsening weather, but it took just 12 minutes to clear back into the United States. Health officials looked at vaccination records, Immigration viewed outdated passports as proof of citizenship, and Customs made a very brief inspection of N2058Y.

The sun sank beneath a cloud deck as we were midway to Long Beach and we turned on both rotating beacons and navigation lights. With the heavy traffic between San Diego and the Los Angeles area, we called Long Beach Approach Control (120.5 mc) over San Juan Capistrano and asked for a radar surveillance approach to the Long Beach Airport.

"N2058Y, remain on top and report on a 190° radial from Orange County VOR on 108.8," replied the controller. We were very definitely back in "civilization" and far from the leisurely VFR flights over the blue water and palm trees of Baja.

Perhaps it was the result of a week of flying in Baja, but we landed in the first few hundred feet of the huge jet runway at Long Beach and had to taxi up to the first turnoff.

We checked the new Cessna *Skyhawk* carefully after parking on the brightly lighted line at Air Oasis. Despite the rocks, gravel and soft spots on the Baja runways, we found no nicks on the propeller and only a little black paint chipped from the back of the blades. On some takeoff or landing, we had sandpapered the paint off the rear tiedown ring. Aside from that, after 20 hours of flying time in Baja California, N2058Y showed no ill effects.

And on the plus side of the ledger, Baja made an exciting flying destination. We'll certainly be returning. ◆

THE UNITED STATES

Hawaiian pilots carry extra gas in planes because it's unavailable at smaller airfields. Here author's wife refuels Cessna 172 at Kona Airport, Hawaii (which now has fuel)

Because of its irregular terrain, Lanai Island makes good check point for pilots flying on V-2 Airway. Maui Island can be seen beyond the Auau Channel

Island of Hawaii is easy to spot from the air—it's the largest in the chain

Kahului Airport on Maui Island has paved runways and plenty of parking area for private aircraft. In background is 10,000-foot Haleakala mountain

Lightplane flies above coastline of Oahu's north shore

Pineapple fields form lush setting for flight over Oahu

Hawaiian pilots learn how to spiral up through volcanic fume, fly "cross-country" over open ocean. They're a rare lot but growing in numbers

Flying In Our 50th State

I t'll be many a year before lightplane pilots can take off from the mainland and fly the 2,636-odd miles to Hawaii, the farthest removed of the two noncontiguous states. There's too much ocean and no stopping-off places in between.

Nevertheless, general aviation flying in Hawaii, though small at present, is on the increase. Student pilots have tripled in the past seven years, and more and more business and pleasure aircraft are being shipped over by cargo jet. This seems a paradox when one considers the common fear of overwater flying—almost all flying in Hawaii is over water —and the fact that Hawaii's two airlines have such frequency of service as to make private flying almost impractical. But there it is—the increase, though modest when compared to general aviation's expansion in the other 49 states, is perceptible.

Hawaiian pilots get to know the ocean intimately. The longest straightline distance flyable by lightplane is the 355-mile overwater route from northern Niihau Isle to South Cape on Hawaii Island. Unless the sky is unusually clear, none of the state will be visible on this flight, though the plane will pass 50 miles south of Honolulu.

On the flight to Kauai, 100 miles north of Honolulu, a lightplane pilot on a typical day will be out of sight of land for at least 30 minutes—definitely long enough to get completely lost unless plotting and radio navigation procedures are in top form. It does not help when tradewind reports differ on each island and the mid-channel forecast is a guess with wind generally blowing across the heading.

Wind and weather fluctuation from island to island increases the chances of getting lost. Ordinarily, a lost pilot calls for help and waits for the Hawaii Air Guard's F-105 jets to scramble and vector him in on radar. This is always a sure way to get home. Unfortu-

By ROBERT WENKAM | *AOPA 179385*

nately, several planes have been lost between the islands—two in recent years without a trace.

In spite of these factors, there are some insurance companies who refuse to insure Hawaiian pilots for mainland flying because they consider them inexperienced. "It's too easy to fly in Hawaii," an insurance agent told one 300-hour pilot. "All the Hawaii pilots do is fly from island to island. They have no landmarks for practicing pilotage and working with check points. They have only nine omni stations in the entire state!"

Of course, it is true—there are no landmarks to check while flying across the ocean, and that's all the "cross-country" flying possible in Hawaii. Many times ocean haze will cut visibility to a point where it is not possible to use the horizon as a reference point for VFR flying. Looking straight down is no value when the bottom is a featureless ocean. Honolulu FAA considers this IFR.

Mark Twain reported Hawaii to be the "prettiest chain of islands anchored in any ocean." Should he have seen them from 10,000 feet, he would have topped his claim with an exclamation point. There are few sights more beautiful to the private pilot. From the air Hawaii literally floats on the water, and many-hued islands of red and green ringed by silver surf on an azure sea take on the aura of another world.

The tourist resort of Kaanapali with its private airstrip is only 40 minutes from Honolulu. Honolulu International Airport, one of the world's busiest, has seldom been closed by weather for more than an hour. Hawaii enjoys VFR flying almost every day of the year.

While increases in private aircraft shipments foretell greater expansion in coming years, in the entire state only five business-owned private aircraft exist, and there are only 200 lightplanes (142 of which are privately owned) and about 200 active pilots. There are eight flying clubs, some with only one plane and a half dozen members on neighboring islands.

The reason for this situation is that Hawaii is airline-minded. The two island airlines (whose longest route is only 300 miles) flew 1,293,356 interisland passengers last year—more than the state's total population. Island airlines have never had an accident of any sort. Their safety record is perfect.

Viscounts, DC-6B8's, Convairs and F-27's have street car schedules. On the average, every hour of the day an airliner departs for every city in the state. This frequency of service tends to discourage business flying in Hawaii. Local businesses with their financial stake in local airlines will generally buy an airline ticket rather than invest in the higher efficiency of operating their own aircraft.

Economic savings may be convincingly proven for a Honolulu firm with sugar plantations on every island and top personnel traveling almost continuously on airline schedules. But time is not so valuable to Hawaiian executives. The Hawaiian way of life is no "rush and bustle." There is a lot to say for the slow and easy Polynesian manner.

Every major island city boasts its own state-operated airport, with modern facilities, terminals and paved runways. Yet general aviation is finding operating space steadily decreasing.

The former Kailua Sky Ranch, on windward Oahu, is now a subdivision. The only

field Honolulu had that was suitable for student training, the old military strip at Kipapa, is now in sugar cane with plans for subdividing.

As the usual aviation stepchild, the lightplane pilot finds it difficult to buy gas outside of Honolulu. At the smaller fields, no service of any kind is available—except restrooms in the terminal during airline hours. At Kahului,

Maui Island, a key is available by calling Senator (Doc) Fleming. At Lihue airport on Kauai Island, a slip says the gas pump key is available in Honolulu—100 water miles away unless you can find the mechanic, who never seems to be around.

All state airports are now operated by the Airports Division of the State Department of Transportation. There are now 12 state air-

High point was spot landing contest at Kamuela Airport on Hawaii Island. This Cessna 175 carrying Pilot Elsie Miyasato (AOPA 175095) lands too soon to score

The winner! Dottie Reese, student pilot, receives a lei and a kiss from AOPAH president Bob King (AOPA 101862)

ports, and three new private landing strips for resort areas available for public use with permission. The monthly rental for state-owned T-hangars is either $15 or $18.75.

Honolulu has two fixed base operations—Murrayair, which is also a *Cessna* distributor, and Pacific Flight Service, which is a *Cessna* and *Piper* dealer and which rents both types of aircraft.

Retired Qantas Airlines pilot Eric Holloway operates Executive Flight Service out of Murrayair flying two 310's and one *Nayak*, and across the ramp, Hawaiian Air Tours flies four De Havilland *Doves* on charter and interisland tours. The Royal Hawaiian Air Service operates two 310's and a *Skymaster*, primarily between Honolulu and Hawaii Island. Ringo Airways flies an Aero Commander, and Valley Airways flies a Piper *Apache* and a Beechcraft *Baron*, primarily on Maui Island. Pan Pacific Aero operates two *Aztecs* and one *Apache*. Andrews' Flying Service keeps two veteran T-50's flying to Molokai and the isolated leper colony at Kalaupapa.

Absence of weather observation points to windward, and widely varying wind and pressure areas, covering thousands of square miles over the Pacific, give Hawaiian weather rapidly changing characteristics.

On Honolulu's 12,380-foot Runway 8-26, it may be raining to seaward with clear skies over the mountain end. This is all very frustrating to the Weather Bureau and makes local forecasting an extremely hazardous task.

Pilots become quite skilled in combining the terminal forecast, their own common sense, what they see outside the window, and remembrance of things past. Even so, no one knows what the weather in Hilo is like until touchdown.

Trade-wind weather changes very rapidly, and while conditions very seldom drop below VFR minimums, the particular airport location may affect flying procedures considerably. A typical Hawaii day may have 24-knot surface winds with clear skies at Kahului Airport, and 28 miles away due east at pandanus-fringed Hana strip, the air will be almost calm with a 1,000-foot ceiling and heavy rain showers slowly drifting in from the sea.

During volcano eruptions the statewide volcanic fume puts almost all flying on an IFR basis. The technique here is to fly to a windward shoreline, spiral up through the fume (visibility straight down is generally assured), then use the fume top as a horizon. Descent is made in clear air windward of the volcano, remaining always alert for cinder fallout.

Unfortunately for the private pilot in Hawaii, the exotic South Pacific and Tahiti are far beyond the range of light aircraft. He is restricted to the Hawaiian chain by the world's longest overwater hops, but the islands do offer him considerable pleasure in exchange.

One can fly among snow-covered cinder cones at 14,000 feet, skirt 1,900-foot molten rock fountains of active volcanoes, trip out for a cruise in usually turbulent-free air with cumulus nimbus skies an unheard-of sight, or, for fun, fly inside 21-mile-circumference Haleakala crater. And, to top it off, you can make a landing at little used Port Allen airstrip on Kauai where you taxi to the white sand beach and have a swim in the best waters in the world—20 feet from your aircraft and only 55 minutes from Honolulu. You will probably be the only person on the beach—if you were foolish enough not to bring along a pretty Hawaiian girl. ◆

Pilots meet on flight line of Murrayair, Cessna distributor, at Honolulu International Airport to begin weekend flight of Aircraft Owners and Pilots Association of Hawaii

One stop was at picturesque Port Allen strip on Kauai's Salt Pan Beach. In background is a sugar cane field

THE AUTHOR

Robert Wenkam, author of "Flying In Our 50th State," is a commercial photographer living in Honolulu. A few years ago, with his wife and small son, he completed a 14,000-mile flight through the United States in a Cessna Skylark.

Bright flowers and native palms grace boardwalk which runs for two miles along water's edge

Bleached bones of fallen trees enhance seascape at northern tip of Jekyll. Across the channel is St. Simons Island

Jekyll Island grass strip borders intercoastal waterway. Pilots' lounge has been built in grove of trees at right

Modern-day Jekyll Island serves not the Morgans and Macys but ordinary tourists—such as these golfers practicing putts at golf course clubhouse. House was built of brick reclaimed from ruins of Joseph Pulitzer "cottage"

SITTING ON
JEKYLL

Author discovers wealth of 'Golden Isle,' off Georgia coast, is something millionaires can't buy

By PAUL HARVEY | *AOPA 49787*

If you'll come with me, please, there is someplace I want you to see.

You'll feel it before you see it.

I remember as my plane was coming in for a landing that Friday night . . . on an island I had never visited before . . . I could feel it. I could smell the sheer seductive fragrance of the marsh grass.

It had been cold—in the thirties—back in Chicago when I took off. Here the soft wind was like a warm caress, the temperature in the eighties. It had been in the nineties by day. And such a few hours away.

There are three islands off the coast of Georgia. Mainlanders in the city of Bruns-

wick call them "The Golden Isles." They are Sea Island, St. Simons Island and Jekyll Island.

This deep south, just barely north of Florida, is steeped in legend. But what I am going to relate now is the truth, nothing added.

Once upon a time, the 100 richest men in the United States formed a club. These were the Cranes of Crane Plumbing and the Mor-

gans and the Macys and the Rockefellers and the Vanderbilts, the giants of industry and the merchants of astronomical wealth. They wanted a place to get away from it all.

They sent scouts, mostly their family lawyers, all over the Americas seeking a Shangri-La, an Eden on earth. They were looking for the one perfect place where they might build a colony of millionaires, indeed, billionaires,

57

where their privacy would be protected, where the climate was as nearly perfect as climate can be.

The searchers finally agreed upon an island where pirates of the Spanish Main had once found sanctuary, where Blackbeard reportedly hid his wealth. An island of rare beauty and mild climate . . . ancient live oaks draped in lace-like negligees of Spanish moss . . . broad white sand beaches. An island only nine miles long and perhaps a mile wide.

There these families of great wealth built their "cottages." A "cottage," understand, might have 20 bathrooms, but they called them cottages. A huge central club with spacious dining rooms was built and ornately furnished with materials brought in by boat to Jekyll Island. They brought their own doctors, built a hospital on their island.

And there . . . in 1886 . . . hear this . . . on that one island were the men who controlled one-seventh of all the wealth of the world. The world!

There was a saying among the mainland natives in those days. If one was feeling particularly prosperous, he would say, "I'm sitting on Jekyll."

This was the epitome of all things good. As you or I might say, we're "sitting on top of the world," they would say, "I'm sitting on Jekyll." I'm "doing all right!" I've "got it made," we say today. They said, "I'm sitting on Jekyll."

It was 1886. Times have not changed. But we changed.

The Titanic shattered some of the wealthy families on Jekyll. Taxes ultimately reduced the wealth of the rest. Their young heirs, if still rich, preferred the excitement of Monte Carlo and Miami Beach, and the mansions of Jekyll Island fell into disrepair.

In 1947 Georgia bought the island for a state park. As much as possible of its natural beauty has been preserved.

Today, the modern economic aristocracy, the northern millionaires, have built more modest mansions on neighboring Sea Island. This magnificently lawn-scaped island is an elegant residential area, park-like in its per-

Paul Harvey warms up before one of his daily 15-minute news reports broadcast from Chicago over the ABC network. A news analyst and commentator, Harvey's hard-hitting editorial and human interest broadcasts have been entertaining listeners since 1944. He also writes a syndicated newspaper column for General Features

fection, built around the exclusive Cloister Hotel.

St. Simons Island, where I stayed for a magic night and day at the King and Prince Hotel, is an island which the early Indian tribes considered such a sacred prize that one day they stopped fighting over it and shared it. If the others are parks, St. Simons Island is a garden. Magnificent beaches. Endless woodland drives.

Since the Indian tribes took turns enjoying St. Simons, five flags have flown over the island. Saturday morning I sat under our own flag on the sprawling lawn of the King and Prince and looked out across the Atlantic toward Jekyll Island, and I reflected on those ghosts of a past age, those tycoons of the 1890's who were once "sitting on Jekyll." And I made a discovery.

Though I was not looking for any of the legendary buried treasure thereabouts, with my hands idly sifting the white sand I discovered perhaps the most precious prize of all. Local folks have overlooked it for five generations. Quite by accident, I found it.

Nobody ever gets up before 11 around a resort hotel, except me. I was up at five. I was to speak Saturday night in Brunswick, across the causeway. I was up to watch the sunrise. To inhale the fragrance of the salt marsh again.

I'd learned when those tiny white blossoms bloom, the bass are biting. But I was content just to sit.

I'd learned, too, Brunswick is a sleeping giant. The old cotton port is being opened to vast and varied new industry. This year they're harvesting and processing a good shrimp crop and using even the hulls of the shrimp to make something for shrink-proofing wool. Pine stumps they used to throw away now yield 33 valuable chemicals and more every day. World War II veterans returned with a renewed appreciation for what they had back home, and determined to make the most of it.

Sitting there, hearing the soft warm breeze whisper in the pampas grass . . . lulled by the gentle swish of the palmetto palms and the loveliness of tardy oleander . . . I looked out toward that island where once the wealth of the world converged . . . seeking paradise on earth.

At that instant I discovered that they . . . on their luxurious and carefully guarded island . . . were indeed "sitting on Jekyll." But so was I. So were we.

All of us . . . at that instant . . . the entire population of the Golden Isles . . . without realizing it . . . were "sitting on Jekyll."

For the billionaires—in all their search—had found what? The sun and the sea . . . the warm salt breeze . . . the verdant trees and shrubs . . . the hunting and fishing. That, with good food, was all they had. The sun and the sand and the sea are precisely the same for you and me.

And in that wonderful instant when dawn broke across the eastern horizon, exhilarating realization bubbled inside.

Today all this is part of what Gill Robb Wilson (AOPA 1) calls "The Airman's World." Today the least of us can harness enough horsepower to visit all the exotic places that land-bound men could only dream about.

Here was I . . . with all that the richest billionaire could buy . . . "sitting on Jekyll."

A pleasant place to visit when you are flying down South, in the vicinity of Mobile, Ala., is the eastern shore of Mobile Bay.

One of the interesting features of this shore area is what is locally known as "Jubilee." In a "Jubilee," thousands of fish, crab, and shrimp come right up to the shore. This usually occurs on hot summer nights. People who gather quickly after the first cry of "Jubilee! Jubilee!" have no trouble filling buckets, sacks and even washtubs with these delicacies.

The eastern shore is near Fairhope, Ala. Now in operation 24 hours a day, the new Fairhope Airport (Mobile Sectional) has a 3,200-foot long, paved runway with a 92-foot elevation. Approaches are unobstructed. Facilities include standard two-way radio 122.8, full fueling facilities, tiedown service and hangar.

Point Clear, located midway down Mobile Bay's eastern shore, is a vacation center with a variety of things to see and do the year around. A temperate climate affords year-around enjoyment of boating, fishing, sailing, golf and tennis.

Outdoor sports are popular in the area right through the winter, since not more than a light sweater is required for comfort most winter days. Visitors are welcome at the 18-hole championship golf course at Lakewood Golf Club on the Grand Hotel estate and at several other courses nearby, as well as at yacht clubs on both sides of the bay.

For those who like historic sightseeing, Point Clear is so near Fort Gaines and Fort Morgan, where the Battle of Mobile Bay took place, that shells fell at Point Clear when Admiral Farragut cried "Damn the torpedoes—full speed ahead!" At Fort Morgan, on the tip of a peninsula at the mouth of Mobile Bay, the visitor can stroll through tunnels and climb up ramparts and look out over the scene of the battle. The massive fortification, slave-built with 8,000,000 hand-made bricks, is well preserved.

Fishing and surf-bathing may be enjoyed at the 400-acre Fort Morgan State Park, which covers the tip of the long peninsula

MOBILE BAY'S
Eastern Shore

Makings of a shore dinner—fish, crab and shrimp—come right up shore, and a cry of 'jubilee' hails their arrival. Area around Fairhope and Point Clear contains many historic spots

where the fort stands. The public beach on the Gulf of Mexico is easily accessible, and the free pier at the fort is a popular fishing spot.

A cruise that is popular with visitors takes them to the old forts and to Bellingrath Gardens near Mobile. The gardens, which are open every day of the year, are reported to be beautiful during all four seasons. In the Bellingrath Home, the visitor can see rich furnishings, old English silver and a collection of China and rare porcelain.

With three hotels, two motels and motor courts in the city of Fairhope, and Grand Hotel at Point Clear, the eastern shore of

Mobile Bay is the place to rest, relax and have fun.

On the 400-acre Grand Hotel estate at Point Clear, swimmers and sun bathers can use a white sand beach or an Olympic-sized pool, or they can water-ski on the bay. The hotel also operates deep-sea fishing cruisers, and Rhodes 19 sailboats are available, with instructions if desired.

Nearby streams are reported to have large quantities of bass, crappie, bream and other freshwater fishes, and, in the Gulf of Mexico, an hour or so by cruiser, the fisherman can catch Spanish and king mackerel, cobia, dolphin, yellow fin tuna and sailfish. Quail and

dove shooting are supposed to be good in the area.

There is a special program for children at Grand Hotel—a supervised playhouse, a fishing pavilion where "the Old Timer" baits their fish hooks and identifies their catches for them, and a variety of evening entertainment. There are also planned activities for teenagers.

Dancing under the stars is a regular feature throughout the summer on "Julep Point," which occupies the very tip of Point Clear.

There is a variety of antique and art shops in Fairhope and in Montrose village. Many artists live and work in the area. ◆

Bellingrath Gardens. Among the flowers that bloom there are camellias, chrysanthemums, azaleas and poinsettias

Fairhope Airport is three miles due east of Point Clear and three miles southeast of Fairhope. The airport is lighted, including rotating beacon and lighted windsock

History keeps house in the Acadian country of Louisiana.

Ante-bellum plantation homes recall days

when cotton was king and wealthy planters his aristocracy

LOUISIANA
Bayou Country

By VOLA LAWSON

In our age of industrialization and mobility, interest in the less complex, more gracious life of a younger America is at a fever pitch. Call it a desire for roots or a romantic nostalgia for a bygone era; in any event, the burgeoning public demand for "early American" has driven the price of antiques, and even antique reproductions, skyward.

Business has never been better at historic shrines like Mt. Vernon and yesteryear cities such as Williamsburg, Va. The pilot looking for a "different" vacation or flight will find it when he turns his plane into a time machine and flies to the sleepy land of the Acadians, for there are few trails to the past more picturesque than "Plantation Alley" in the bayou country of Louisiana.

The Shadows, Oak Alley, Belle Alliance, Acadia, Melrose, Belle Helene—these are the names of the palatial Greek-Revival style homes that were built at New Iberia, St. Martinsville, Jeanerette and Lafayette when cotton was king and the wealthy planters his aristocracy.

Hernando de Soto explored and claimed what is now the State of Louisiana for the Spanish crown in 1541, and for the next 250 years it was the prize in a tug-of-war between Spain and France. By the Treaty of San Ildefonso in 1800, Spain ceded Louisiana to France, who in 1803 turned around and sold all of Louisiana to the United States for $15,000,000, or about 4 cents per acre!

After the Louisiana Purchase there was an influx of settlers from the Carolinas, Georgia, Alabama and Tennessee, but the French influence prevailed. The business of the state legislature and the courts was carried on in both French and English until almost 1900.

An aside at this point to define some words that crop up in any discussion of Louisiana: A "creole" is a descendant of the earliest French and Spanish settlers of the state, and creole descent is a source of great pride among the old families. "Cajun" is a derivation of Acadian, the name given the colonial French who migrated into southern Louisiana in the 1750's from the province of Acadia in Nova Scotia. "Cajun" can refer to the descendants of these early French, or to their household language, a form of French adulterated by Spanish, German and southern drawls. Last of our glossary items is "bayou," which can be any slow-moving body of water from a creek to a minor river or river tributary.

In the late 18th and early 19th centuries, sugar- and cotton-rich planters built their magnificent estates in the river valleys and across the coastal plains from Houma and Thibodaux north to New Iberia and Lafayette. Constructed with slave labor and painstaking opulence, these homes were almost uniformly of Greek-Revival style, characterized by the 20 to 30 columns which girded the two-story structures and supported the galleries. Exterior materials varied — brick, frame, plastered brick, stucco. Interiors had quite a job keeping up with all of the exte-

Open today as a museum, this was the home of Louis Arceneaux, the man for whom Evangeline searched after the Acadian expulsion from Nova Scotia

rior grandeur, and so you find hand-carved mahogany banisters and doors, floors of vari-colored marble squares, muraled walls, and 25-foot-ceiling ballrooms.

The plantation homes were built to withstand just about everything, except the neglect of poorer days. The Civil War, the abolishment of slavery's plentiful labor, taxes —all took their toll. Fortunately, there are dozens of survivors that have been carefully preserved or faithfully restored and are open to the public today for nominal fees.

Private pilots can land in the heart of the Acadian country at New Iberia's U. S. Naval Auxiliary Air Station, on the New Orleans Sectional. Operated from 6 a.m. to 11 p.m., the Air Station has an 8,000-foot concrete runway, offers Mobil, 80/87, 100/130 fuel.

After deplaning in New Iberia, you are minutes away from perhaps the most famous of all the ante-bellum plantation homes, The Shadows, located on Bayou Teche. Shaded by Spanish-moss-hung oak trees, The Shadows was once the center of Acadian social life. Built in 1830, it is now owned by the National Historical Society and is open to the public.

Closeby to New Iberia is St. Martinsville, the home of Emmeline Labiche and Louis Arceneaux, the man for whom she searched after the Acadian expulsion from Nova Scotia. This is the legend that Henry Wadsworth Longfellow immortalized in his poem "Evangeline." Evangeline's grave and her lover's home are popular tourist attractions in Evangeline State Park in St. Martinsville. At Morgan City, located south of New Iberia, the rite of the Blessing of the Shrimp Fleet is performed just as it was over 200 years ago.

For information about tours and accommodations, contact the Tourist Bureau, Louisiana Department of Commerce and Industry, Baton Rouge, La. ◆

The august old house behind the lovely young lady is Oak Alley Plantation, built between a double row of live oaks in 1836 by Jacques Telepoher Roman. The first successful attempt at grafting pecans was performed here in 1846 by a slave gardener

This is the Spanish-moss-draped "Evangeline oak" that stands in Evangeline State Park at St. Martinsville as a memorial to the heroine of Henry Wadsworth Longfellow's poem of the same name. Legend has it that the real-life Evangeline was Emmeline Labiche who came with the Acadians from Nova Scotia to Louisiana over 200 years ago

61

Carefree
Island
Hopping

By BOB FARRINGTON | AOPA 152251

Have you ever yearned to follow in the footsteps of famous pilots who hop from island to island in daring "over the ocean" flights?

Well, if you'd like a taste of island hopping without the deep-water danger and would like to have a trip to the birthplace of powered flight thrown in for good measure, make plans to fly down the Outer Banks on the coast of North Carolina.

This string of thin, sandy islands runs from the North Carolina-Virginia border to a point just south of Morehead City, N. C., a distance of slightly more than 250 miles. Initially, they run generally north and south, but they bend off to the west at Cape Hatteras. At that famous, candy-striped landmark, the Outer Banks are nearly 30 miles from the mainland.

Sir Walter Raleigh led the English settlers of the now legendary "Lost Colony" ashore near the small community of Manteo, on the northern section of the Outer Banks, and this would be a great spot for any pilot to headquarter his journey in the area.

The gateway to the "banks" is the Elizabeth City Municipal Airport. Joe Flickinger is the operator there and a valuable source of information on the points to see and the precautions that should be taken. The daring will fly directly from Elizabeth City across the Pasquotank River and Albemarle Sound. Others, this writer included, prefer to island-hop by way of the old Elizabeth City Naval Air Station (scene of World War II blimp operations) and the community of Point Harbor.

The first stop on the "banks" themselves should be the brand new "First Flight" Airport. Situated within a stone's throw of the impressive Wright Brothers Memorial, a 60-foot high gray granite pylon, the paved strip runs parallel to the actual first flight path used by the Wright Brothers biplane. The memorial, a new visitor center, and a prominently placed windsock form a triangle

around the runway which is nestled among the many windblown sand dunes in the area.

Inside the visitor center, as many as 3,000 people a day stop to inspect the exact replica of the Wright Flyer described in The AOPA PILOT last January.

"First Flight" Airport is equipped only to park airplanes. There is neither fuel nor service available.

However, just a few miles away, pilots will find the welcome mat out at Manteo. Bill Henderson (AOPA 107574) is the operator there, and he's been the backbone of the Outer Banks aviation activities for years. Bill is well known to many sportsmen in the East, for he does a bustling air-taxi business between New York, Boston, Philadelphia and the Outer Banks, ferrying fishermen to the fantastic abundance of game fish in the area. The Gulf Stream is just a few miles offshore in this area, creating conditions that have dubbed the region "Gamefish Junction."

Henderson also serves the many year-around residents of the Outer Banks as a dependable contact with the mainland. For years, he has taken a doctor on regular rounds to the more isolated villages. Some of that duty is set aside now, however, with the completion of the new Bonner Bridge, an arching concrete and steel span connecting the two main islands.

RON accommodations in this region are concentrated in the Nags Head-Manteo area. Numerous hotels and motels are open during the long summer season and well into late autumn. Usually, some accommodations are available the year around.

To the south, Hatteras Island has been reserved as a National Seashore Park and Recreation Area. Near Cape Hatteras, the State of North Carolina has constructed a paved airstrip named after famed Air Corps aviator Billy Mitchell. Located several miles southeast of the Hatteras lighthouse near the small fishing town of Frisco, the strip is adequate for most airplanes up to light twins. A tele-

phone booth at the parking ramp brings transportation from the nearby motels, and jeeps can be rented for "do-it-yourself" buggy tours of the sand dunes and fishing spots.

The strong winds that are characteristic of the Outer Banks demand some concentration for a smooth landing, especially at Billy Mitchell Field. More than one newcomer has been surprised by a capricious blast of sea breeze as he drifts down toward the runway. A typical approach is punctuated by a brisk downwind, a sharply corrected base leg, and a power-on final against the wind for a landing. Caution should be exercised as the plane slips down below the level of the nearby sand dunes, for they serve as a natural windbreak and can set the scene for a bumpy landing.

Mitchell Field is the last paved airport for the southbound pilot until he reaches the multirunway facility that serves Morehead City and Beaufort. There are a couple of grass strips at private fishing and hunting clubs in this area, but they should be used only in case of emergency.

This leg of the flight will be made over the quaint community of Ocracoke and some of the most desolate areas of the Outer Banks. There, the long, sandy beaches are punctuated only by an occasional shipwreck, a ragged group of fishermen's shacks, and clusters of multicolored old cars hauled over to the island by the more enterprising fishermen of the region. The rusting remains of some of these "beach cars" can be seen where their owner played a game of tag with the rising tide and lost.

Even the oldtimers on the Outer Banks get a kick out of watching the small herds of wild ponies grazing in the marshlands and dashing across the sand dunes. These four-footed residents apparently descend from Spanish mounts stranded on the islands by ship disasters. The world-famous reefs just offshore have been called the "Graveyard of the Atlantic."

There is a great temptation to land on the

N.C. DEPT. CONSERVATION AND DEVELOPMENT

PHOTO BY CHARLIE KELLY

uninhabited beaches in this area, but it isn't recommended. Only seasoned beach pilots can tell where the sand is solid and where it has been left soft and dangerous by the years of storms and hurricanes in the region.

Dick Rodd (AOPA 256512) and Fred Seitz (AOPA 202811), who run the Coastair Flying Service at Morehead City-Beaufort, use a souped up Piper *Pacer* for their frequent charter flights to the lower beaches of the Outer Banks. Dick says the conventional landing gear of the *Pacer* makes beach landings safer and easier for him, and the extra power of the 150 h.p. engine enables him to carry three paying customers and their gear to the best fishing spots early every morning with room to spare for the fish in the late afternoon return flight.

Coastair has marked the beach off into zones and charges according to zone selection for this "take 'em out in the morning—bring 'em back in the evening" service.

Morehead City also serves as the home base for the largest deep-sea fishing fleet on the North Carolina coast, so it is well worth an overnight stay on the vacation schedule.

This is the stepping-off point for the Outer Banks flyer. The islands to the south of Morehead City are used as a gunnery range by the Marine pilots stationed at the nearby Cherry Point Marine Air Station. As a matter of fact, the Morehead City-Beaufort Airport rests right on the edge of a large restricted area centered by Cherry Point. However, a direct telephone line to the Cherry Point tower is available at Morehead City-Beaufort for the filing of a flight plan through the zone, and the Marine controllers are usually will-

Cape Hatteras Lighthouse, tallest in America, overlooks surfcasting beaches in the Cape Hatteras National Seashore on North Carolina's Outer Banks islands. Over 30 different species of salt water gamefish are taken from surf, deep sea and inlet waters along the North Carolina coast

ing to approve a VFR flight through the area at 2,500 feet and above.

A slight in-shore detour to accommodate the zone restrictions will send the Florida-bound pilot on to Wilmington, N. C., and southward down the beaches.

Both the seasoned pilot and the novice can find adventure "island-hopping" on the Outer Banks of coastal North Carolina. Normal precautions for cross-country flying and adherence to the advice from the operators at Elizabeth City, Manteo and Morehead City will prove sufficient for a safe journey into this world of fishing, swimming fun and unexcelled scenery. ◆

Fred Seitz and Dick Rodd at the Morehead City-Beaufort Airport are typical of the courteous operators in the Outer Banks area who are invaluable sources of good advice on "Banks flying." Their Coastair Service operates a regular run on the Banks

A modern twin taxis up to the ramp at Billy Mitchell field. Within a stone's throw are towns with quaint names such as Whalebone Junction, Frisco and Waves

By JANE MAHON

Fly And Hunt
In North Carolina

Good hunting is accessible on the Eastern Shore, even for the big-city dweller, if he flies a plane. In North Carolina, there is abundant hunting for many kinds of game. For information regarding seasons on game throughout North Carolina, you can write the North Carolina Wildlife Resources Commission, Box 2919, Raleigh, for "1964-65 Hunting & Trapping Regulations."

Now for the types of hunting:

GAME ANIMALS

The tidewater lowlands are reported to provide excellent deer hunting from the Dismal Swamp in the north to the Waccamaw area in the south. Raccoons are abundant in the tidewater area, and Dismal Swamp offers excellent bear hunting. Airports in the Dismal Swamp area are Elizabeth City Municipal and Edenton Municipal.

Dare county and the area surrounding Lake Mattamuskeet are good for hunting deer and bear. Airports serving Dare county are First Flight, Manteo and Billy Mitchell. The Mattamuskeet area is served by Mattamuskeet and Engelhard airports.

In the Sandhills, there is good hunting for deer. Grannis Field is in this area.

On the Piedmont, there is good deer shooting in the Uwharrie Wildlife Management area and in the hardwood forests located in the Camp Butner area. Raccoons are also found on the Piedmont. Albemarle Airport is in the Uwharrie Wildlife Management area, and Raleigh-Durham and Wilkins are in the Camp Butner area.

There is good hunting for bear in Washington, Tyrell, Craven, Columbus, Carteret and Gates counties. Airports are: Craven county, Simmons-Nott; Columbus county, Leggette, Rogers Field and Whiteville Municipal; Carteret county, Beaufort/Morehead City.

In western North Carolina, the best of the bear hunting is in Yancey, Haywood, Mitchell, McDowell, Caldwell, Avery, Swain and Graham counties. Wild boar is found in Graham, Clay and Cherokee counties. General aviation facilities in western North Carolina are Asheville Municipal, Asheville Airpark, Franklin and Sossamon airports, and Andrews-Murphy Air Park.

Opossum are fairly common throughout North Carolina.

Four organized fox hunts that are accessible by private plane are:

The Moore County Hounds, Southern Pines—fox and drag, three times a week with occasional bye days (Pinehurst-Southern Pines Airport).

The Sedgefield Hunt, Greensboro-High Point area—fox, twice a week (Hendersonville-Meyer Airport).

The Mecklenburg Hounds, Charlotte—fox and drag, twice a week (Brockenbrough Field, Carpenter and Douglas Municipal airports).

Triangle Hunt, Raleigh — drag, weekly (Raleigh-Durham and Raleigh Municipal airports).

Arrangements to participate in these hunts can be made through the Hunt Secretary or the Master of Hounds of each hunt.

GAME BIRDS

The best of the quail hunting is found in the counties that stretch from tidewater up to the lower Piedmont. The best dove hunting is supposed to be in approximately the same area, on the Coastal Plain above tidewater across the Piedmont to the foot of the mountains. Wild turkey is also found in this area. Washington Municipal and Mattamuskeet airports serve the area.

Some of the best grouse hunting is found in the southwest in Cherokee, Clay, Graham and Swain counties.

Canada geese and American brant provide the big bird shooting in North Carolina. The best of the duck hunting is in Currituck Sound and south down the coast along the inner side of the Outer Banks. Large flights of wild geese winter in these waters. The best brant shooting is along the Outer Banks in the Hatteras and Ocracoke areas. The small sora rail and the large king rail favor freshwater marshes like those of Currituck Sound.

The 50,000-acre Federal refuge at Mattamuskeet has two areas set aside for controlled shooting. Application forms for this can be obtained from the Wildlife Resources Commission, Box 2919, Raleigh, or from the office of the Protector, Mattamuskeet Wildfowl Refuge, New Holland.

Shooting on the Cape Hatteras National Seashore Park is regulated by the National Park Service. The office of the Park Superintendent, Manteo, can provide current details regarding guides, regulations and fees.

COMMERCIAL PRESERVES
FOR FOWL

The commercial shooting preserves release pen-raised but flight-trained ring-neck pheasants, chukar partridge, bob white and coturnix quail. Hunters pay a fee—usually $25 a day—to take a limit over a season that runs from the beginning of October to the end of March. Most of the public shooting preserves are located on the Piedmont section. A special hunting license good only on

State offers good facilities for the flying hunter. Most game areas easily accessible by lightplane

BELOW: *Quail hunting in the Sandhills. The best quail hunting is in the counties that stretch from tidewater up to the lower Piedmont*

ABOVE: *Waterfowl hunters on the North Carolina coast. Canada geese and American brant provide the big bird shooting in North Carolina*

BELOW: *Hunter poses with trophy at Mann's Harbor. The best of the bear hunting is in western North Carolina*

the Preserves is $5.25 for both residents and nonresidents. Preserves accessible by private plane include:

Greensboro — Bennett & Darden Game Farm, Box 6147 (Claiborne H. Darden), quail, chukar. Airports: Air Harbor, Greensboro-High Point.

Greenville—Pitt Game Bird Farm, Bethel Highway (M. F. Jolly), pheasants, chukar, quail. Airport: Pitt-Greenville.

Pinehurst — Pinehurst Shooting Preserve, Pinehurst, Inc., quail. Airport: Pinehurst-Southern Pines.

Raleigh — Raleigh-Durham Shooting Preserve, Rt. 6, Box 269A (Charles A. Smith), pheasants, chukar, quail, ducks. Airports: Raleigh-Durham, Raleigh Municipal.

Reidsville — Jones Brothers Game Farm, Rt. 6 (Ernest H. or James L. Jones), pheasants, chukar; Stony Creek Hunting Preserve,

Box 6 (M. J. Gilmore), pheasants, chukar, quail. Airport: Warf's.

Siler City—Chatham Game Bird Farm & Shooting Preserve, Box 83, pheasants, quail. Airports: Siler City, Gilmore No. 2.

MANAGED HUNTS

Managed hunts for deer, bear, boar, wild hogs, squirrel, grouse, raccoon, dove, quail, rabbit and fowl are conducted by the North Carolina Wildlife Resources Commission on 19 publicly owned areas from mountains to coast. All managed hunts are within the regular hunting seasons. There are special hunts for bow and arrow shooting as well as for hunters using firearms. Applications and complete information for the various types of hunts are available from the North Carolina Wildlife Resources Commission, P. O. Box 2919, Raleigh.

PACKAGE HUNTING

Package hunts accessible by lightplane include:

Currituck Sound — Walnut Island Lodge, Grandy, waterfowl.

Hatteras Island — John E. Herbert, Rodanthe, waterfowl.

Kitty Hawk—Walter D. Perry's Cherokee Inn, Kill Devil Hills, waterfowl.

Lake Mattamuskeet—Mattamuskeet Lodge, New Holland, waterfowl.

Marion—Lake Tahoma Steak House (W. B. Gibbs), U. S. 70 N.W., bear and deer hunts.

Here are some of the Airport facilities:
Air Harbor *(Winston-Salem Section), 6 mi N of Greensboro. Runway: 2,400 feet, sod. Fuel, major repairs, tiedown and transportation available. Hours attended: daylight.*

Albemarle *(Charlotte Sectional)*, 1 mi SE of Albemarle. Runway: 3,200 feet, sod. Fuel and minor repairs available. Hours attended: daylight, nights by prior request.

Andrews-Murphy Air Park *(Charlotte Sectional)*, 2 mi W of Andrews. Runway: 4,900 feet, sod. Fuel, hangar, minor repairs available. Hours attended: 8 a.m.-6 p.m.

Asheville Airpark *(Charlotte Sectional)*, 3 mi NW of Asheville. Runway: 1,800 feet, 800 feet paved, remainder sod. Fuel, repairs, hangar available. Hours attended: 24, 7 days.

Asheville Municipal *(Charlotte Sectional)*, 11 mi S of Asheville. Runway: 6,500 feet, asphalt. Fuel, hangars, tiedowns, major and minor repairs, restaurant and transportation available. Hours attended: 24.

Beaufort/Morehead City *(Norfolk Sectional)*, ½ mi NE of Beaufort/Morehead. Runways: three 4,200 feet, paved. Fuel, tiedowns, minor repairs, courtesy car available.

Billy Mitchell *(Norfolk Sectional)*, 3½ mi SW of Frisco. Runway: 2,400 feet, paved. Fuel, telephone available.

Brockenbrough Field *(Charlotte Sectional)*, 6 mi N of Charlotte. Runways: 2,600 and 1,500 feet, sod. Fuel, hangar, tiedowns, Unicom, major repairs available. Hours attended: daylight (owner's house on airport).

Carpenter *(Charlotte Sectional)*, 10 mi SW of Charlotte. Runways: two 3,000 feet, asphalt treated. Fuel and major repairs available. Hours attended: daylight, 7 days.

Colerain *(Norfolk Sectional)*, 2 mi S of Colerain. Runway: 2,800 feet, sod.

Douglas *(Charlotte Sectional)*, 5½ mi W of Charlotte. Runways: 7,500 feet, 5,000 feet, paved. Fuel, hangars, tiedowns, Unicom, and major and radio repairs available. Two-way radio required. Hours attended: 24.

Edenton Municipal *(Norfolk Sectional)*, 3 mi SE of Edenton. Runways: 3,200 and 4,800 feet, paved.

Elizabeth City Municipal *(Norfolk Sectional)*, 4 mi SW of Elizabeth City. Runways: 4,300, 4,300 and 2,800 feet, sod. Fuel and repairs available. Hours attended: daylight.

Engelhard *(Norfolk Sectional)*, ⅛ mi S of Engelhard. Runway: 2,000 feet, sod. Hours attended: daylight.

First Flight *(Norfolk Sectional)*, 1 mi W of Kitty Hawk. Runway: 3,000 feet, paved. Hours attended: park attendant at Wright Memorial, ½ mi NW.

Franklin *(Charlotte Sectional)*, ½ mi E of Franklin. Runway: 2,700 feet, sod. Fuel available. Hours attended: daylight.

Gilmore No. 2 *(Charlotte Sectional)*, 5 mi SE of Siler City. Runway: 3,300 feet, sod. Hours attended: none.

Grannis Field *(Charlotte Sectional)*, 4 mi S of Fayetteville. Runways: 5,005, 4,800 and 4,165 feet, paved. Fuel, hangar, repairs available. Hours attended: 24.

Greensboro-High Point *(Winston-Salem Sectional)*, 8 mi W of Greensboro. Runways: two 6,500 feet, paved. Fuel, hangar, tiedowns, major and minor repairs, Unicom available. Two-way radio required. Hours attended: 6:30 a.m.-11:30 p.m.

Halifax County *(Norfolk Sectional)*, 4 mi SW of Roanoke Rapids. Runways: two 3,000 feet, one paved, one sod. Fuel, hangar, minor repairs available. Hours attended: daylight (nights on request).

Harrington *(Norfolk Sectional)*, 2 mi SW of Lewiston. Runway: 4,800 feet, sod. Fuel available. Hours attended: irregular.

Hendersonville-Meyer *(Charlotte Sectional)*, 2 mi ESE of Hendersonville. Runway: 3,000 feet, sod. Fuel, hangar, repairs available. Hours attended: daylight.

Leggette *(Charlotte Sectional)*, 3 mi N of Tabor City. Runway: 3,000 feet, sod.

Manteo *(Norfolk Sectional)*, 1 mi NW of Manteo. Runways: three 3,300 feet, paved. Fuel, storage, tiedowns available. Hours attended: daylight, others on request.

Marion Field *(Charlotte Sectional)*, 2½ mi N of Marion. Runway: 3,600 feet, sod. Fuel available. Hours attended: none.

Martin *(Norfolk Sectional)*, 4 mi E of Severn, 4 mi N of Murfreesboro. Runway: 2,800 feet, sod.

Mattamuskeet *(Norfolk Sectional)*, ½ mi W of Fairfield. Runway: 3,600 feet, sod. Fuel, hangar available.

Pinehurst-Southern Pines *(Charlotte Sectional)*, 4 mi N of Pinehurst. Runways: 4,500 and 3,200 feet. Fuel, hangar and major repairs available. Hours attended: 8 a.m.-sunset.

Pitt-Greenville *(Norfolk Sectional)*, 2 mi NW of Greenville. Runways: three 5,000 feet, paved. Fuel, tiedowns available. Hours attended: daylight.

Raleigh-Durham *(Charlotte Sectional)*, 14 mi NW of Raleigh, 13 mi SW of Durham. Runways: 7,500, 4,500 and 4,500 feet, paved. Fuel, repairs, weather information, hangar, tiedowns, food, transportation available. Two-way radio required. Hours attended: 24, 7 days.

Raleigh Municipal *(Charlotte Sectional)*, 3 mi S of Raleigh. Runways: two 2,400 feet and one 1,900 feet, paved. Fuel, hangar, tiedown, transportation, minor repairs available. Hours attended: daylight.

Siler City *(Charlotte Sectional)*, 2 mi SW of Siler City. Runway: 3,000 feet.

Simmons-Nott *(Norfolk Sectional)*, 3 mi SE of New Bern. Runways: 4,807 and 4,000 feet, paved. Fuel, repairs, weather info, hangar available. Hours attended: 5 a.m.-7 p.m.

Sossamon Field *(Bryson City Municipal, Charlotte Sectional)*, ½ mi SW of Bryson City. Runway: 2,265 feet, sod. Fuel, hangar, tiedowns, minor repairs available. Hours attended: daylight.

Warf's *(Winston-Salem Sectional)*, 4 mi SW of Reidsville. Runway: 2,600 feet, sod. Fuel, hangar, major repairs available. Hours attended: daylight.

Washington Municipal *(Norfolk Sectional)*, 2 mi N of Washington. Runways: three 5,000 feet, concrete. Fuel hangar, tiedown, transportation, major and minor repairs available. Hours attended: 24.

Weyerhaeuser County *(Norfolk Sectional)*, 2 mi W of Plymouth. Runway: 2,500 feet, sod. Fuel, taxi, weather information available. Hours attended: daylight. Open by prior request.

Whiteville Municipal *(Charlotte Sectional)*, 3 mi S of Whiteville. Runway: 3,400 feet, sod. Fuel (80), tiedowns, weather information, charter service, taxi available.

Wilkins *(Winston-Salem Sectional)*, 6 mi NE of Durham. Runways: 3,200 and 2,600 feet, sod. Tiedowns, fuel available. Hours attended: 8:30 a.m.-dark.

◆

Like romantic little islands? There's one off Florida's Gulf Coast beyond the mainland at Fort Myers that may be just what you have in mind. It's called Sanibel Island, famous (in a quiet way) for its treasure of seashells which abound on the beaches, and also for the many forms of winged wildlife —roseate spoonbills, egrets, herons and hundreds of varieties of migrating birds which are found from month to month, varying with the seasons.

No lost colony of Atlantis this. Sanibel is easily accessible by water or air, but, in spite of its proximity, the island is never overcrowded with tourists even in the height of the winter season. Flying above San Carlos Bay, three miles from the Florida mainland you will see Sanibel Island as a vaguely shaped crescent, extending 14 miles from east to northwest. Near the eastern tip on the southern shore, you'll spot the island's only landing strip, owned and maintained by the Casa Ybel Hotel but open to all. Turf surfaced, the strip is 2,600 feet long, running east-west with clear approaches. Like all turf strips, this one is rather difficult to see from the air and for better recognition it is outlined by rows of white rocks. Gasoline (80 octane) is available. Two-way radio is required.

At the east end of Sanibel strip a taxiway turns off to the right and leads to a small parking area where limited tiedowns are provided. If you stay in one of Casa Ybel's several beach cottages, you can taxi right up to the rear of the cabins and tie down.

Natives like to speculate on the reason for the island's bounty of shells—about 400 varieties in all. They say it's because Sanibel lies east-west while most islands run north-south. Thus, so the story goes, great masses of shells are washed up on the island's northern and southern shores with every tide. Whatever the reason, collectors are delighted at the result, and you'll find that, no matter how great your indifference is now, before a day is out at Sanibel you too will be out combing the beaches for specimens that cannot be found anywhere else along our coasts. Junonias, angel's wings, pear conches, pectins, and spiney rock oysters are a euphonious few of the species you're likely to find.

Winter vagabonds find relaxation in a tropical setting at this Florida offshore island

Sanibel Island

One of the highlights of the year is the annual Seashell Fair in March at which collectors show their rare and exotic specimens, and a live exhibit of unusual deep-sea animals is presented. The event has been covered in many national magazines.

If fishing rather than shells is your forte, Sanibel can accommodate you. In late fall the great kingfish move southward and prove to be great sport in Sanibel offshore waters. The fighting champ of the Gulf, the tarpon, will also provide some stiff competition. Surf fishing usually is quite good for trout and mackerel. Boats for fishing, water skiing and skin diving are available at Casa Ybel's own docks.

It's been said that birds are more populous than people on Sanibel Island. They're seen everywhere—along the shore, on the water, in the air, in rookeries. There is a national wildlife refuge of 2,685 acres in the middle of the island, established to provide a winter habitat for migrating ducks and other birds at the southern end of the Atlantic flyway. In summer it is a nesting site for mottled ducks, black-necked stilts and gallinules as well as the more common herons, egrets, anhingas and pelicans. There is an observation tower in the refuge where visitors equipped with binoculars are known to spend hours watching the birds.

Accommodations on Sanibel vary from cabins to motels to hotels, all of which are good but not too numerous. Casa Ybel, one of the largest, can accommodate about 100 people in its cottages. Most of them are air-conditioned and have kitchens and screened porches. They vary in size and have from one to five bedrooms. In the center of the cottage colony is Ybel Lodge with a spacious guest lobby, dining room, cocktail lounge and shops of all kinds.

As usual, the AOPA Flight and Travel Department can handle flight planning and reservations for you, making the whole trip as carefree as possible. If you're suffering from winter doldrums (February being most conducive to this malady), now is a good time to gas up the plane and head south. ◆

Casa Ybel Hotel has ocean in front and 2,600-foot landing strip behind. Taxi strip (right) leads from strip to small parking area behind hotel

From the air Sanibel Island looks like a giant crescent, 14 miles long. Its eastern point (shown in photo) is only three miles from Florida mainland

PHOTO BY HANS GROENHOFF

PHOTO BY KENNETH E. CHELLIS

AOPA Flight Department publishes a
report on Florida attractions, written
especially for the vacationer who flies

The
Sunshine State

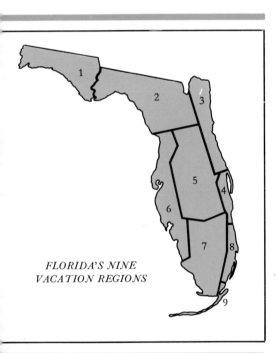

*FLORIDA'S NINE
VACATION REGIONS*

If a poll were taken among AOPA's members to determine the most popular vacation area in the United States, it's a sure bet that Florida would be at—or at least near—the top of the list. AOPA's Flight Department tallied nearly 1,500 requests for information and flight routing to the Sunshine State last year [1960], a factor which prompted the department staff to prepare a special report on the state's attractions written especially for the tourist traveling by private plane. Called "A Flying Vacation to Florida," the report is available to any AOPA member who requests it. (Report updated in 1965.—Ed.)

The following lists a few of the resorts covered in the Flight Department report divided into regions (see map). Recommended airports appear at the end of each listing. The Flight Department credits the Florida Development Commission and its Aviation Department for help in compiling extensive information on the resorts and their nearby airports. For further information on airports, consult the Mobile, Jacksonville, Orlando and Miami sectional charts and the AOPA Airport Directory.

REGION 1: Northwest Florida
Pensacola. A Gulf port, Pensacola has one of the nation's finest natural harbors. You will find the waterfront interesting, especially when ships of the red snapper fleet are in port. Things to see: U.S. Naval Air Station, ruins of Fort San Carlos and Fort Barrancas, Pensacola Beach on Santa Rosa Island for yachting, sailing, water skiing, swimming, Greyhound racing from May to September. Pensacola Municipal Airport.

Marianna. Three miles north is Florida Caverns State Park which contains Florida's largest cave as well as a golf course, picnic and camping facilities. Marianna Municipal.

Panama City. Famous for both fresh-water and salt-water fishing. Nearby is St. Andrews State Park, and "back country" hunting territory. Sailing races June to September. Fannin Field.

REGION 2: North Florida
Tallahassee. The State capital, home of Florida State University. Things to see: Capitol Center composed of government buildings, Killearn Gardens State Park. Tallahassee Commercial and Tallahassee Municipal.

Chattahoochee. On the Apalachicola River at the Georgia border, it is near the Jim Woodruff Dam which backs up waters of two converging rivers to form a 37,500-acre lake; boating, fishing and camping areas. Chattahoochee Airport two miles NE (no services).

Apalachicola National Forest. Largest of the Florida national forests, the area abounds in wildlife including black bear and panther; excellent fishing. Has several recreational areas, largest of which is Silver Lake Recreation Area. Apalachicola Municipal Airport.

REGION 3: Upper East Coast
St. Augustine. Oldest permanent settlement in the United States, founded in 1565. Churches dating from the 18th century and narrow streets lined with typically Spanish houses are highlights. Fairchild Airport.

Daytona Beach. Florida's only year-round resort. Ocean-front accommodations located along the "Cinderella Strip" on the new South Atlantic Ave., away from congested and overcrowded areas. Speed records for automobiles have been made on famous Ormond-Daytona Beach, 23 miles long by 500 feet wide. Daytona Beach Municipal Airport.

REGION 4: Indian River Region
Jensen Beach. Attractions include a protected ocean beach and river for fishing and bathing. Spectacular sight is watching giant sea turtles weighing up to 2,000 pounds crawl out of the ocean after dark to lay their eggs. Witham Field.

Stuart. Southern terminus of Indian River located here. Important as a commercial fishing and sport fishing center; House of Refuge Museum perpetuates the seafaring and life-saving lore of the locality. Witham Field.

REGION 5: Central Florida
Silver Springs. (See photo.) Principal at-

traction is glass-bottomed boat ride over pools of 14 groups of springs filled with hundreds of plant varieties and 25 different species of fish. Silver Springs Airpark.

Lake Apopka. State's second largest freshwater lake, good for bass. Rustic cypress cottages overlook lake; fishing, boats, guides available. McDonald Field.

Kissimmee. Commercial center of the Kissimmee Valley, Florida's cow country. Annual rodeos are popular, "Boatacade" is held annually in October, good hunting and fishing on Kissimmee River. Kissimmee Municipal Airport.

Lake Wales. Home of the Mountain Lake Sanctuary and Singing Tower as well as "Spook Hill." Tower provides carillon selections on the hour. "Spook Hill," where parked cars appear to roll uphill, attracts many tourists. Lake Wales Municipal Airport.

REGION 6: West Coast

Venice. Located on Manasota Key, the city boasts relaxation in a tropical atmosphere as its main claim to fame, and features one of the most beautiful beaches on the west coast of Florida. Restaurants, shopping facilities and golf courses are nearby. Venice Municipal Airport.

St. Petersburg. Bordered on three sides by water, the city offers facilities for every type of outdoor activity. Waterfront Park contains a municipal pier jutting 2,400 feet into the bay, a solarium, swimming pool, bathing beach and three yacht basins. To the west, the Holiday Isles offer five fine beach resorts. Two major league teams—the St. Louis Cardinals and New York Yankees—train here in the spring, there are Greyhound races December to April, and the St. Petersburg to Havana International Yacht Race in March. St. Petersburg-Clearwater International Airport, Albert Whitted Municipal.

Tampa. (See photo.) Florida's busiest port and commercial center plays host annually to the Florida State Fair held in midwinter. One of the features of the fair is the Gasparilla Festival, named in honor of the legendary pirate Jose Gaspar. Tampa International Airport, Vandenberg and Peter O. Knight.

Naples. Renowned for fishing, Naples' municipal pier extends 1,000 feet into the Gulf of Mexico where anglers catch snapper, sheepshead, grouper and multiple other varieties. Caribbean Gardens is high on sightseers' lists—tropical trees, plants and flowers gathered from all over the world are found here. Naples Municipal Airport.

REGION 7: The Everglades

Everglades National Park. Many species of rare birds, tropical flora, game fish and broad mangrove forests are found in this, the largest remaining subtropical wilderness in the United States. From the Royal Palm Ranger Station near the park entrance a road leads through the park 30 miles to Flamingo on Florida Bay. The Tamiami Trail skirts the northern border. Accommodations include a 60-room motel with restaurant as well as 54 campsites. Everglades City Airport lies at the western side of the park, Miami International and Tamiami Airports can be used when entering from the eastern side.

REGION 8: Lower East Coast

West Palm Beach. Metropolitan hub of a resort area which extends 40 miles up and down the coast. Miles of protected waterways provide yachting, cruising, racing and fishing; one of the most popular events of the year is the Silver Sailfish Derby held in late January and early February. Several fine beaches are conveniently at hand across Lake Worth. Norton Gallery, an art museum, has a notable collection of rare jade. Palm Beach with its impressive array of luxurious winter estates is connected by a causeway. Palm Beach International Airport.

Fort Lauderdale. A city of islands, bays, canals and inlets with more than 150 miles of waterways. Fishing, sightseeing by boat, swimming at superb public beaches, and a great variety of after-dark activities attract the tourist. Fort Lauderdale-Hollywood International, Ft. Lauderdale Executive and Bradley Field (latest report 1962).

Miami and Miami Beach. Twin, but separate, cities on Biscayne Bay where the principal business is still entertaining tourists. Swimming at six municipal facilities, fishing (Metropolitan Miami Fishing Tournament held from mid-December to mid-April), horse- and greyhound racing, golfing at 12 courses in the area are popular pastimes; there's a wide range of night clubs for after-dark amusement. Sightseeing attractions include the Fairchild Tropical Garden, Miami Serpentarium, the Monkey Jungle, Musa Isle, Seminole Indian village and the Seaquarium featuring performing porpoises and sea lions. Miami International Airport.

REGION 9: The Florida Keys

Key Largo. The first and largest key in the chain contains several resorts, among them the Ocean Reef Club and Yacht Harbor which has its own airport.

Tavernier. Named for a pirate, this popular fishing resort on Key Largo is a reminder that pirates once flourished in these parts. Skin divers still hunt for treasure presumably buried in the Keys. Seven miles west of Tavernier, near Islamorada, is the Theater of the Sea, a display of porpoises, sea turtles, sharks, etc.

Key West. Tourism, sports fishing, commercial fishing and the U.S. Navy installation provide the principal sources of income for this tropical island. Streets are narrow and the pace is slow in the city where the Spanish language is still heard. The Conch Train Tour provides a pleasant way to see the sights of Key West, among them the U.S. Naval Station, the Municipal Aquarium and the Key West Lighthouse. Swimming is a year-round activity, for Key West is said to be the only frost-free city in the United States. Key West International Airport. ◆

Looking west over Silver Springs, one can see the 3,000-foot sod runway of Silver Springs Airpark. Field provides 80 octane fuel, tiedowns and transportation to and from motels, according to operator John Henderson. Note glass-bottom boats on marina in foreground MOZERT PHOTO

Coastal Aviation, Inc., fixed-base operation at Tampa International Airport, maintains this modern terminal building for private and executive pilots. Building is equipped with pilots' lounge, snack bar, briefing room and weather teletype machine

A subtropical island off the South Carolina coast offers air travelers the rare treat of an unspoiled Deep South paradise—miles of virtually deserted beach, hunting, fishing, swimming, golfing and luxury motel accommodations, all within 12 minutes (and free transportation) of a 3,000-foot airstrip.

The island is Hilton Head. It is separated from the Carolina mainland by Skull Creek, bounded on the east by the Atlantic Ocean and on the north by Port Royal and Calibogue Sounds. It is a 30,000-acre wonderland, a virtual jungle of sabal palms, towering oaks, pines and magnolias, inhabited principally by pheasant, quail, chukar (a swift-darting bird imported from India), deer, wild pigs and occasionally sleepy alligators.

There is little to do on Hilton Head but enjoy yourself.

The Sea Pines Plantation has carved out of the edge of the jungle room for a motel (the William Hilton Inn) and a golf course designed by the man who made President Eisenhower happy at the Augusta National, home of the Masters. There's all the oceanside or woodland recreation you could ask for.

Hilton Head Island has been described as a sports-oriented retreat which, because not too many have found out about it yet, is virtually an "island Rip Van Winkle," slowly awakening from a long, deep slumber.

The fact is that Hilton Head Island is as old as nature, and yet new. The island's fantastic history goes back thousands of years. But its development is new. The chamber of commerce says the first settlers (Indians) date back at least 4,000 years. Two ceremonial shell rings, still evident, are said to date back 3,800 years, about 800 years before work started on the Great Pyramid of Egypt.

More recently, Spain landed two explorers on the island—eight years after Ponce de Leon discovered the Fountain of Youth at St. Augustine, Fla. It is said that at least two fabulous treasures were buried on the island. If they have ever been found, history has not recorded the event.

The island got its name from William Hilton, 17th century English explorer who returned to his native land and reported of the island with exuberance:

"The air is clear and sweet, the country very pleasant and delightful, and we could wish that all they of our English Nation, who wish a happy settlement, were well transported thither."

At that time the only way to Hilton Head Island was by boat, and so it remained until 1953, when a car ferry was put into operation. A bridge followed, in 1956, and the island became more accessible.

But still it has not become accessible enough to be spoiled by the onrush.

A major development on the island of recent vintage is the Sea Pines Plantation, which operates the William Hilton Inn and the golf course. The course was designed by George Cobb, a consultant for the Augusta National, and he insisted, in the developing process, on a first-class course. The course is famous for its 15th green, a built-up point overlooking the blue Atlantic. Other greens jut into a virtual jungle of palms, oaks and pines. Golfers are subjected to an unusual hazard, albeit a minor one—alligators. The sleepy creatures simply lie on the banks and behave themselves. A sign implores: "Do not molest alligators; be careful of deer crossing

road." There is no precedent for alligators molesting golfers.

The Sea Pines Plantation plans within a year to have constructed two criss-crossing, 4,500-foot paved runways for private air travelers.

Meanwhile, there is a 3,000-foot turf strip on the north end of the island. This strip is on the Savannah Sectional, and is maintained by the South Carolina Aeronautics Commission. It is fenced in and has landing lights, but night landings are not recommended. (Savannah, with jet runways, is only 30 miles away.) There is a windsock, tiedown space,

and free telephone. A call to the William Hilton Inn will bring free transportation. The strip is unattended and has no fuel.

Rates at the Inn, for modified American plan which includes breakfast and dinner, are $20 to $24 double during the winter (November through February) and $31 to $35 during the remainder of the year. The Inn offers a "special golf week" for those who love the links—special rates for a week on the modified American plan with unlimited golf on the Sea Pines course during the period. There are 80 rooms and reservations are necessary.

◆

A Cessna Skylane comes in for a landing at Hilton Head's turf airstrip. The field's windsock is at right. Although the strip has boundary lights (at left of windsock), night landings are not recommended

PHOTO BY FREDERICK C. BALDWIN

PHOTO BY FRANK J. MILLER

ABOVE *The William Hilton Inn, located right on the oceanfront, offers free pickup from the airstrip, just 12 minutes away*
RIGHT *The 15th green of the Sea Pines Plantation's golf course is on a built-up point overlooking the Atlantic Ocean. Hilton Head golfers are apt to run into an unusual hazard on the course—alligators. There's never been any trouble with the gators bothering the golfers; in fact, a sign on the course reads: "Do not molest alligators"*

Fly 'Where The Air Is Clear and Sweet'

Hilton Head, a sleepy little island just off the coast of South Carolina, has hotel and motel accommodations, a first-class golf course and a 3,000-turf strip on the north end of the island

Fly And Play Golf In
GEORGIA

Georgia and golf are closely connected in the minds of many because of the famed Master's Tournament in Augusta. The Master's is one of the major tournaments of the world for golfers. In fact, practically all of the foremost golfers of the last 20 or 30 years have played in it. Golf fans come from all over the country to watch it. Enthusiasts who want to fly to the event will find good terminal facilities at Augusta's two airports, Bush Field and Daniel Field, both on the Savannah Sectional.

Bush Field, seven miles south of Augusta, has two asphalt runways, one 8,000 feet in length and the other 5,300 feet. Services available are fuel, ground transportation, minor repairs, beacon and runway lights, weather information, Unicom, hangars and tiedowns. Two-way radio is required. The airport is

attended 24 hours a day. Daniel Field, in western Augusta, has two 4,100-foot asphalt runways. Here available services include fuel, ground transportation, major repairs, runway lights, weather information, Unicom, hangars, tiedowns. Hours attended are 7 a.m. to 7 p.m.

The golfer can play at a large number of good courses throughout Georgia before or after watching the Master's. For these flying enthusiasts, information on some of these courses, starting in the north and working southward, is given below.

Cleveland
Skitt Mountain Golf and Country Club, seven miles south of the city on U.S. 129, is a 6,385-yard, 18-hole course with regular USGA holes. It is reported to be in excellent

condition. The club has a swimming pool, bowling alleys, free picnic tables and free fishing.

Gainesville
Chattahoochee Golf Club is on Tommy Aaron Drive, one block off State Highway 60 and five miles north of downtown. It's a 6,461-yard, 18-hole course, and caddies, bag carts, electric carts, rental equipment and locker facilities are available.

Atlanta
Bobby Jones Municipal Golf Course at 384 Woodward Way, N.W., is an 18-hole, 6,300-yard course. It is reported to be tough and hilly. A creek has to be crossed five times. John A. White Golf Course at 1053 Cascade Circle, S.W., is a 3,193-yard, nine-hole course

PHOTO BY BOOKMAN'S STUDIO

PHOTO BY GEORGIA DEPARTMENT OF INDUSTRY & TRADE

ABOVE *Golf is free for motel guests at Jekyll Island, beach resort off the coast at Brunswick, Ga. Many of the holes overlook the Atlantic Ocean*
LEFT *Valdosta Country Club has an 18-hole golf course. Several tournaments are held during the year. Adjacent to the golf course is a club swimming pool*

and is reported to be one of the toughest nine-hole courses in the state.

Washington
Washington-Wilkes Country Club, 4 miles east of the city, is a nine-hole, 3,300-yard course. Caddies are available. There's a 16-acre lake with a sandy beach and a club house.

Griffin
Griffin Municipal Golf Course in the city park is an 18-hole course which reportedly is kept in excellent condition the year around.

Pine Mountain
Callaway Gardens Golf Course, an 18-hole, 5,982-yard course, is reported to be an exceptionally fine course noted for its excellent year-around condition, wide fairways and minimum of rough. A man-made island tee on the ninth hole makes for a shot across a lake. Callaway Gardens is a resort, and you can stay there as long as you want to enjoy the golfing and other recreations.

Blakely
Town and Country Club, two miles south of town on Highway 27, reportedly is a well-kept and very interesting course. Holes 7, 8 and 9 play across, and by, a lake.

Albany
American Legion Golf Course in Albany is a 2,900-yard, nine-hole course, privately owned but played as a daily fee course. Radium Springs Country Club on U.S. 19 has a 6,125-yard, 18-hole course.

Tifton
Tifton Country Club, a 3,250-yard, nine-hole course, is four miles southeast of town. It is open every day the year around and welcomes tourists.

Douglas
Douglas Golf Club, a 3,136-yard, nine-hole course, is reported to be one of the best nine-hole courses to be found. It is a rolling course with a lake hazard, sand traps around each

green and available electric golf carts and caddies.

Cairo
Cairo Country Club, northwest of the city limits, has a 6,800-yard, 18-hole championship course with a PGA listing. A swimming pool, 16-acre lake and club house are available to the tourist golfer.

Thomasville
Glen Arven Country Club has an 18-hole, 6,350-yard course.

Valdosta
Valdosta Country Club, north of the city on U.S. 41, has a 6,500-yard, 18-hole course. Greens and fairways are maintained throughout the year. The course has two well-trapped lake holes. There's a pro shop and locker-room facilities. The Jack Oliver Tournament is held there annually on Labor Day weekend.

Jekyll Island
Jekyll Island Golf Club, a 3,300-yard, nine-hole course, is reported to be one of the finest nine-hole dune courses in the world. An 18-hole course is reported to be under construction. Jekyll Island is a year-around beach resort where you can also swim, fish and relax.

Here are some of the airport facilities available to pilots visiting.

Albany — *Albany Municipal (Mobile Sectional), 4 mi. SW of city. Runways: 3 asphalt, 4,900, 5,000 and 3,600 feet. Services available: fuel, taxi, beacon and runway lights, weather, Unicom, hangars, tiedowns. Hours attended: daylight.*

Atlanta—*Atlanta (Birmingham Sectional), 8 mi. S of city. Runways: 3 asphalt, 5,505, 7,860 and 7,220 feet. Services available: fuel, major and minor repairs, beacon and runway lights, weather, Unicom. Two-way radio required. Hours attended: 24.*

Atlanta — *DeKalb-Peachtree (Birmingham Sectional), 8 mi. NE of city. Runways: 3 asphalt, 4,000, 3,750 and 3,400 feet. Services*

available: fuel, courtesy car, taxi, rental cars, major and minor repairs, beacon and runway lights, weather, Unicom, hangars and tiedowns. Two-way radio required unless waived by prior permission. Hours attended: 24.

Atlanta—*Fulton County (Birmingham Sectional), 7 mi. W of city. Runways: 5,200- and 4,000-foot asphalt, 2,632-foot sod. Services available: fuel, major repairs, bus, taxi, car rentals, beacon and runway lights, weather, Unicom, hangars and tiedowns. Hours attended: 7 a.m. to 11 p.m.*

Blakely — *Early County (Mobile Sectional), 2 mi. SE of city. Runways: two 2,050-foot turf. Services available: fuel, minor repairs, tiedowns. Hours attended: irregular.*

Cairo — *Cairo-Grady County (Birmingham Sectional), 3¼ mi. NE of city. Runways: 2 2,100-foot turf. Hours attended: none.*

Cleveland — *White County (Charlotte Sectional), 3 mi. SE of city. Runway: 2,400-foot sod. Services available: tiedowns. Hours attended: none.*

Douglas — *Douglas Municipal (Jacksonville Sectional), 2 mi. S of city. Runway: 3,500-foot asphalt. Services available: fuel, runway lights, hangar and tiedowns. Hours attended: irregular.*

Gainesville — *Gainesville Municipal (Charlotte Sectional), 1 mi. SW of city. Runways: 2 4,000-foot asphalt. Services available: fuel, courtesy car, taxi, minor repairs, beacon and runway lights, Unicom, tiedowns. Hours attended: daylight.*

Griffin—*Griffin-Spalding County (Birmingham Sectional), 1 mi. S of city. Runways: 3,300-foot asphalt, 2,200-foot sod. Services available: fuel, courtesy car, major and minor repairs, beacon and runway lights, weather info, Unicom, hangars and tiedowns. Hours attended: 8 a.m.-dark.*

Jekyll Island *(Jacksonville Sectional), on W side of island, 6 mi. SE of Brunswick. Runway: 1,900-foot turf. Services available: courtesy car, weather, tiedowns. Hours attended: none.*

Pine Mountain—*Callaway Gardens (Birmingham Sectional), 2 mi. S of city, 30 mi. N of Columbus and 85 mi. SW of Atlanta. Runway: 3,100-foot sod. Services available: fuel, courtesy car, beacon and runway lights, Unicom, hangars and tiedowns. Hours attended: on call.*

Thomasville—*Thomasville Municipal (Jacksonville Sectional), 7 mi. NE of city. Runways: 2 5,000-foot asphalt. Services available: fuel, courtesy car, taxi, major repairs, beacon, runway lights (on request until 10 p.m.), weather, Unicom, hangars and tiedowns. Hours attended: 24.*

Tifton—*Henry Tift Myers (Jacksonville Sectional), 1 mi. SE of city. Runway: 3 5,000-foot asphalt. Services available: fuel, courtesy car, rental car, major repairs, beacon and runway lights, hangars and tiedowns. Hours attended: 8 a.m.-dark (on call 24 hours).*

Valdosta—*Valdosta Municipal (Jacksonville Sectional), 3 mi. S of city. Runways: 4 asphalt, 4,644, 4,120, 5,600 and 4,500 feet. Services available: fuel, taxi, minor repairs, beacon and runway lights, weather, Unicom, tiedowns. Hours attended: 8 a.m.-6 p.m.*

Washington — *Washington-Wilkes County (Savannah Sectional), 5 mi. NW of city. Runway: 3,400-foot asphalt. Hours attended: none.* ◆

Master's Course in Augusta, Ga., site of the Master's Tournament (which was played April 8-11 in 1965). The Master's is an invitational tournament sponsored by a private organization, but golf fans come from all over the country to watch it

By BEN H. RYAN, JR. | *AOPA 82882*

Dog Island was a detour for Gladys and Ben Ryan this time, but it won't be next time

Dog Island, Florida

Our first encounter with Dog Island was a small advertisement in the PILOT early in the spring of 1963. The island airstrip situated in the Gulf of Mexico sounded intriguing enough for us to send for more information.

By the time the literature arrived, the urge to take a long cross-country in our new Mooney was almost unbearable. One thing after another delayed our embarking, however, until late in October. Better late than never, though, so, after putting in for vacation, we waited patiently for the September PILOT and its AOPA Weathercast, flying the route a hundred times on the charts in the meantime.

From previous experience we knew this area would be cool at this time of year, so we picked Miami as our ultimate destination, with a short detour for a few days to see what Dog Island was really like.

Anyway, the forecast looked favorable—our first encouragement in months.

The day of departure arrived with a big blue sky dotted with scattered puffs of fleecy white clouds—VFR all the way to our first stop, Huntsville, Ala.

After two delightful days seeing the sights around Huntsville, hosted by our friends the Jim Keats, we took off bright and early Monday morning for Dog Island.

Our flight plan was VFR Huntsville to Montgomery to Dothan to Teresa Intersection via V7W. Flying south of Dothan we experienced the famous "automatic rough" in the engine as we flew over swamps for the first time. Then, at 7,500 feet, coming up on Teresa, there off our right wing was Dog Island, Fla., shimmering in calm blue waters and bright sunshine, just as advertised.

Since Gladys is quite squeamish flying over water, and I had enough automatic rough for awhile, we descended, following the coast to the west until we were over the tiny fishing village of Carrabelle, Fla. Here we swung out over St. George Sound to look for our landing strip.

If you want to see some of the most beautiful natural beaches in the world, this is the place. The sand is so white it first looks like snow. The sun, reflecting off the floor of the gulf, enhances the contrast of blues, greens

Aircraft parking and tiedown area at end of 2,800-foot sod strip at Dog Island, Fla., is adjacent to mainland ferry slip and small boat docks

LEFT: *Calm, blue waters and facilities for water sports bring many boaters as well as flyers to Dog Island, off the Florida coast*

RIGHT: *An hour's ferry ride from Carrabelle, Fla., lies Dog Island, seen here on the horizon. The 1,800-acre island has its own flight strip and is reportedly an ideal retreat for those who want to get away from it all for a few days*

and whites to present scenery equal to that of the most famous beaches of the world.

We came in over the strip at about 3,500 feet, continued our descent, turned west to see a little more of the island, and then went back across the strip again at about 500 feet to examine the runway.

The runway is 2,800 feet long, running north and south. Soil was dug from a nearby lagoon and spread on the runway during construction to provide a firmer surface than just sand would afford. There's a power line running along toward the south end of the runway, but it is very thoughtfully buried where it crosses the approach. We later learned that a few pilots have complained about these wires, after failing to notice the section that's buried.

Sure enough! Upon taxiing to the parking area and spotting some tiedown ropes, we no sooner cut the switches than an unshaven beachcomber, wearing khaki shorts and G.I. shoes, hopped out of a Volkswagen truck, stuck out a big fist and welcomed us to Dog Island. This was our first meeting with Jeff Lewis, ex-Air Corps pilot, ex-flying school operator, ex-bank vice president, and currently president of the Dog Island Company.

Since this area of Florida is mainly a summer resort, Gladys and I were two of only nine people on the 1,800-acre island. This, however, added to the excitement of "discovering" a new and mysterious island hideaway. The solitude reminded us of one of those movie thrillers that take place on an island deserted in the off season.

Jeff quickly had our Mooney tied down and our bags on the truck and was driving down a white, sandy, pine-tree-bordered lane toward the Hut. The Hut is a quonset-type building which is situated about 50 feet from the surf and serves as a snack bar, general store, post office, dance pavilion and general island headquarters.

To the east and still on the beach sits a new eight-unit apartment house—and here was another pleasant surprise. Since we had our choice of all eight, we chose an apartment on the second floor for a better view of the surroundings. Inside, everything was brand new and tastefully decorated. The kitchen was equipped with new G.E. appli-ances and a breakfast bar. A heat pump was provided for either heating or air conditioning, and there was a balcony outside the sliding glass window wall. The view of the gulf and beach from this tiny balcony was very imposing.

While we got acquainted with the apartment, Jeff primed the pump to activate the water system and turned on the hot water heater (for the wrong apartment, as it turned out). Later, we met at the Hut to purchase some supplies. The variety was limited because of its being the slow season, but we had missed lunch and were not too fussy at that particular moment. As a matter of fact, soup, baked beans and hamburgers washed down by a cold beer, with the surf off the balcony for dinner music—all after a pleasant day of flying—well, I can recall more elegant meals that I have enjoyed much, much less.

The next morning broke bright and clear. Although it was too cool for swimming, we enjoyed exploring the beach, taking pictures and gathering shells, found here in abundance. Further back from the beach, the pine trees yielded huge cones for our Christmas decorations. The fishing is said to be good, both in the surf and the sound, but our lack of equipment forced us to forego this pleasure.

Around noon, Jeff was going into Carrabelle via his Volkswagen and the ferry, so he invited us to go along. The 25¢ ride takes about an hour, and, since it was windy and cool with spray blowing, we sat with Jeff in the truck. Here he found time to talk not only about the background of the island but about himself as well.

This is a fellow who has done what probably every man in the world has dreamed of. He gave up the rat race, bought an island, and made a brand new career for himself doing as he pleases. Being a banker myself, I had a difficult time concealing my envy by the time the ferry docked.

In Carrabelle, Jeff dropped us off at a little cafe where we lunched on some excellent crabmeat. Later we walked around town, took a few pictures, and worked our way to the docks to catch the last trip back.

Once on the Island again, we strolled over to the Hut for a few more supplies and to make arrangements for some 100 octane gas.

Both 80 and 100 octane are available, despite the fact that the Airman's Guide Directory of Airports says otherwise (must get that AOPA edition).

As we topped the tanks, the crisp, cool evening descended upon us, and a big, round moon rose out of the gulf. We made our way back to our quarters to finish off the remaining supplies and retire early. Believe me, that's not at all difficult to do after spending the day outdoors in bright sunshine and the sea air. I was unconscious the moment my head touched the pillow, with the sound of the surf outside and the pleasant expectation of good flying weather in the morning.

After a light breakfast the next day, we gathered our things together and were transported back the short distance to our airplane. Since 87 X-ray had stood outside for a day with a couple of empty tanks and since we were not too sure about the possibility of water from the fuel truck, we took some extra time in draining all sumps. Our fears were unfounded, however, so we finished our walkaround inspection and hopped in. The engine runup was completed while taxiing out to the runway, as the surface is quite sandy.

For practice and insurance, we did a soft field takeoff. In order not to suck up a lot of sand with the prop, we didn't hold the brakes for full power, but we soon had 60 m.p.h. IAS, dropped full flaps, eased back on the yoke, and left the turf. The runway surface is as good as any grass strip I've seen, and unless they've flown on nothing but long paved runways, most pilots would have no problem at all with Dog Island.

Swinging around to the right, and climbing over the eastern end of the island, we saw the outline of a championship golf course in the making. Then, after circling out over the sound, and waving to a couple of shrimp boats inbound from a night's work, we ran out of excuses to linger any longer. Back to the business of filing our flight plan with Tallahassee radio, and on to Miami.

Maybe it's just the wind and snow outside, but we're ready to go back on a moment's notice. Dog Island isn't as we expected it to be—and that's why we're hoping to get back—but it won't be just a detour next time.

◆

BIG SPRING
STATE PARK

By BILL E. BURK | *AOPA 161522*

Got a weekend or a vacation you'd like to spend flying somewhere away from it all and spend next to nothing doing it? Then get out your Tulsa Sectional and head for the Ozarks—to be precise, the airport at Big Spring State Park, three miles south of Van Buren, Mo.

Big Spring is Missouri's only state park with an airport. It was put there on a trial basis as the result of much urging by the Swamp Angels, a Southeast Missouri pilots' club. One of the Swamp Angels, Roy Radford, a fixed-base operator at Popular Bluff, Mo., donated a lot of his own time in clearing the approaches.

The Big Spring Airport is located in a spectacularly beautiful natural setting. An approach from the north takes you down a wide valley, with rising hills on both sides and the crystal-clear Current River below. Some 800 feet below a high hill to the east, the Big Spring airport is nestled on the west bank of the river.

The ride from the airport through Big Spring State Park is exciting. You are surrounded by the river on the left side of the road and by high hills of virgin timber on the right. An occasional boat motors downstream. Now and then you see the famous Current River float boats, filled with people, speeding down the stream. Rates on these sightseeing trips are surprisingly low.

Big Spring has everything for the flyer who wants to shuck it all, even for just a weekend. It's only a short hop from Memphis, Little Rock, Kansas City or St. Louis. It has a large public lodge with a restaurant overlooking the beautiful river. It has Big Spring, largest in the U. S., pumping 864 million gallons of ice-cold water a day—seemingly right out of the ground. It has a tent area and low-cost lodges rent for $3 a day and up. There is a playground for children; a museum for the family; and plenty of bass and bream for the sportsman.

My wife and I spent four days and three nights at Big Spring and our total lodge and dining bill was $22.50, including souvenir T-shirts we bought the boys. The most wonderful thing about it all is that there are no telephones in the lodges.

When the airport was first opened in 1961, ground transportation was a drawback. This has been worked out by lodge concessionaire E. B. Newton.

All you have to do is circle over the lodge, a half-mile south of the airport, and a car will be waiting at the strip when you land. If, by some chance, this fails, passing motorists—and there are many between March and November—are usually glad to give pilots a ride. If you intend to get a lodge, however, it's best to make reservations in advance.

The sod strip is 2,400 feet long, 200 feet wide, runs north-south, and has good, clear approaches at both ends.

The popularity generated by the airport at Big Spring has pushed Joseph H. Frets, Missouri's airport commissioner, to ask for more airports in the state's colorful Ozark playgrounds. ◆

Missouri's only state park with an airstrip, Big Spring is located in the Ozarks on the banks of the Current River. The park's lodges rent for as little as $3 a day

ABOVE *The 2,400-foot airport at Big Spring State Park, about three miles from Van Buren, Mo. The strip is on the Tulsa Sectional*

BELOW *Big Spring's restaurant is located in this public lodge overlooking the Current River*

MISSOURI'S
Lake OF THE
Ozarks

Huge, dragon-shaped lake is a boating and fishing paradise and

fast becoming the leading resort of the central United States

By ALAN HOFFSOMMER | *AOPA 57445*

The sparkling blue waters of the Lake of the Ozarks wind their way through the picturesque hill country of south-central Missouri, creating a huge, dragon-shaped lake which is fast becoming the leading resort spot of the central United States.

This sprawling recreational area was formed by the construction of Bagnell Dam on the Osage River in 1931, inundating some 66,000 acres of land.

Averaging a depth of 150 feet over some 129 miles of main channel and with a shore line of 1,372 miles, this lake is a boating and fishing paradise. Some 500 resorts and fishing camps are scattered along the coves and rocky peninsulas which add to the rustic beauty of this rugged country.

The Lake of the Ozarks is equidistant between Jefferson City, the state capital at the northeast, and Springfield, Mo., to the southwest. It is roughly divided into eight major sections — Gravois Mills, Hurricane Deck, Camdenton, Bagnell Dam, Osage Beach-

Grand Glaize, Versailles, Eldon and Headwaters.

For the pilot, there are landing strips at Eldon, Camdenton and Osage Beach-Grand Glaize. The Grand Glaize-Linn Creek Memorial Airport is located in the heart of the lake area and is the most convenient for those wishing to fly in. With a 2,900-foot runway, it can handle aircraft up to the DC-3 class, and gas, oil, car rental and complete repair facilities are available. Naturally, those lucky enough to be flying seaplanes can take their pick of many natural coves and anchorages to beach their seaplane for a fun-filled vacation of fishing and camping.

Although the normal tourist season runs from May through September, many of the resorts are open the year around. Those wishing to visit the lake area during June, July or August should make sure they have reservations at the resort of their choice. For a list of resorts and motels, write the Chamber of Commerce, Lake Ozark, Mo., or the Mis-

souri Division of Resources and Development, Jefferson City, Mo.

Focal point and main tourist attraction is Bagnell Dam and the adjacent Lake Ozark "strip." A guided tour of Bagnell Dam, which cost $30,000,000 to build, is given seven days a week from 8:30 a.m. to 4 p.m. There is no charge for this tour, and it is a very worthwhile experience. The strip, as it is commonly called by residents, abounds with gift shops, motels, restaurants, boat and seaplane ride concessions, along with various other entertainment provided by local residents. Country music shows, a house which defies gravity, museums displaying everything from clocks to antique autos, horseback riding, water-ski shows and underwater ballets are found not only along the strip but elsewhere throughout the lake area.

Fishing, of course, takes top billing as the choice of sports, and there is no closed season either on the lake or the river below the dam. A nonresident fishing permit costs $5, with a

78

ABOVE *Three young ladies reflect on the beauty of the sightseeing flight they have just completed over the lake area by floatplane*

BELOW *A seaplane ready to take up the next load of sightseers, while a helicopter waits in the background. This service is offered by many docks around the lake area*

ABOVE *Water skiing is popular on the Lake of the Ozarks, and a number of boat docks employ professional instructors to teach the beginner*

PHOTOS BY THE AUTHOR

10-day permit available at $3. These permits may be purchased from the many sporting goods stores around the area, or from the State Conservation Commission at Jefferson City. Float fishing, which originated in the Missouri Ozarks, is one of the most popular forms of fishing. According to his desires, the visiting Izaak Walton may arrange to float-fish for a half day or two weeks. There are commercial guides, cooks and camping equipment available at several locations. The cost for a day's trip will average between $15 and $20 per day, the fisherman bringing his own tackle. A variety of fish may be caught in these waters, and the angler may go after perch and bluegill, black bass, white bass, crappie, jack-salmon, carp, catfish, and a few trout. The spoonbill catfish is the largest species, and some have been taken from the river measuring six feet long.

Boating and water sports are on the increase all over the country, and enthusiasts come from far and wide to enjoy the wide range of boating activities offered by the Lake of the Ozarks.

Those with their own boats will find that the 129 miles of main channel offer the boater something different from going around in circles as is required on most lakes. Water skiing is always popular, and a number of boat docks employ professional instructors to teach the beginner.

If you don't have your own boat, almost any size or style boat can be rented by the day or week. A most delightful experience may be had by renting a houseboat which sleeps six people and provides a home afloat with cooking facilities. Here, you can cruise along the lake, stopping whenever and wherever you wish.

Another popular sport is that of Scuba diving, and several places sell or rent equipment. For those who have never had the experience of communing with the fish on their own level, lessons are offered under the watchful eye of a qualified instructor. The experienced

Scuba diver will find many rough fish to spear during season.

Several events are held annually in the lake area: Hillbilly Days, the J Bar H Ranch World Championship Rodeo, the Lake of the Ozarks Dogwood Festival, Heart of America Square Dance Festival and the International Square and Round Dance Festival. The Fourth of July is celebrated by a colorful fireworks display at Bagnell Dam and is sponsored by the Lake of the Ozarks Yachting Association. Several gun shows are held each year during the summer season.

Like most resort areas, attire is informal, and the visitor should bring swimsuits, shorts and slacks. Few people dress for dinner in the evening, except for the more formal affairs. Equipment to be taken depends upon whether you want to spend your time fishing or in just loafing around, visiting the various places of amusement.

Whatever your choice is, you may be sure you can find it on the Lake of the Ozarks! ◆

DUDE RANCH FLY-IN

Rancho de los Caballeros, Wickenburg resort with its own landing strip, is weekend destination of California fly-in club

A distinguished, graying executive reaches for the telephone. "Tell everyone I will be out of town today," he instructs his secretary. In a nearby garage a burly man in grease-stained coveralls wipes his hands. "That's all for today," he says, "got to get going." In a hospital a surgeon checks out. "No more calls for the weekend," he tells his exchange. "I'll be unavailable." "Where am I going?" exclaims a young salesman to an inquisitive neighbor. "Why this is the weekend of the fly-in. I wouldn't miss it!"

This is a typical scene around Santa Monica, Calif., on five or six weekends each year when the Santa Monica "Fly For Funsters" club prepares to take off, usually at noon Friday, for varied and often far-ranging destinations. [See "It's Travel That Sells Them," Nov. 1963 PILOT—Ed.] The Rancho de los Caballeros, Wickenburg, Ariz., a dude ranch that has its own landing strip, was the destination

By JOANN ROE

recently when my husband Ernie Burkhart (AOPA 235405) and I went along in our Cessna 210.

A thin layer of fog hung stubbornly over the Los Angeles basin as we climbed out on instruments, but the mist slid by in wisps, and before we reached our EEL, we broke out into brilliant sunshine.

The approach to the Rancho de los Caballeros strip is over the swimming pool. We circled the ranch once and when we landed, Bob Gunnell (AOPA 183439), who organizes

Entrance to Rancho de los Caballeros, Wickenburg, Ariz. Ranch has its own swimming pool, golf course, skeet range, and facilities for numerous other outdoor sports

Bob Gunnell, who organized the fly-in to the dude ranch, is on hand on horseback to greet his fellow "fly for funsters" as they land at the Rancho de los Caballeros strip

the "fly for funsters" outings, was waiting on horseback to greet us.

So began one of the most enjoyable, and exhausting, weekends I've ever spent. It takes initiative and a certain spirit of adventure to fly, and the Santa Monica flyers apply the same energy to their "ground" hobbies. An hour after we were ensconced in our cabins, I found myself in blue jeans on a horse bound for a desert cookout four miles away. Before we arrived at the cookout site, night fell with remarkable suddenness and I was ducking wicked-looking cactus along the trail, as well as admiring the outline of an occasional saguaro against the darkening sky.

"Boy, smell that coffee," exclaimed our cowboy guide as we approached the hollow in the hills below Vulture Mountain where the ranch staff was ladling out beans and steak, salad and hot bread to the dudes. We lost no time getting in line and joined the "fly for funsters" around the campfire. A guitar player held forth with "Home On The Range" and "I'm An Old Cowhand," and we joined in with enthusiasm, if some lack of harmony.

After breakfast the next morning, some of our group in 10-gallon hats and cowboy boots climbed into their planes to look over the desert surrounding Wickenburg. Others went out on horseback for a chuckwagon lunch in the desert. Ernie and I wandered over to the skeet range where Dallas Gant, owner-manager of Los Caballeros, was showing novices how to shoot. I'd never shot skeet but thought I was pretty hot with a rifle and so expected to do pretty well. Banging away with a shotgun is nothing like taking a careful bead with a rifle, and I crept away from the skeet range after missing 24 out of 25 pigeons.

Lunch tasted wonderful, especially outdoors beside the pool. After eating, we headed for the golf course.

"Must be a real job to keep up these green grass fairways out here in the desert," I remarked to my caddy.

"Well, it's not so bad," he replied, "we just let them go in midsummer and reseed in the fall when the weather cools off."

Golfing on the desert has some unique angles, though. For instance, the ball rolls so far on the hard ground that you have to consider this factor in gauging your drives. The greens were tricky, too, as coarser grasses crept into the turf, and as far as getting into the rough was concerned, every rock resembled a golf ball and you need an eagle eye to spot old Spalding 7.

The evening schedule called for hors d'oeuvres at 6:30, dinner at 7:30. Los Caballeros had turned over a private dining room to our group and Gil Gunnell, Bob's wife who had masterminded the fly-in arrangements, gave out numerous trophies and awards, some of them hilarious. To my amazement, I received a trophy for women's low in the golf "tournament." My ego was shattered a few moments later when I discovered only two women had entered the tournament. After dinner a cowboy orchestra appeared, beating out the twist and bop, instead of the hoedowns you might expect. And, of course, there were the inevitable hangar-flying sessions around the room.

After a hearty Sunday morning breakfast of hotcakes and strong coffee, we went back to the skeet range, determined to plug those elusive black pigeons. Will power had little influence on accuracy, however, and my score was no better than before. Trying to cram fun into every last moment, several other fly-in guests and I swam in the ranch pool and soaked up the incomparable Arizona winter sun. As Ernie and I ate a leisurely poolside lunch, we could see some of the Santa Monica flyers taking off for home.

Reluctantly we packed our gear into the ranch stationwagon to return to the airstrip. Climbing out from the strip, we circled once or twice for a last look at Rancho de los Caballeros, waggled our wings to our fly-in friends still lounging by the pool, and then set our course for Blythe and Santa Monica. ◆

PHOTOS BY THE AUTHOR

Four 'Places To Fly' In Arizona

Some of the fly-in dudes from Santa Monica's "flying for funsters" at the cookout in the desert on their first night at Rancho de los Caballeros. After supper the group gathered around the campfire for some singing and guitar music

Although it's only a few minutes from landing to the greens of the Wigwam, lightplanes don't normally land right on the first green as Downie had this Cessna 172 do for this photo. The par 71 golf course is one of the attractions for visitors

Luncheon at the Wigwam is served around the pool. Guests can swim during entire November to May season; pool temperature is maintained at 80°

Litchfield Park Airport is only four blocks from the Wigwam, has 4,500-foot paved strip, sells fuel. About 300 of the resort's guests fly in to Litchfield every year

Balmy winter climate and top-notch golf course

attract tourists to the Wigwam—an inn, bungalows

and country club 15 miles west of Phoenix

WIGWAM In The Sun

By DON DOWNIE | *AOPA 18841*

The Wigwam in Litchfield Park, just 15 miles west of Phoenix, Ariz., began in 1918 as a two-room adobe house. Its purpose was to provide overnight accommodations for business visitors, as, in those days, it was almost a full day's travel from Phoenix. As when it first opened, the Wigwam is owned by the Goodyear Tire and Rubber Company. However, now it incorporates an inn, bungalows, a country club and will accommodate over 180 sun-loving visitors from November to May.

Aside from the balmy winter climate, the main tourist attraction of the Wigwam is its adjoining 6,414-yard, par 71 golf course. Other outdoor activities include swimming, horseback riding, lawn sports, tennis and archery.

The 4,500-foot, hard-surfaced Litchfield Park Airport, just four blocks (and a quick phone call) from the Wigwam, has 80/87 and 100-octane fuel. The airport averages 100 transient aircraft each month, while 272 Wigwam guests flew their own aircraft to the strip last year.

Pilots flying into Litchfield Park should note that the traffic pattern is below 1,600 feet m.s.l. (field elevation is 1,062 feet) because the airport is under the normal downwind leg of nearby Luke Air Force Base where

active jet training is in progress. The airport has six sets of lights on the main flight strip. There is neither rotating beacon nor taxi lights.

The airport is maintained by Goodyear for guests of the Wigwam and is also used by March Aviation as a base for agricultural operations. The traffic pattern is always to the south—away from Luke AFB—and visitors are requested to take off away from the resort area, weather permitting. Extensive early morning agricultural flying should be expected.

For the past 10 years, the manager of the Wigwam has been Reade Whitwell, a private pilot since 1947. He reports that the resort caters to conventions between November and the Christmas holidays. In recent years, special programs for families with children have been developed for both the Christmas and Easter holidays, with at least a third of the guests during these weeks being youngsters.

Tourism is now the fourth largest industry in Arizona (behind manufacturing, farming and mining), and reservations are suggested during the Wigwam's half-year season.

The history of the Wigwam and adjoining Litchfield Park dates back to World War I when a critical shortage of long-staple cotton developed. After the U.S. Department of Agriculture determined that the soil and climate of southern Arizona were suitable for

cotton, Goodyear conducted successful experiments. Soon they contracted to purchase or lease some 40,000 acres of undeveloped land in the area, named after Paul W. Litchfield, former board chairman of Goodyear.

The Wigwam was opened to the public in 1929 and served as officers' quarters during World War II. The resort was modernized in 1961 with the addition of lounges for conferences and guest cottages in Indian pueblo style. Also, there are four experimental "bubble" houses designed by architect Wallace Neff and built by Goodyear of air-foam structure in which thick layers of cement are sprayed over a huge inflated rubber bubble. After sufficient cement and reinforcing steel are in place, the bubble is deflated and the structure is complete.

Manager Reade Whitwell points out that the staff numbers 130 to 135 full-time employees during the season. "We don't use college students since our busy season is in the winter."

The golf course, open year 'round, has another 25 people on the staff to keep its grass, water hazards and sandtraps playable. Starting times are never required, and the course is open seven days a week. For the first time in its history, the U.S. National Seniors Open Tournament will be held here in November. ◆

REMUDA RANCH–
Out Wickenburg Way

Western guest ranch has 4,000-foot airstrip

Remuda Ranch staff member watches a private plane come in for a landing on the ranch's 4,000-foot dirt strip. Strip has Unicom, is half-mile from guest bungalows

Deplaning guests are met by Remuda Ranch car and other guests already on horseback. Ranch is operated from October to May, has own swimming pool and tennis courts and hundreds of acres to explore on horseback

The Wickenburg, Ariz., Chamber of Commerce, which calls itself the Round-up Club, calls the Wickenburg area "The Dude Ranch Capital of the World." It backs up its claim with the piece of information that there are no less than eight dude or guest ranches nearby.

One of this number that has its own landing strip is Remuda Ranch. Its 4,000-foot dirt runway was completed last year, has Unicom (122.8), is open 8 a.m. to 6 p.m. A phone call from the field will bring a car from the ranch, a half mile away.

Beyond the main lodge and the guest bungalows stretch Remuda's 1,800 acres, which, combined with a neighboring ranch's acreage, provide over 22 square miles of unfenced riding land for guests to explore on horseback.

Remuda has morning and afternoon horseback rides, with fast and slow groups to fit the abilities of the guests. There are also breakfast, lunch and dinner rides out to a chuck wagon in the desert, and, several times a week, moonlight picnics around a campfire to the accompaniment of a guitar. Some of the specialties of Remuda are sourdough pancakes, beer biscuits and prickly pear jam, and spareribs and hamburgers a la charcoal.

Although horseback riding is the mainstay of Remuda's activities, the ranch also has its own pool, tennis courts, and pool and Ping-pong tables. Guests at Remuda Ranch have the privileges of Wickenburg Golf Club, which charges a nominal green fee and has rental clubs. Twice a week there's a square dance, either at Remuda or one of the neighboring ranches. Remuda also provides transportation into nearby Wickenburg, where in stores wearing Old West false fronts, tourists can buy saddles, western clothing and souvenirs.

Remuda has a special, supervised program for guests' children from 8 a.m. to 8 p.m. The children have their own dining room and play room with counselors to supervise their meals and activities. Remuda has special children's amusements, rides, square dances, hikes, and a special school and state accredited teacher. Each child can bring his own books and an outline of what his class is to accomplish during his absence, which is supervised by the ranch's teacher.

Remuda Ranch is open from October 1 to May 1. Rates are "Arizona plan," which includes room, meals, all ranch facilities and entertainment and all horseback riding fees. During the regular December 15 to April 10 season, rates average about $25 single, $42 double, per day. Off-season rates are $16 per person per day. ◆

LAKE HAVASU
In The Desert

Trailer-park oasis is built around 6,500-foot paved flight strip

Dock and refueling facilities at Lake Havasu, originally an auxiliary field for Kingman Air Force Base, later a test site for outboard motorboats

Overall air shot of airport and improvements at Lake Havasu. Trailer park and recreational center with pool are at lower right; motel is at extreme right on shore of inlet. In background, hotel and city streets

The broad airport at Lake Havasu (Site 6) on the Arizona side of the Colorado River dates back to World War II days when it was the number six auxiliary field of Kingman AFB. Since that time it has been operated on a limited basis by a number of private owners.

Today things are different. McCulloch Motors, producers of Scott Outboard Motors and many defense industry items, purchased the property, first as a test site for their outboards. Later a trailer park, swimming pool, clubhouse and laundromat were installed. Many pilots are among the trailer owners. Now Lake Havasu City is a complete city, with industry, commercial and professional enterprises, homes, hotels, apartments and many recreational facilities, and Lake Havasu City Airport has played a key role in its growth.

The main strip at the airport is 6,500 feet long and paved, and two crossing runways are 6,000-foot compacted gravel and 2,800-foot compacted dirt. The main strip can handle all aircraft except large jetliners. The Lake Havasu City airport is the fourth busiest civil field in Arizona in annual traffic volume, exceeded only by Sky Harbor in Phoenix, Tucson Municipal, and Deer Valley with its glider activity. The airport has all-night runway lighting, 80 and 100 fuel and Unicom 122.8. Fueling and servicing are available all day, and there is no charge for landing, parking

By DONALD CHASE

PHOTOS BY DONALD CHASE

or tiedown. There are no hangars. A U.S. Weather Bureau station will soon be established, and a new passenger terminal building is in the planning stage.

Fishermen, water skiers, boating enthusiasts, tourists and vacationers from all over the West fly in for weekends on Lake Havasu. Many of them keep boats and trailers there. They can park their airplanes and be out on the lake in a matter of minutes—Lake Havasu City field is almost completely surrounded by the blue waters of Lake Havasu.

J. A. Nicholson, vice president, sales administration, of the company that's handling the desert subdivision, reports that 10,000-square-foot lots, complete with lights, water and sewers, start at $2,300.

For pleasure pilots and flying clubs wondering where to go next, Lake Havasu City has come up with the answer. ◆

LAKE TEXOMA
State Park

Nothing does more for amicable relations between states than to name a town located on a common border after both. Thus, on either side of the line that divides California from Mexico we have Calexico and Mexicali. Texas and Arkansas showed their compatibility by each begetting their own Texarkana.

Fortunately for the Chambers of Commerce of Colorado, New Mexico, Arizona and Utah, there isn't a town within miles of their common boundaries—the only place in the United States where four states meet —for what would the Post Office think of setting up shop at a Mexutaricolo or Colarizutamex?

One of the more famous combined names belongs not to a city but to a lake bordering on both Texas and Oklahoma. This is Lake Texoma, said to be one of the largest manmade lakes (93,080 acres) in the United States. Lake Texoma, with its 580 miles of shoreline, was formed when the Army Corps of Engineers built Denison Dam on the Red River. Though most of the land surrounding the lake is Federally owned, the State of Oklahoma leased 2,600 acres between Madill and Durant for Lake Texoma State Park, a recreational area that has received as many as 6,000,000 vacationers in one year.

One would think tourists had paraphrased the U. S. Travel Service's slogan to "See Lake Texoma First" and had taken it to heart! A broad range of activities and variety of accommodations undoubtedly are the reasons for the appeal.

If you're a fisherman, Lake Texoma could be your natural habitat. Fishing has open season all year long and boats and outboard motors may be rented at more than 30 points on the lake. Guide service is available at the marina, and for the "dock-sitter," Lake Texoma's donut-shaped enclosed pier makes the wait for a bite more comfortable. The catch? Black bass, channel cat, crappie, white bass, apalucian, spoonbill cat and other varieties.

The second most popular sport at Lake Texoma is waterskiing. Lessons are available for the novice, and the lake has been the scene of many competitive ski events of regional and local ski clubs. For swimming, there are several sand beaches along the lake and a pool near Lake Texoma Lodge.

PHOTOS BY OKLAHOMA PLANNING AND RESOURCES BOARD

Less exerting but just as much fun is the "Idle Time" excursion boat that gives regularly scheduled tours of the lake to visitors during the summer and which is available on a charter basis for groups.

Other than water sports, there's golfing on a nine-hole course, trap shooting, horseback riding, tennis, shuffleboard, badminton and baseball.

Accommodations run from a bed-sitting room in Lake Texoma Lodge to an individual cottage to dormitory type arrangements at Bay View Lodge. Campsites are also available, equipped with picnic tables and grills. Since the Lodge and its adjuncts are state-owned, rates are quite reasonable—the highest twin bedroom charge is $13.50, while a single can be had for as little as $5 a day.

Lake Texoma State Park has an additional attraction for pilots—its own airport, one of three state park airports in the State (others are at Lake Murray and Sequoyah). "Our airport, which is 2,500 feet hard-surfaced, is maintained by the state park personnel, but is operated by the Texoma Lodge," said Boyce Harkey, Lodge manager. "We have a Unicom system located at the front desk in the Lodge. The strip is lighted by automatic farmer type lights.

"Transportation is available by station wagon between the Lodge and the strip. Gas is available at the tiedown area and is furnished by the park service at the same location."

The Lodge is open winter and summer. When hunting season starts in the fall, hunters come from many surrounding states to take advantage of the good supply of duck, geese and quail. Hunting is restricted to Tuesdays, Thursdays and Saturdays during the months of October, November and December.

Sightseeing attractions in the area include Platt National Park near Sulphur, Okla.; Lake Murray State Park near Ardmore, Okla.; Denison Dam, that holds back Lake Texoma, near Denison, Tex.; Devil's Den Park near Tishomingo, Okla.; and Eisenhower State Park located on the south shore of Lake Texoma near Denison, Tex. ◆

AT TOP *Waterskiing is one of the most popular sports at Lake Texoma, second only to fishing*

LOWER *Lake Texoma Lodge with a view of the lake and Roosevelt Bridge beyond. The lodge has 106 rooms, but manages several housekeeping cottages and cabins elsewhere on the lake. All facilities were built by the state*

LEFT *When guests fly in to Texoma in their own planes, they are met at the 2,500-foot strip by the Lodge station wagon. Pilot contacts desk clerk via Unicom*

Port Isabel-Cameron County Airport, 12 miles northwest of Port Isabel, has four paved runways, 8,000, 5,315 and two 5,000 feet

Padre national seashore area is vacationing flyer's paradise. Some of the Southwest's best fishing is found in the gulf and the Laguna Madre, the narrow bit of water between the island and the mainland

Treasure hunters have a field day on the Padre Island beaches. Many masts, floats and all types of cargo have been washed in with the tides. The mast these men are examining is reputed to have come from a ship built during the American Revolution

PADRE ISLAND

Off-Shore Texas Treasure

By CHUCK WOLFE | AOPA 216547

Beachcombing — Texas style — is only one of the magnets drawing the flying vacationer to the newly created Padre Island National Seashore Area. With each tide the Padre beach is coated with an endless variety of treasure and flotsam that hold such fascination for the landlubber. And if one is to believe the stories of buried treasure (and many sober Padre devotees do), you can search for the true treasure hunter's top reward: pieces of eight.

Padre is named for a Catholic priest who formerly held title to the sandy island. Serving as a natural breakwater for the mainland, Padre Island extends over 100 miles from Corpus Christi to Port Isabel near the mouth of the famous Rio Grande. Never more than 10 or 12 miles wide, Padre pinches to a few hundred feet at many points.

Wildlife on the island ranges from coyotes and rattlesnakes to fox, deer and wild hogs. Fishing is good, both in the gulf and in Laguna Madre, the narrow body of water that separates Padre from the mainland. Marlin, tarpon, snapper and other fish are caught in numbers, and most of the motels and resorts either operate fishing boats or arrange for the services of a nearby charter operator.

Padre is still pretty much an unspoiled wilderness. Near Port Isabel in the south and

at Corpus Christi in the north, there is building going on to house the visitors. In between, the island is traversed by only the most hardy with experienced guides.

At the southern tip of Padre, across the causeway from Port Isabel, a free public recreation area is provided. Camping, swimming, and fishing areas are being added to daily. Resorts, motels and private beach houses extend several miles to the north. When the populated area thins out there are miles of unspoiled beaches.

In the public camp area a museum displays many items which have washed up on the beach. Anchors, chains, timbers and ships' masts delight the visitors. Imagination runs wild as you view a mast from a ship which sank nearly 200 years ago.

Within the immediate vicinity of the Padre Island resorts are a great many other attractions for the visitor. Port Isabel State Park greets visitors with the old lighthouse built in 1817 and used as recently as the early 1900's. During the Civil War the lighthouse played a big role.

The Magic Valley of Texas starts at Padre Island and is world famous as a vacation paradise, retirement land, and leading citrus-growing region.

Mexico is just a few minutes' flight or drive,

and most will want to spend some time enjoying a visit south of the border.

For those flying to Padre's southern tip a number of landing fields are available. The airport closest to Padre Island is Port Isabel-Cameron County. This airport, 12 miles northwest of Port Isabel, has four runways, 8,000, 5,315, and two 5,000 feet. All are paved. Among services available are 80 and 100 fuel, minor repairs, beacon and runway lights on request, courtesy car, weather information, hangars, tiedowns, possibly Unicom 122.8 by now. Other facilities include charter and food (light snacks). The airport is attended during daylight seven days, and the operator, Ray L. Sandlin, is on call 24 hours a day. Nearby lodges that will pick you up are Miramar Motel, Sandy Retreat, Sea Island and White Sand.

Other fields in the area include Brownsville, a port of entry, and Harlingen.

Padre Island is on the Corpus Christi Sectional. Now that the Government is developing the island everyone is looking for a big boom in visitors. The climate is cool in summer from the ocean breezes and warm in winter. Combine these advantages with good fishing and hunting (animal and treasure), and you can see why more pilots are heading south—to Padre Island. ◆

89

The NATIONAL PARKS

Travelog photographer-lecturer takes you on a tour of 13 national parks in his Cessna 172, ranging from the rockbound coast of Maine to the magnificent Teton range of Wyoming

By JAMES W. METCALF | AOPA 212766

"Jim," Gil said to me, "the film is needed very badly, and you are perhaps the only man in the business able to produce it. I certainly hope that you'll give the project considerable thought." The speaker was Gilbert Grosvenor, chairman of the National Geographic Society's lecture committee and a member of their editorial staff.

The film he referred to concerned a very comprehensive photographic coverage of our national parks. He had singled me out because I'm one of the few pilots in a very small field: the production of travelog lecture motion pictures. These films are shown during the winter season on lecture platforms throughout the United States and Canada, and by the National Geographic Society to audiences in Washington, D. C.

Just a little research into the national parks as a possible film subject revealed that it would be a big bite to chew. After giving it some thought, I decided that ordinary ground transportation was out of the question. With more than 10,000 air miles to cover, my Cessna 172 was the only answer. My log book covering this assignment records some of the

most interesting and pleasant flying I've ever undertaken.

If you include Hawaii, Alaska and the Virgin Islands, there are 31 national parks belonging to the United States. They are administered by the National Park Service, and they represent to many people the most beautiful part of scenic America.

Obviously, it would be impossible to film them all and present them sensibly within the 90-minute format to which the travelog lecture is limited. With the help of Conrad Wirth, director of the National Park Service, and other members of his staff, we narrowed the list down to 13 parks, representing every characteristic of scenery, geography and climate that the widespread park system has to offer.

Touring the national parks by air is a unique vacation idea that I'd unhesitatingly recommend to any qualified pilot, but it should be pointed out that the idea is not without certain drawbacks. For instance, some of our parks do not have airports close by. Getting to them and around in them after landing may involve renting a car for a few days, but

we never found this to be much of a problem. With a little research, and a few prior arrangements regarding hotel accommodations and ground transportation, the average pilot and his family can have a two- or three-week flying vacation to the parks they'll remember for the rest of their lives.

Just a word about overflying the national park areas. Under FAA regulations, the pilot can fly at 1,000 feet above uninhabited areas, and most sections of the parks fall within this category. However, the idea behind the forming of the parks in the first place was to preserve for all Americans, and for all time, the scenic wonders with which this country has been so lavishly blessed. This entails preserving them from the creeping encroachment of civilization, the building of railroads, highways, and even the establishing of airports and the necessary airlane approaches. The pure wilderness aspect of the parks could obviously not be preserved if roads were built through them, and the same sort of thinking can apply to low-flying aircraft. The National Park Service, therefore, requests that aircraft remain at least 2,000 feet above any park

ABOVE *People visit Yosemite National Park time after time to view scenes such as this one of Mirror Lake. More than a million persons visit this California beauty spot every year*

BELOW *An aerial view of the 14,000-foot Grand Teton mountains as seen from the author's Cessna 172 near Jackson Hole, Wyo.*

area, and this appears to be a reasonable altitude from which to do one's sightseeing and picture-taking.

The present National Park Service policy for aircraft is that "the use of low-flying aircraft within the parks is restricted to investigations, protection, rescue and supply services. Roadless parks in Alaska and such other parks that may be specifically designated by the Director are exceptions to this policy. Rail and bus terminals and airports, except for already designated landing areas, shall be located outside of park boundaries."

For weeks we pored over our research material on the parks, drawing up an itinerary for our film-shooting schedule. Then we moved to WAC and Sectional Charts. Many days prior to our departure we had the flight plan for the first part of our trip all laid out.

N5771A's crew had been cut in half from our usual complement, due to my wife's major operation and my son's college commitments. This meant that our 13-year-old daughter, Brooke, moved up from back-seat observer to copilot and assistant navigator.

Acadia National Park

It was clear and fine the day we took off on the first leg of our visit to Acadia National Park, far to the northeast on the rockbound coast of Maine. From home base in southern Michigan, it figured out to almost 1,000 miles exactly. For days we had been looking forward to a leisurely nine- or 10-hour flight. Shortly after we took off, however, Detroit Radio started giving us bad news about a low pressure area over southern Ontario that was supposed to have moved hours before. Like most lows, this one had not read the weather forecasts and just sat there. As a result, 71A had to alter course to the south and we sort of sneaked into Acadia by the back door and via the heavily travelled air routes around Boston.

Most of Acadia National Park is located on Mt. Desert Island. After seeing it from the air there is no question why they call it the "rockbound coast." The island is deeply indented with coves and bays, and Somes Sound, which nearly cuts the island in two, is said to be the only true fiord on the U. S. Atlantic coast.

Just to the north of Mount Desert Island on the mainland is Bar Harbor Airport, its three hard-surfaced runways standing out against the deep green forest like a giant figure "4." Cars can be rented here from Bar Harbor Airways, Inc., and it's a short eight- or 10-mile drive along Route 3 to Bar Harbor, Me. It, too, is on Mount Desert Island, but outside of the park boundaries. Attractions at Bar Harbor include a "Little Theater," art colony, the town's lovely old homes and quaint shops.

Acadia National Park offers many miles of fine roads (most of them former carriage drives of the wealthy), excellent camping facilities, hiking trails, the scenic Otter Cliffs, Thunder Hole and Anemone Cave, the bottom of which is colored wine red by anemones growing in saltwater pools. More than one park ranger here has been convulsed by some tourist asking directions to "Enema" cave! Sailing and fishing are both popular here. There are many fine hotels, and the local seafood is usually excellent.

Great Smokies National Park

If you ever fly to the Great Smokies Na-

Jim Metcalf ground checks 71A at Jackson Hole Airport, beneath the towering mountains of Grand Teton National Park

tional Park, try for an ETA on a bright spring day in June. On a really clear day (a rarity in this region, unfortunately), you'll see a carpet of color below your wingtips, for at this time of year the mountains are ablaze with rhododendron, dogwood, azaleas and laurel.

Our flight from Acadia National Park was made on a beautiful day and covered more than 1,000 miles down the eastern slopes of the Appalachian Mountains. Near Asheville, N. C., we turned northwest to Knoxville and, even at 8,500 feet, the flowering mountains below were spectacular. The route lies 292° off the Asheville VOR and takes one near Clingman's Dome which, at 6,643 feet, is the second highest mountain in the East.

Of special interest here are the "balds." Many of the Smokies' crests are practically bare rocks, a phenomenon which is something of a puzzle. Some scientists say that excessive evaporation, caused by altitude and winds, killed the trees. The local Cherokee Indians believe that their ancestors cleared the tops as lookouts for a monster that was carrying away their children.

Colorful as well as interesting are the rhododendron "slicks" that one flies over, bright patches of pink and rose and, in many cases, looking so slick and smooth that the flier comes to feel that he could practically land

LEFT *Metcalf's daughter Brooke wades in the Pacific Ocean in Olympic National Park. The "stacks," or rocky offshore islands of the Pacific coast, make Olympic National Park one of the Northwest's great scenic attractions*

BELOW LEFT *Metcalf's daughter mounts a horse for descent down the slopes of Mount Le Conte in the Great Smoky Mountain National Park*
BELOW RIGHT *A satisfactory way of exploring Bryce Canyon National Park is on horseback. This photograph, made by Mrs. Metcalf, gives you an idea of the awe-inspiring formations to be seen along a Bryce Canyon trail*

PHOTOS BY MATILDA METCALF AND U. S. NATIONAL PARK SERVICE

on them. However, a worse place for a landing would be hard to find. The foliage here covers most of the mountains in an impenetrable tangle. More varieties of trees are found on these slopes than in all of Europe.

Just short of the Knoxville VOR we closed 71A's flight plan and veered west to McGhee-Tyson Airport (Charlotte Sectional) serving the Alcoa-Maryville area. This is a major installation with three runways of 5,000 feet in length or more. Either hangarage or tiedown can be arranged, and the airport has rental cars and a limousine which you can use to get to Gatlinburg, Tenn., where there are several hotels and motels in all price ranges. The park headquarters are located in Gatlinburg, as well as a most interesting museum. Most of the side trips out into the park start here.

One of the outstanding trips is the trail ride to the top of Mt. Le Conte. Horses can be rented in the town, or the path can be hiked by the vigorous. Flame azalea and mountain laurel brighten the trail. You'll most likely spend the night in Jack Huff's Lodge with its rustic cabins and roaring log fires at night in the fireplaces. Be sure to take the short walk out to Cliff Top. You'll be rewarded by a vast panorama and, unless it's unusually clear, you'll see why these mountains have always been called "The Great Smokies."

Everglades National Park

The flight south from Knoxville is a simple, seven-hour trip over easily navigable terrain, about half of which lies in Florida. There's an airport within sight almost all of the time, and in the Miami area there are several at which you can terminate your trip. A 40-mile drive south along U. S. Highway 1 and Florida 27 brings you to the entrance of Everglades National Park. Two miles south of the entrance is the first of several scenic turnoffs featuring self-guiding trails, exhibits and other facilities. Don't miss the Royal Palm area and the Mahogany Hammock. Thirty-eight miles from the entrance at the southern end of the only highway that traverses the park is the Flamingo area. Here are restaurants, a motel, a beautiful marina with sightseeing boats and a very complete campground.

Most people living north of Florida have completely erroneous ideas of what the true Everglades are like. Actually, the region is a mosaic of many interesting things, each strongly influenced by the tropical climate. Plants of the temperate zone meet those of the torrid zone, fresh water meets salt, and land meets sea. Following the shorelines and growing upon keys (islands) in open water, mangrove forests form almost impenetrable thickets. Outstanding among the features of the park are the rookeries of birds.

The Everglades have been called the widest river in the world, slowly draining the Lake Okeechobee area just to the north. There are vast regions of flat, open grasslands dotted with islands called hammocks. On some of them the colorful Seminole Indians have lived for generations. If you have time, by all means arrange for an unusual type of "air" craft trip to visit one of them: the craft in this case being a propeller-driven airboat which zips with amazing speed across the shallow stretches of water.

Big Bend National Park

The next leg of our filming trip was a long one: 1,700 miles from Miami to Big Bend National Park. We decided to break it right in the middle and spent the night in colorful old New Orleans.

The next morning, we flew west across the rest of Louisiana and deep into the heart of Texas. You could make a career out of flying across this state; we seemed to fly forever before getting out of it! We landed at Starns Airport just north of Alpine, Tex., located on the El Paso Sectional Chart. Car rental facilities, however, are more complete at nearby Marfa-Alpine Airport, located just a few miles east of the Marfa Omni. And believe me, Big Bend is one national park where a car is a must! The nearest good, attended, all-weather airport, whichever you choose, will be more than 70 miles away from the road bordering the park on the north. The Del Rio Sectional Chart shows some closer airports like Terlingua, but beware of these. I've seen them, and they were intended for flying mountain goats and are attended only by wild burros.

Big Bend National Park is well worth the trouble it takes to get there. It gets its name from a great sweeping curve made by the Rio Grande. Here indeed is remote isolation. The park surrounds the wild and ruggedly beautiful Chisos Mountains, but in spite of its wilderness location, there are good campgrounds and comfortable stone cottages at The Basin, right in the heart of Chisos.

The best way to see this unusual park is from the back of a horse. From the elevation that is the south rim of the Chisos, you can experience the sensation of the utter immensity of sky and land. As you gaze southward into old Mexico it is said that "you can see the day after tomorrow."

The Big Bend country is desert country and would be ideal for a winter vacation. At any season, though, it is a rugged, stunningly beautiful land. Its physical grandeur, however, has been a deterrent to exploration and settlement, and as a result, history has largely

bypassed Big Bend. The impact of Big Bend on those who visit it was well told in 1895 by a U. S. Treasury agent who came to establish a port of entry at nearby Boquillas. He wrote that "Nowhere else have I found such a wildly weird country. . . . Never have I beheld such a display of glorious color as falls at sunset on the bald head of the Chisos Mountains 25 miles away. First orange, then pink, then crimson and, last of all, purple tints on the mountains' dark background."

Carlsbad Caverns

Here is one national park that cannot be seen very well from the air. Most of it is about 800 feet under ground.

The closest airport is the Carlsbad Caverns Airport in White City, N. M., about 10 miles and 220° from the Carlsbad (N. M.) VOR (Roswell Sectional Chart).

The airpark has a 3,200-foot E/W paved runway, hangar space, and 80/87 fuel. If you circle the town, genial Jack White (AOPA 216110), whose father founded White City, will probably meet you at the strip before you're ready to tie down. When we touched down, Jack waved a greeting from the wind tee he was just finishing. White will gladly arrange for transportation and a motel (there are none within the park itself). It's only a short drive through the New Mexican desert to Carlsbad Caverns.

The caverns were discovered because of bats whose built-in "radar" brings them unerringly home to roost in the caverns every morning. Millions of bats live here and at dusk they come streaming out of the natural entrance in a great cloud. From a distance, the bats look like a great plume of smoke—and that's exactly what the cowboy who discovered these caverns thought they were!

There are two ways to get into Carlsbad Caverns. The natural entrance requires a modest hike of a few miles, not at all difficult, but there is also an elevator that will take you quickly down into the heart of the caverns. The temperature there never varies from a coolish 56°F., so a light sweater or other wrap should be worn.

Carlsbad Caverns are renowned throughout the world for the spaciousness of their rooms and passages and for their great variety of stalactites and stalagmites. To illustrate, a single room within the caverns has a floor as expansive as 14 football fields and a ceiling as high as a 22-story building.

The formations here range in structure from delicate to massive; some resemble needles, others huge chandeliers. In the Big Room are the famed Rock of Ages and the Giant Dome, the latter looking for all the world like the Leaning Tower of Pisa.

The King's Palace is perhaps the caverns' most ornate chamber. Here the paved trail levels off beneath thousands of stalactites, glittering like jewels in the dim light. Each of these downward-hanging stone lances was forged by water seeping from the ceiling, leaving behind a tubular mineral trail. One seven-foot pendant, as slender as a soda straw, is known as the King's Bellcord.

Among caverns, Carlsbad is king. Not even the mightiest cathedrals of man can match this wonder of nature.

Yosemite National Park

From Carlsbad Caverns, we flew west and spent the night at Tucson, Ariz., in a nice rontel, located conveniently in the shadow of the control tower. Early the next morning, we arranged for a radar departure and headed for California and Yosemite National Park.

I had long looked forward to Yosemite and to landing at nearby Mariposa (Calif.) Airport, located on the San Francisco Sectional. Nestled high up in the western foothills of California's Sierra Nevada, Mariposa Airport is only a few minutes from Yosemite in one of the rental cars available at the field.

Yosemite National Park is a photographer's dream: domes and granite rocks in the valley, snowfields on the High Sierra, groves of giant sequoias, alpine meadows, lakes, waterfalls and majestic mountains everywhere.

Nowhere in the world are there waterfalls of such variety within a single area as in Yosemite Valley in the spring and early summer. Each has its own particular beauty, but perhaps the most overpowering, when in full flow, are Yosemite Falls, whose combined height of 2,425 feet makes them the second highest in the world.

Yosemite National Park, in the heart of the Sierra Nevada, is an area that can be described only in terms of beauty. Today, more than a million people every year spend summer, spring, autumn or winter vacations here, for Yosemite is a year-round park. It is easy to understand why people come back to Yosemite again and again.

Grand Canyon National Park

Just south of the Grand Canyon Airport, which is located on the Prescott Sectional, a prominent knob sticks up a hundred feet above the surrounding terrain and serves as a handy landmark.

At 6,400 feet elevation, the Grand Canyon Airport was the highest field I'd ever landed on. This, combined with temperatures in the 90's, called for slightly different approach techniques, and I kept plenty of power on all the way down. With almost two miles of north-south runway to play with, however, there's not too much trouble involved in "flying it on."

Located on the south rim, the Grand Canyon Airport sells fuel, has hangar and tiedown facilities and operates Unicom on 122.8. [This field is closed from Nov. 1 until April 1. A new $2,000,000 all-weather airport is presently under construction seven miles north of the present airport. During the winter months, pilots can now land on the north rim of the Grand Canyon at either the Marble Canyon Airport, which has a 3,800-foot dirt runway, or at the Cliff Dwellers Lodge Airport, with a 3,400-foot dirt strip. Both of these strips are on the Grand Canyon Sectional.—Ed.]

The Grand Canyon is one of the major wonders of the world—a gorge in the earth one mile deep, 10 miles wide on the average from rim to rim, and 50 air miles long. Its vastness swallows sound; any motion against this giant backdrop, except that of cloud shadows, passes unnoticed.

The park has such a great range of altitude that it is possible for the thermometer at Phantom Ranch, at the bottom of the canyon, to register 50°F., while a freezing blizzard is raging on the rim. It also accounts for the great variation in plant and animal life found between the bottom of the canyon and its rims, reflecting a gradual progression from a climate like that of a Mexican desert to a climate like that of southern Canada.

This is the reason why you will miss so much of the canyon if you confine your sightseeing and exploring to the rims. Even though you have only a day or two, plan to take one of the shorter mule trips or a brief hike into the canyon on the Bright Angel or Kaibab Trails. Looking into the canyon is one kind of thrill; looking out of it is an entirely different kind of experience!

If you have at least two days to spend in the canyon, arrange for the overnight mule trip down to Phantom Ranch. If possible, avoid the months of July and August for this adventure; it was 124°F. at the bottom the day we went down! But, at any season, Phantom Ranch is a little oasis where a tree-shaded pool and a good meal await you. After breakfast the next morning, you start the return trip which follows a different, but equally colorful, route back up to the top of the rim. As you take your last look at this incredible chasm you'll experience an uplifting of the spirit and a deep sense of humility. Like all who view Grand Canyon's majesty, I find endless freshness in what naturalist John Burroughs called "the world's most wonderful spectacle, everchanging, alive with a million moods."

Zion Canyon National Park

The flight from Grand Canyon to Zion Canyon National Park is as scenic as the West has to offer. The shortest course lies slightly west of due north and, if you take it, you will have to plan on using altitudes of at least 12,000 feet. Much of this country is well over 10,000 feet, and in some parts of it the pilot will have to climb to 14,000 in order to keep in touch with the widely scattered omni stations.

The scenic route, however, will be slightly longer but can be flown at lower altitudes. We took off to the east, skirting the south rim of Grand Canyon and following that rim in a great, sweeping curve to the north. Ahead lies the Painted Desert shimmering in brilliant shades of pink and orange. It was here that we picked up the 295° radial of the Tuba City VOR and turned northwest, crossing the Colorado River where it comes out of Marble Canyon. The route passes over the forested Kaibab Plateau and it's about here that you begin to run out of omni.

Ahead lies some of the most rugged terrain this country has to offer, but it can be flown easily in good VFR weather. With the 34th edition of the Grand Canyon Sectional Chart, the U. S. Coast and Geodetic Survey began an experiment in indicating the most feasible VFR routes through these mountains by a line of diamond-shaped markers. One of these lines is intercepted just south of Kanab, Utah, and we found it easy to follow the indicated route west to St. George.

Here we turned northeast, following a highway to Hurricane, where another diamond-shaped marker trail blazes the way north to the airport at Cedar City, Utah. The Cedar City Airport, on the Grand Canyon Sectional, is at an elevation of 5,620 feet and has two paved runways, both of which are over 5,000 feet in length. There's daily bus service from the airport at Cedar City to Zion National Park, some 30 miles away.

In Zion Canyon are spectacularly deep, narrow canyons, sheer rock walls and masses. The highly colored finger canyons on the western edge of the Kolob Terrace are the end result of great opposing forces in nature: uplifting of the earth, faulting and erosion.

Perhaps more than any other single feature, the lavish display of color in the exposed sheer-wall formations sets this area apart from all others. Zion Canyon is the color photographer's paradise.

Bryce Canyon National Park

From the Cedar City Airport, Bryce Canyon is a scant 52 miles, but here again the most direct route is not necessarily the easiest or safest. Lying astride this course is Brian's Head, looming up more than 11,300 feet and requiring a climbout of about 8,000 feet within the first 15 miles after takeoff from Cedar City.

Probably just as fast and certainly more interesting is the route north over the little town of Parowan, Utah. Even here you'll need at least 10,000 feet in order to pick up the Bryce Canyon VOR, only 30 miles from Parowan on a 100° heading.

Bryce Canyon Airport is at a high elevation, some 7,586 feet, but the paved runway is just about that long, too, and landing presents no unusual problems. If you are going to want your tanks topped off, it's a good

idea to tell Bryce Canyon Radio beforehand. They'll have the gas boy from the nearby Pink Cliffs Motel all ready for you. And be prepared for another surprise as you taxi in. At the edge of the ramp sits what is probably the largest, if not the only, log-constructed airplane hangar in the U. S. A.! It's operated by the FAA, and most of the time there's plenty of free hangar space available.

Two little gems await you at Bryce Canyon. One is the canyon itself, and the other is Bryce Canyon Lodge. The lodge has comfortable log cabin accommodations, made cozy at night by roaring fires in the fireplaces. There is an excellent dining room, staffed by a group of college students working their way through school. After dinner they put on some of the most unusual stage presentations I've ever witnessed; their "state show" will make you want to stand up and cheer. After breakfast, they all gather in front of the lodge to "sing away" the departing bus loads of tourists.

Within the 56-square-mile area of Bryce Canyon National Park stands the jagged edge of the Paunsaugunt Plateau. Here are exposed the famous Pink Cliffs of Bryce Canyon, carved in Wasatch limestone. Below the plateau rim stand miniature cities, cathedrals, spires, windowed walls, endless chessmen, shaped by rain, frost, and running water working through alternate strata of harder and softer limestone. These rock sculptures challenge the imagination not only with their fantastic forms but with their color, a riot of pink and red and orange blended with white and cream. Here and there strips of lavender, pale yellow and brown appear.

You may stand anywhere along the rim and look down into what appears to be a community of houses, schools and theaters, with inhabitants of various sizes and shapes.

BELOW LEFT *"The Window" forms a natural lookout from the basin area of the Chisos Mountains in remote and rugged Big Bend National Park, Tex., near the Mexican border*

BELOW RIGHT *Not yet open to the public, Wetheral Mesa—in Mesa Verde National Park —contains some fabulous cliff dwellings. This southern Colorado park contains many attractions for the tourist*

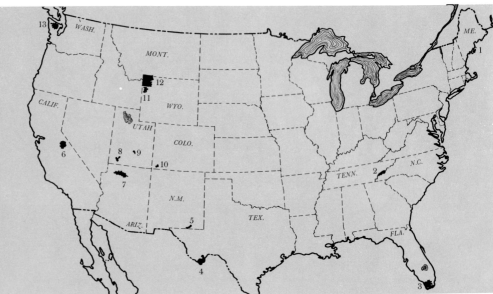

But you will never experience the sensation of mystery and awe that hangs over this amphitheater until you have ventured into it on one of the many trails that wind through its weird depths. This can be done either on foot or horseback, but, by either method, it's a trip you'll make with your mouth hanging open in wonder. Bryce Canyon National Park is, without any reservation, one of the most jewel-like areas on the face of the earth.

Mesa Verde National Park

The area between Bryce Canyon and Mesa Verde, Colo., contains some of the wildest, most desolate country in these United States. I've flown it both direct and by way of Hanksville, La Sal and Dove Creek omnis to the north. Either route involves overflying about 200 miles of forbidding, uninhabited mountainous desert, and great care should be taken with planning and weather selection. Water and survival gear should most certainly be part of the cargo.

There are no insurmountable altitudes; in fact, the toughest part of the flight is right at the beginning, getting enough altitude to pass over Barney Top which rises to an elevation of 10,700 feet. An early morning departure, before the heat of the day thins out the atmosphere, will help in this regard.

Your flight will take you once again over the mighty Colorado. As you pass over this canyon-laced country, keep your eyes open for ancient cliff dwellings tucked beneath overhanging ledges. There are hundreds of them, but they are not always easy to see. It's hard to believe that hundreds of years ago man lived and even flourished in this inhospitable land.

There is a nice airport at Cortez, Colo. (Grand Canyon Sectional), with a 5,900-foot runway, and available fuel, hangars, and tiedowns. As you end your flight there, your downwind leg takes you parallel to Mesa Verde. As you stand at the tiedown area, you can see the 7,000-foot wall of prehistoric cliff dwellings just to the south, that at one time supported one of the most unique civilizations the western hemisphere has ever known. The escarpment rises high above the surrounding country like a giant green table, which is precisely what the Spanish words "Mesa Verde" mean.

Mesa Verde tells a fascinating story of what life in prehistoric America was like. For about 1,300 years agricultural Indians occupied the mesa and surrounding regions and, from the hundreds of ruins that remain, archeologists have compiled one of the most significant chapters in the story of prehistoric America.

Mesa Verde is the only national park designed to protect and preserve the works of man. There are hundreds of ruins areas in the mesa, only a few of which have been excavated. Abandoned for many centuries, they have been weakened by natural forces, and maximum protection must be given these fragile artifacts.

The culture of these once nomadic Indians developed here at an astounding rate. At first it was very simple but progressed through crude pithouses to virtual cities of many apartments or cliff dwellings made of true coursed masonry.

The end came quickly for Mesa Verde. Beginning in the year 1296, a severe drought struck the region and for the next 24 years hardly a drop of rain fell on the land! One by one the springs dried up and the people were in serious trouble. They migrated to the south, leaving behind their silent cities, to which they were never to return.

Grand Teton National Park

A last-minute photographic assignment took us from Mesa Verde back to Bryce Canyon, and it was from there that we headed north to Grand Teton National Park, Wyo., and the fabulous Jackson Hole country. Once again we took advantage of the diamond-marked VFR pathway through the mountains to Salina, Kan., and from here on it is easy going to Nephi and Salt Lake City. The first threatening weather of the entire trip put us down for the night at Pocatello, Idaho, but the little cold front that lashed the town with rain and high winds that night left everything clear for us the next morning.

We've always found it pays to get all advice possible from local pilots, and it certainly paid off here. They suggested a heading of 060° out of Pocatello, slowly climbing to about 12,000 feet. Just as you begin to run out of range of the VOR, you should have the 15-mile length of Palisades Reservoir within sight and shortly should be able to pick up Dunoir omni. Jackson Airport, on the Pocatello Sectional, lies 25 miles southwest of it on the 215° radial.

How I envy you your first sight of Jackson Hole from the air! The broad, flat valley of the Snake River lies before you and, at the far north end, Jackson Lake shimmers like a sapphire. The magnificent Teton range rises abruptly to the west, and unless you're careful, you'll overfly the airport, preoccupied with the beauty of it all.

Jackson Hole Flying Service operates the field which has the distinction of being the only airport within a national park. It's a friendly, hospitable place with two runways (6,300-foot paved; 3,000-foot gravel). You'll be tied down and on your way to see the park before you know it.

Jackson Lake Lodge is one of the finest places to stay in the entire park system. It was built at a cost of more than $6,000,000 by John D. Rockefeller and is operated on a nonprofit basis by Jackson Hole Preserve, Inc. It was, in fact, Rockefeller who made this park possible, for he bought up 52 square miles of this region and gave it to the American people as a gift.

The word "teton" means breast in French and the name was given to the mountains by an early French fur trapper who obviously had been away from home too long. They are, however, mountains of great beauty, and for sheer imposing majesty are in a class by themselves. Whatever other beauties of lake or stream or forest or meadow attract your eyes for the moment, these mountains dominate the entire landscape.

One of the distinctive charms of the park is the great diversity of things to do. You can find some of the finest fishing of the west here, and you can camp out. You can swim, water ski and go boating. You can take a raft trip down the Snake River, go horseback riding or take lessons in mountain climbing. You can just rest, you can hike and you can fly. And boy, how you can fly. No country was ever more tailor-made for flying than this.

If you should visit the park without your own plane, by all means hire the boys at Jackson Airport to take you up for a sightseeing trip. If you use your own plane and are not used to mountain flying, seek their expert advice before you take off. Remember, these mountains are big enough to make their own weather, and a real mountain storm can be a terrifying thing if you happen to get in it. Even in good VFR weather, one should not venture too close to such precipitous slopes because of downdrafts.

Yellowstone National Park

Before leaving Jackson Airport for Yellowstone National Park in northwest Wyoming, place a phone call to Old Faithful Inn in that park and inquire about the next eruption of the famous Old Faithful Geyser. They can often call it pretty close, and if you can time your arrival there to coincide with the eruption, you'll have an introduction to Yellowstone that you'll not soon forget.

At the north end of Jackson Lake, you'll pick up U. S. Highway 89 which leads to Yellowstone Lake about 25 miles further north. As you go, keep on the lookout for elk in the high mountain meadows. They summer here, and in the fall, hundreds of them migrate through the area. At Yellowstone Lake, the highway swings west and you'll shortly find yourself over the geyser area.

It was precisely here that I had one of the closest squeaks of my flying career. As I circled blithely around, watching the great thermal activity below and waiting for Old Faithful to erupt, my engine suddenly slowed down and almost quit entirely. Instinctively, I grabbed for the carburetor heat control and yanked it out. Just at the last second and with a great deal of sputtering, the motor caught and finally smoothed out again. To my amazement, I found that I had to keep it well out all the time, while flying in this area.

You've probably already guessed what had happened. The great thermal area below sends so much moisture aloft that carburetor icing is a real threat. Fly a half mile away from it and the threat is gone.

Still shaking, we landed at West Yellowstone Airport just outside the park boundaries in Montana.

Yellowstone is the largest (3,472 square miles) and the oldest national park in the United States, having been founded in 1872.

It was here, in fact, that the very idea of a series of parks belonging to the people of the country was first expressed.

Within its several geyser basins, Yellowstone harbors more than 10,000 thermal features. About 200 geysers, myriads of hot springs and bubbling mud volcanoes, and brilliant pools and terraces make it the most extensive and spectacular thermal area in the world.

But Yellowstone is not only the mighty surge of Old Faithful's periodic eruptions, nor the angry convulsions of the Black Dragon's "cauldron." It is also the Grand Canyon of the Yellowstone River, 24 miles of twisting, sheer rock walls 1,200 feet high, tinted with red and every shade of yellow known to man; it is Yellowstone Lake, whose blue waters are fed by snow from the forested mountains that surround it. Finally, Yellowstone is the best-loved park of many Americans because of the number and variety of wild animals—bear, moose, deer, wapiti, pronghorn, coyote, bison and others—that roam mountainside and meadow in one of the greatest wildlife sanctuaries in the world.

Olympic National Park

From West Yellowstone we back-tracked as far as Pocatello, preferring the scenic valleys of the Snake and Columbia rivers to the high mountainous areas of the direct and shorter route. We stayed overnight at Pendleton, Ore., with friends living nearby, and early the next morning we took off into amazingly clear skies. Down the valley of the mighty Columbia River we flew, and long before arriving at The Dalles dam, we saw the snowcapped heads of Mount Hood, some 30 miles to the south, and Mount Adams, 40 miles north in Washington State, standing bright above the horizon.

After clearing the Cascade Range and just east of Portland, we left the gorge of the Columbia and turned north into Washington State. There, gleaming tall and white in the distance, was Mount Rainier. And what a distance! At more than 100 miles away we began taking pictures of that 14,000-foot mountain and continued shooting away at it until we were too close to include it all in the viewfinder.

We learned later that the weather and

visibility of that day was something of a climatological freak. I know people who have visited Mount Rainier (it's a national park, too) half a dozen times and have never seen the full mountain because of cloud cover.

The Great Northwest has a beauty all its own. There is much more flat land here than we had been used to seeing over the past several weeks, but there are always the mountains. As you fly north over Puget Sound, the northern end of the Cascade Range fades off into British Columbia, and close by, to the west, are the Olympic Mountains.

We were headed for Port Angeles and Clallam County Airport which serves the city. On the Bellingham Sectional, the Clallam County Airport has two paved runways, one over 5,000 feet long. They have fuel, hangar and tiedown facilities and handle minor repairs.

Olympic National Park has perhaps more diversity of climate and geography to offer than any other area in the country. The wettest climate in the continental United States prevails on the west side of the Olympic Peninsula. Yearly precipitation exceeds 140 inches in some sections. Mount Olympus and all of the high country in the western side of the park probably receive much more than that, but mostly in the form of snow. In contrast to the wetness of the west side, the northeast side of the peninsula approaches aridity and is the driest place on the west coast outside of southern California. The Olympic Peninsula is almost an island, being nearly surrounded by water. Because of the wetness and mildness of climate, an extraordinary growth of rain-forest has developed in the western valleys of the park. Sitka spruce and western hemlock dominate this forest, but the Douglas fir and western red cedar are also common. Many exceed a height of 200 feet; in fact, the largest known individual tree of each of these four cone-bearing species is found in the rain forests of this park.

Mosses carpet the forest floor and upholster tree trunks and fallen trees, while draperies of clubmoss hang from the branches. The whole place appears to be filled with a warm, green light.

The Olympic seashore is a fascinating place, being one of the last primeval reaches of the Pacific coast. It looks today much as it did when it was discovered in the 16th century. Physically it has changed little. The waves still rush through the "stacks," or rocky off-shore islands, and crash onto the beaches. The tides come as of old, the forest stands, and life goes on just about as it has for uncounted millennia. It is a place where modern Americans can still catch the feeling of the wilderness of the old Pacific coast.

The park is crowned by Mount Olympus, a glittering jewel of ice fields and glaciers almost 8,000 feet high. It can best be seen from Hurricane Ridge. As you travel the ridge, women in your party may turn around at the sound of a shrill wolf-whistle and fail to see any wolves at all. What they will see, if they are quick about it, is the golden Olympic marmot, a large rodent-like animal that makes its home in these high mountain meadows.

The last leg of our trip took us from Olympic National Park clear across the northern part of the United States back home to southern Michigan. Our national park assignment had been one of the finest trips a flying photographer could possibly dream up. ◆

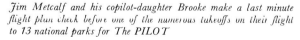

Jim Metcalf and his copilot-daughter Brooke make a last minute flight plan check before one of the numerous takeoffs on their flight to 13 national parks for The PILOT

May to October in California's High Sierra Mountains brings good flying weather, good fishing weather and thinking men who combine the two without spending a "fort full of fins" for the excursion.

Eight of these good flyer-type men took advantage of their travel opportunity and used a Hiller 12E belonging to Whirl-Wide Helicopters of Fresno to compress a three-day pack trip into 12 healthy hours of fishing fun which was neither expensive nor time consuming.

They took off from Fresno in the morning and returned that evening with full limits of fighting rainbow trout. Their flight to Spanish Lake, 45 statute air miles east (80°T) of Fresno Air Terminal, was easy with a non-supercharged helicopter, and the fish gave more appeal to a flight that would be interesting in itself.

For those not familiar with Fresno's three runways (9,236, 2,960 and 4,550 feet) and full ILS facilities (it's an alternate airport for San Francisco and Los Angeles jet flights), it is easily accessible in flat, open country and is on the Mount Whitney Sectional chart. Fresno is also the heart of the richest agricultural country in the world, surpassing even the famed Nile River Valley and its historical fame. It is also the home of the Fresno scraper, a dirt-moving tool without which the Panama Canal would not have been built.

But to get back to the fishing party. Eight men will not fit into a Hiller; it rebels at the total of their normal weight, let alone the extra necessary weight they had gained as an excuse to go fishing. Six traveled from Fresno by station wagon to Yucca Point on the road to Cedar Grove (a well-known end-of-the-road spot on Highway 180 east of Fresno). Yucca Point, famed for the magnificent flowering Yucca plants, also has an asphalt heliport installed by the Forest Service.

In the meantime, Harry Rogers, who spends most of his waking hours flying mountain missions in a 'copter, had flown direct from Fresno to Spanish Lake with two of the party and all the food for lunch. He then returned to Yucca Point for the rest of the party. There were 15 gallons of gasoline and oil stowed in the back of the station wagon as mountain insurance.

From the heliport, the flight to Spanish Lake is almost true north over Rodger's Ridge, which bulks out at 9,500 feet. The

Avid, modern-day fishermen (from left) Harry Rogers, Brad Quinn and Del Runyon (AOPA 252601) pose in front of the Hiller 12E that lifted them to remote rainbow-trout-filled lakes in California's High Sierra Mountains

PHOTOS BY DEL RUNYON

By HARTT PORTEOUS | AOPA 244603

Gone Fishing - By HELICOPTER

Fresno, Calif., sportsmen find fishing's the greatest in remote High Sierra lakes that are readily accessible only by rotorcraft

rugged grandeur of this flight will impress the hardiest of mountain flyers, and it is topped on the east—one-half mile—by 10,440-foot Spanish Mountain, which serves as a good direction signal—something you check on, but which Rogers disregards with a hand-familiar glance.

The early-morning air is usually smooth here, and the afternoon air is still good, though lighter, but in weather this is no place for the inexperienced. In fact, you'd not go out in weather. In the winter and late spring, thunderheads will build up to 60,000 feet or more and will look beautiful only from Fresno Air Terminal, which almost never experiences thunderheads. But at this time of year the weather is usually "go" in the mountains.

Until midsummer, snow is still on the ground, the air is crisp, clean and cold, and the water in Spanish Lake and its sister, Little Spanish Lake, is almost ice laden, and loaded with cold fish—fighting fish! And there is a meadow not 400 yards from the lakes which will accommodate a fleet of 'copters.

The Hiller can take three men, including the pilot, over this country with ease, but, if you've not flown before in a helicopter in rugged country, it may take you a few minutes to get used to the lack of speed and the rough country in which no airplane can land.

"There are places for a rotorcraft to land—if only you can see them," says pilot Rogers, who can show you the spots on the six-minute trip over Rodger's Ridge and down to Spanish Lake at 8,700 feet. The fact that you can force-land on these spots might mean you spend all night there before rescue. And the nights are cold. The protection you carry is in the heavy clothes on your back, a fly-casting rod, a small box of tackle and your bated breath—much less than the equipment you'd carry on a three-day pack trip by mountain trail.

The reason the fishing is superb here is that it is not easily accessible to the usual vacationing fisherman, and it doesn't take long to get a limit of shimmering rainbow trout.

Del Runyon (AOPA 252601), a multi-engine pilot, explains the fishing. "On my first cast with a four-pound monofilament line, a Super-Duper on the end, I hooked a fish. I wasn't prepared for the fight and lost him. But then on successive casts with a ³/₁₆-ounce Andy Recker Wobbler, a No. 5 Flat Green Fish, and a Colorado Spinner, I bagged a fighter each time. Fantastic! You don't need boots, but a net would be helpful. There are lots of underwater snags."

After taking off the fat accumulated so carefully for the trip, it's easy to put it on again with food kept hot in containers packed in Fresno's famous Iran Restaurant—Chicken a la Shah, rice in grape leaves, delicate goats' milk cheese, hot-cooked peda bread with melted butter, and, for some, there was pomegranate wine. The flyers thought the food, served thus in the mountains, was as good as the fishing, and the Hiller lifted all of this new bulk back to Yucca easily.

At a total cost of $30 each, these men feel they may become regular flying mountaineers of the future, for modern seven-league fishing boots are within the reach of most everyone with skill enough to read the Mount Whitney Sectional, and more lakes will become accessible with the newer, supercharged Hillers and Bells that Whirl-Wide has added to its stable. ◆

ABOVE *Little Spanish Lake, high in California's Sierra Mountain range, proved to be a fisherman's paradise to 'copter-traveling group of Fresno anglers*

BELOW *Circles on this map mark the takeoff and landing spots for Hiller 12E helicopter that carried Fresno sportsmen to inaccessible lakes in the Sierra Mountains*

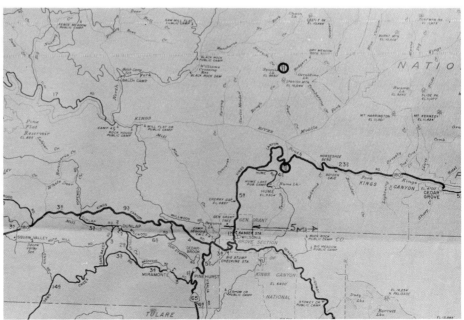

Did you ever cherish a kaleidoscope of great dreams, wealth, glorious adventure, dashing men and fair ladies? Does the fading glory that was a saga of Americana whet your imagination? Then a flying visit to the "ghost towns" of the far West is for you.

A true "ghost town" has the shells of a few buildings still standing, with no "living" person in residence. More common, however, are a few well-preserved buildings and a handful of hardy old-timers; remnants of a boom town that once housed thousands of prospectors. These remaining residents have one thing in common; they don't like being called "ghosts."

By comparison to the pioneers who traveled these "glory trails" by mule, oxen, wagons or afoot—often through bitter cold or extreme heat—a flight through this picturesque, colorful wilderness is a breeze. However, we'll guarantee that such a tour will not be uneventful.

Many of the flight strips near the famed "ghost towns" are primitive. If you're lucky, you'll find a bladed piece of rocky ground, a windsock of sorts and perhaps a set of tiedowns. There will be no fuel, no rental car, no attendant and, worst of all, usually no telephone to call a cab that doesn't exist in town anyhow.

When you plan to land at one of these out-of-the-way airports, you buzz town—and do it right. If you don't come down to the minimum legal limit, no one will take any notice and you'll have a long walk in from the airport. However, if you circle low enough to attract attention, you'll probably be met after landing by a sheriff's car. A ticket for low flying? No; he's probably the only transportation available in a too-small-for-a-taxi town and he'd "be right obliged to drive you back to town."

Visitors flying into the legendary towns of Goldfield, Beatty and Austin, Nev., must be prepared to take "pot luck" on just about everything; marginal airports with tricky high-desert winds, ground transportation, meals and lodging. If you like the niceties of omni and Unicom, rental cars or cabs, weather reports on the half-shell, hangar space and maintenance, then stick to the broad paved runways of Reno, Tonopah or Las Vegas. But you'll miss much of the color and friendliness of the "old West" if you don't fly into some of these smaller "mostly ghostly" towns.

In six windy days, three of us made a ghost-town tour in a brand new Beechcraft *Musketeer*, N2360Z, furnished by the Norman Larson Company of Van Nuys, Calif. It was a family trip back into Western history, with 14-year-old daughter, Dana, sharing the back seat with at least a half-dozen cameras.

Whether or not you're a fan of the Western movie or TV series, a visit to these famed mining towns is made even more interesting if you have browsed through a few history books. The two preflight books that we used were Nell Murbarger's "Ghosts of the Glory Trail" (Desert Printers, Palm Springs, Calif.) and "Nevada's Turbulent Yesterday" by the late Don Ashbaugh (Westernlore Press).

On a good part of our trip, we could have retitled Mr. Ashbaugh's book "Nevada's Turbulent *Today*." We had planned this tour to fit in with the Easter week of school vacation. Frankly, it was the wrong week for lightplane flying in Nevada, and we had high surface winds, blowing dust, moderate to extreme turbulence at all altitudes and a good view of the notorious "Sierra Wave." If nothing else, this unstable weather proved that the *Musketeer* is a rugged four-placer whose excellent aileron control makes it simple to stay right-side-up. Under these conditions, the

ample cabin ventilation system was most appreciated.

We had planned to head up California's Owens Valley with a stop at Bridgeport, near the well-preserved ghost town of Bodie. That was out of the question with the "Sierra Wave" working and Notams cautioning both transport and light aircraft of extreme turbulence. So we went the other way around and headed toward Las Vegas, certainly not one of Nevada's ghost towns.

Rather than waste a night on the bright lights, we landed within sight of Las Vegas on the 4,500-foot gravel strip at Jean, Nev., a former mining town now producing white lime and red sandstone for roofing material.

Even though we circled twice, no one at the combination gas station-garage-cafe-and-motel came to the field. We taxied back to the corner of the flight strip nearest the buildings, chocked the wheels with rocks and walked the hundred yards to the office.

"Sorry, we didn't hear you land," explained Manager Virgil Poole. "The wind was making too much noise."

When we asked about tiedowns, Poole explained that the strip had just been redragged and the tiedowns had not yet been replaced. "But we have plenty of five-gallon cans filled with cement," he added. "Just a second and I'll have one of the boys drive down with a half-dozen of them."

As in every other Nevada landing spot, we paid our "landing fee" through the route of the "one-armed bandit." (For our younger readers, that's a slot machine.)

Jean is one of those small places just off the crowded freeway where people seldom stop except for fuel or a bite to eat. "We do get an occasional plane who's short of fuel for 'Vegas," explained Poole.

The food was good, accommodations adequate and most reasonable, and we listened to the wind howl before catching that usual first-night-out's full sleep.

The main tourist attraction at Jean, aside from the slot machines, is the rusting 20-ton steam tractor, originally one of three purchased by the Pacific Borax Company in an effort to replace the "20-mule-team." One of these three exploded with "a boom heard half way across Nevada." The Jean tractor was salvaged after 50 years at Emery's Landing by "Pop" Simon, old-time owner of Jean. The remaining tractor is now a shutter-bug attraction at Furnace Creek in Death Valley.

Over a cup of very black coffee the next morning, old-timer Tom Keeler, who came to Jean in 1910, told us a little about the country.

"The 'junkies' are wrecking all the old ghost towns," he said vehemently. "When the mines close down and can't afford to keep a watchman, these two-legged vultures come in with their trucks and scavenge all the iron. If it's too heavy to pick up and haul away, they'll use blasting powder to break it up. I've seen big flywheels and gears broken up just for the little value of the metal. It's a damn shame."

With the wind still howling, we "promoted" a car from Manager Poole and drove the 7½ paved miles to Goodsprings, a former lusty mining town that once produced lead, zinc, copper and gold. It is better known to pilots as the location of the LF nondirectional Goodsprings homing beacon. Today, some 30 families live here and old-timers cordially point out bullet holes in the woodwork in the lobby of the hotel.

By RUTH AND DON DOWNIE | AOPA 188441

"Stokes Castle" at Austin, Nev., built in 1897 by Anson Phelps Stokes. The eastern mining financier lived in the structure for several years

Sheriff W. L. Schuh picked up the Downies at the airport after their low pass over Austin and showed them around the town

SEEING THE 'OLD' WEST BY PLANE

Part of the "downtown" district of the old mining town of Goodsprings, Nev., which was visited by the Downies. Some 30 families now live there. It is also the site of an FAA L/F marker beacon

Ghost towns and early-day mining camps are visited by the Downies in a lightplane.

We did a double take on one back-bar sign which read, "Notice, We do not serve miners."

When the wind subsided to perhaps 20 knots, we returned the car with thanks, untied the *Musketeer* and took off after a very brief roll. As soon as we could reach Las Vegas Radio, we asked for present and forecast weather. Apparently it wasn't going to get any better for the next couple of days, so we eliminated a side trip to Searchlight and headed north along U.S. Highway 95 with a destination of either Beatty or Tonopah.

Pilots in this area are cautioned to pay strict attention to the restricted areas of the Atomic Energy Commission at Yucca Flats, where the first atomic bomb was triggered. Restricted area R-4808 is listed as "continuous and all altitudes," which roughly translates into "stay out!"

However, on the legal side of the highway, you can peer into the forbidding Yucca Flats area from 8,500 feet and see where "the bomb" was fired.

Since the fabulous "ghost town" of Rhyolite adjoins Beatty, and it was getting uncomfortably rough in the air, we elected to go into the FAA's 5,500-foot gravel emergency field at Beatty. We circled town, some eight miles away by road, gunned the engine a few times at minimum legal altitude and headed directly toward the airport. A *Cub Cruiser* was tied down in a ranch adjoining the airport, so we circled low overhead just before landing, hoping for a ride into town.

The wind was a stiff 20 knots plus gusts and at 90° to the runway. Here the easy-landing characteristics of the *Musketeer* were most appreciated. After landing, we taxied back near the FAA shack and the tiedown area. The full-swivel nose-wheel of the *Musketeer* makes precise parking over tiedowns a simple procedure.

Once 60Z was safely tied down, we looked around at the nothingness and waited. Nothing happened. There was a new power line to the airport, a $250,000 to $300,000 omni station nearby—but no telephone to town. So what to do now?

Since we really wanted to visit Rhyolite, just a few miles west of Beatty, we locked the *Musketeer* and started to walk toward the farm house with the *Cub* in the front yard. This "ghost town" tour might be conducive to the New Frontier's 50-mile hike, but we were lucky.

A charming young lady and her two small children drove up in a pickup truck before we had trudged more than half a mile. Certainly, she'd take us into town, but we took a back road once we reached "the city" because she hadn't yet received her driver's license.

We checked later with Mrs. Barbara Brant, who with her husband maintains the ranch near the airport where Dr. H. Markham (AOPA 123946) keeps his *Cub*. They reported driving pilots into town "two or three times each month."

A taxi or a rental car in Beatty? No, but our unlicensed chauffeur suggested that we talk with County Commissioner Ralph Lyle at the Texaco station. We explained our temporary transportation problem and he helped us borrow a family second car.

Rhyolite is only a five-minute drive from Beatty. The history of each of these famed "ghost towns" is a book in itself; to condense each to a paragraph is pure sacrilege. We would reread the local portion of "Ghosts of

Ruins at the ghost town of Rhyolite, Nev., where gold was discovered in 1904. By mid-1907 three railroads served the city. Now, the nearest rail connection is at Las Vegas, more than 100 miles to the south

the Glory Trail" each evening to take the place of a conducted tour—which didn't exist.

Gold was discovered in Rhyolite in August 1904. By 1906, the population, counting transients, was 10,000. By mid-1907, three railroads served the Rhyolite terminus, "the Dearborn Street Station" of the West. Both the station and the famed Bottle House, constructed of 51,000 quart bottles, are open to the public, and souvenirs may be purchased.

The first mail to arrive in Rhyolite from Goldfield took three weeks by stage. We made the same trip in the *Musketeer,* with a detour over the ghost towns of Gold Point and Lida, in only 36 minutes. There is a good dirt strip at Lida junction and the old FAA emergency strip at Bonnie Claire.

It's wild, wonderful, beautiful and rugged country. Most "ghost towns" have much history in common: an errant burro wandering off and the owner stumbling across a gold nugget or spotting a vein of rich ore while in search of the animal. Following the "strike," there was the brief formality of filing a claim, an assay in the nearest town usually followed by a drunken spree, a new stake (financing) and back to work—followed by almost everyone who had heard and believed the prospector talking in the saloon.

Then came the oxen or mule teams; tents were set up, and a town laid out. When enough lumber arrived, a few permanent buildings were erected. If the supply of ore held up, the speculators, "girlie houses," more saloons, per-

haps a newspaper and more and more people arrived. The new town achieved status by the size of its post office. Schools and a few churches were built, and the never-ending game of trying to wrest the county seat away from another town began. Since mining was the sole reason for these towns, there was a mass exodus when the ore gave out, the market price for metal became too high or freight charges took too large a slice of the profits.

In these cities, constructed largely of wood and tent-cloth, fire was an ever-present danger. With such a transient pattern, it was amazing to us that these mining nomads took the trouble to erect stone and marble buildings, use beautiful woods and leaded stained-glass windows shipped around the Horn and from San Francisco. Many of these masonry buildings remain today, a tribute to the finer sensibilities (a description probably grounds for shooting "in self defense") of this breed of "crude, rough, tough, gutsy pioneers."

At Goldfield, the visiting pilot has a choice of three airports. There's a close-to-town strip, 1,800 feet long at an altitude of 5,850 feet with a cemetery directly off the north end of the field. Then there are two mile-long bare spots in the sagebrush some five miles north along Highway 95.

After checking with the Tonopah omni station, we made a very close fly-by of the two strips; we found that the one nearer the highway was deeply eroded, but there was no "X" on the strip. However, the second strip had

a windsock, looked smooth and usable, so we circled and landed uphill, into the wind.

We taxied to the end nearest town, chocked the wheels with rocks and waited. Nothing happened, even though we had done a fair job of making a "low pass" over town before heading for the airport. Since we were better than five miles out of town and a half-mile from the highway, we mentally tossed coins to see what to do next.

But leave it to the Old West. A county road grader, towing a husky truck, turned into the road going to the flight strip and soon pulled up alongside. H. E. Hanson stuck his head out of the cab and asked if we were in any trouble.

"No," we answered, "but how do you get into town?"

"I'll take you," he offered. "You'll find a couple of tiedowns at mid-field next to the windsock."

We taxied back, rolled between heavy stakes and soon had 60Z safely tied down. It is good desert insurance to tie down your plane anytime you leave it since a small, vicious "dust devil" can blow by and wreck a plane with great efficiency.

Mr. Hanson unhooked his grader from the truck and we all piled aboard. He took us on a short "Cook's tour" of the colorful mine "tailings" and then dropped us in town where we met Ed Denton, secretary of the local Elks Club and an enthusiastic town booster.

Since he was on duty alone, Mr. Denton

couldn't show us around town, "but there's Henry Dahlstrom (AOPA 227631) who owns the Union Station and garage." Dahlstrom keeps his *Tri-Pacer* safely out of the weather in a hanger at Tonopah. Dahlstrom was born in Goldfield and told us a little about the town, once Nevada's top gold producer.

He lent us a pick-up truck for a self-conducted tour of the sprawling mining area. Goldfield's "diggings" were the best preserved of any we visited, due primarily to the fairly active community that still remains. There was a minimum of vandalism in evidence, and most of the "glory holes" have been carefully fenced so that you have to work at it to fall down a deserted mine shaft. The color of the rocks in the "tailings" are so subtle that they are virtually impossible to put on color film in true register.

After two hours of admiring the glory that was once Goldfield, we returned the pick-up, and Mr. Dahlstrom drove us back to the airport.

"I usually use the close-in strip," he said, "but I'm familiar with the country and my plane is usually lightly loaded. When I took over as County Commissioner the first of this year, we had plans to lengthen it, but we found that someone else had title to the property and we are checking now to see if we can get it back."

Next stop was Tonopah and a return to the "civilization" of an FAA station, a lighted airport with four runways (two 4,400 feet long and two about 9,000 feet long), hangars, gas out of a pump, telephones and rental cars.

However, there were surprises even in Tonopah. As we taxied in, a pert young lady with a bright red beret signaled us up to the gas pumps. With its 60-gallon fuel capacity, this was the first fuel we had added to the *Musketeer* since leaving Van Nuys.

"We're open for gas 24 hours a day, seven days a week," she said with a grim grin.

The Tonopah FAA station covers a large, sparsely populated area. In talking with FSS Chief William H. Lowe, we found that the station handles remote transmissions to Beatty omni, Bishop, Calif., radio, and by the time this is printed, Coaldale omni, all with single channel receivers tuned to 122.2. For some unexplainable reason these remote stations do not monitor the emergency frequency, 121.5. Neither does the Tonopah station yet have a VHF ADF—a very handy gadget for pinpointing lost aircraft. However, the nearby Chestnut Radar Control Center is frequently used to help track lost planes.

Despite the lack of equipment, coupled with the transmitter location in a valley where line-of-sight communication is frequently impossible, Tonopah Radio does a most efficient job. A quick look through their file of "saves" is enough to make your hair turn grey, for here were modern-day ghosts in the making. This is no place for night or IFR flight except by well qualified pilots in fully equipped aircraft, including adequate oxygen. Dark nights in this lonesome desert area are the same as IFR.

Tonopah is now bustling and brassy, yet it retains a feeling of the rip-roaring pioneers who founded the town at the turn of the century. The five-story Mizpah Hotel boasts of "atomic slot machines—the jackpot fallout is terrific."

Before taking the rental car back to the airport the next morning, we drove around town and admired the architecture of what must

have been some of the finest homes in a fabulous era. The ever-present "Boot Hill" was in a sad state of neglect; headboards missing, fences toppled and a pitiful few plastic flowers among the empty beer cans.

From Tonopah we headed north over Highway 82 and circled the well-preserved buildings of Belmont, where the brick courthouse, built in the middle 1870's, still stands. There were no suitable, or legal, landing spots, so we had to be content with a set of air-to-ground pictures made in considerable turbulence. We resisted the temptation to land on a nearby road, because this would have invalidated the aircraft insurance, and flew on over the towering Toquima Range, just south of snow-covered peaks reaching to almost 12,000 feet.

This route took us over Manhattan, now a town with a handful of inhabitants. Manhattan is virtually unique in that a 3,000-ton, 400-foot dredge was used from 1938 to 1948 to extract gold from the area by placer mining. The orderly ridges of gravel left by the dredge are easily seen from the air.

Our next landing was at Austin where, according to a tourist pamphlet prepared by the local Lion's Club, "a horse kicked loose a piece of rock, revealing rich silver ore, in 1862." If you approach Austin from the east, you won't see the town until you're right on top of it. Austin is built in a steep canyon and has a once-in-a-while flight strip immediately west of town. This strip is not on current charts, was eroded and unsafe during our visit. The regular oiled 6,000-foot airport is seven miles out of town, so we let down through the canyon and circled back again for a good "low Western pass."

We had just tied the *Musketeer* down when the sheriff drove up. He smiled and introduced himself as W. L. Schuh. "Would you like a ride into town?" he asked.

As we climbed into the car, Mr. Schuh explained that there was no telephone at the airport, but that fuel could be obtained in town at the Chevron Station owned by Joe Dory (AOPA 181625) who keeps his *Navion* in one of the two hangars on the airport.

Sheriff Schuh told us that Austin now has some 225 year-round residents, but had once had a population of over 10,000. We had lunch in the International Cafe, the oldest hotel in Nevada. This building was originally erected in Virginia City in 1859-60 and moved piece by piece to Austin a few years later. Its original dance floor is mounted on springs, perhaps indicative of some really jumping parties.

Here was a truly western spot, but tinged with a bit of Hollywood humor. The sheriff called our waitress "Kitty." She replied, "Yes, Marshall Dillon." The young man riding with the sheriff was promptly dubbed "Chester," even though he didn't limp.

The citizens of Austin have thoughtfully numbered 16 historical buildings to correspond with their small tourist brochure. Unique is the outside second-story movable stairway, constructed because cloudbursts carried huge boulders down the main street of town—and also could be lifted at night to keep intruders away.

The Austin brochures says, ". . . many of its old buildings have fallen down, but in most respects Austin is much the same today as it was in the 'sixties. It has not been modernized and its famous old Main Street is not lined with garish honkey-tonks. It is, in itself, an unspoiled relic of Nevada and the West in the days of their greatest fame and glory."

Next stop, Virginia City, "Queen of the Comstock Lode." We "drove" over Highway 50 to Fallon, detoured around a restricted area used by the U.S. Navy for jet training, and headed for Reno's Municipal Airport. Spectacular lenticular clouds made a picturesque, turbulent sunset and we were relieved when the *Musketeer* was safely tied down.

Within five minutes, we had a Hertz car—with that ever-lovin' AOPA 20% discount—and were on our way up the scenic 22-mile skyline drive to Virginia City. From a number of modern motels on the outskirts of town, we picked the Virginia City Motel ($6 per couple and $8 for three). Owners Andy and

Ella Paskey advised that our choice of landing in Reno instead of Carson City had been correct. "Even though Carson City is a little closer, there are no rental cars available and the one-way cab fare is $15," said Mr. Paskey.

Virginia City is not just a ghost town, it's a national tourist attraction. Its past included a population of 70,000 people in the district and a total of nearly one billion dollars worth of silver and gold taken from the ground with silver leading in volume three to one. Still not missing any bets, the town is proud of its 500 weddings a year and advertises that it is "a lot cheaper for a potential divorcee to spend six weeks here than in any of the big towns of the state."

Yes, Virginia City was—and is—quite a

town.

Our week of wind was still blowing, and we coasted the *Musketeer* up the turbulent ridge winds after takeoff, circled Virginia City for aerial photographs and headed down the railroad and highway toward Hawthorne. We crossed the azure waters of Walker Lake, where cut-throat trout can be caught all year, circled the U.S. Navy's ammunition bunkers surrounding Hawthorne and landed on the broad 6,700-foot up-hill runway. [Hawthorne now has two bare runways, 4,000 and 4,800 feet long.—Ed.] There's a Unicom on 122.8—temporarily located at the El Capitan Casino—that will provide transportation should you not care to walk the few short blocks to town.

With a telephone on the field, it was only

ABOVE LEFT *Famed mining town of Virginia City, Nev., from the air. Virginia City is not a ghost town—it is now a national monument. Nearly a billion dollars worth of gold and silver was taken from its mines. At one time the district had a population of 70,000 people. Now, about 500 weddings a year are performed here and the town is advertised as being "a lot cheaper for a potential divorcee to spend six weeks here than in any of the big towns of the State"*

ABOVE CENTER *Austin, Nev., as seen through the windshield of the Downie Musketeer on a "low pass" over town (a signal for a landing). The airport at top left in the photo is unusable and the principal airport serving the community is seven miles to the southwest and marked on the Reno Sectional Chart*

ABOVE RIGHT *A Nevada ghost town, Belmont, as seen from the air. The old brick Nye County courthouse was built in the middle 1870's and abandoned in 1903. Unless you want to make an illegal highway landing, the best way to visit Belmont is to take a rental car 40 miles north from Tonopah*

RIGHT *Although established during mining boom days, Tonopah, Nev., is by no means a ghost town. Here, the Musketeer (from which this photo was taken) was landed at an airport with an 8,900-foot paved runway, lights, hangars, rental cars, etc.*

FAR RIGHT *This little donkey is still pulling his own weight —extracting silver from tourists. Donkeys, which may have been ancestors of this little fellow, are given much credit for assisting prospectors in the gold and silver strikes in the West. Author Downie, as you can see, already has paid the 10-cent fee and is getting on with the picture taking at Rhyolite*

a few minutes until a Cessna 182 owner, G. L. Kitchenmaster, drove up to top our tanks. He drove us through town with a stop for lunch and explained that the famous ghost towns of Bodie, Aurora and Masonic were within driving distance. Rental cars may or may not be available from local garages.

Since the bright lights of Hawthorne would add little to our "back-country" tour, we took off with an hour of daylight remaining and headed down the highway to the small town of Mina. There's a well-maintained 4,200-foot sod strip within easy walking distance of town. We circled twice at a rather low altitude, rolled out and landed. Two sets of tiedowns were plainly marked and we parked over one of them. (We carried a tie-

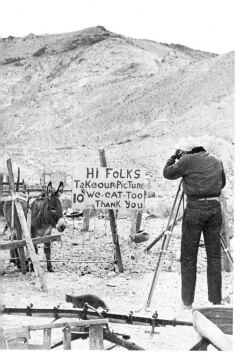

down kit, but did not have to use it on the entire trip, since some sort of tiedowns were always available.)

Before we had even chocked the plane, a green Jeep pulled up and G. A. Peterson, a retired mine owner, stepped out. He had been out on the adjoining dry lake driving golf balls.

"If I hadn't come over, there would have been any one of six people here to pick you up," he explained.

Mina has a unique way of lighting its airport. Mr. Peterson pointed out that this Mineral County airport has no lights, but if you buzz town after dark, anywhere from three to 12 cars will collect at the airport to outline the flight strip. They will slant their lights at a 45° angle to the runway with the lights shining up-wind. Thus, the pilot merely lines up on the rows of lights shining away from him and lands into the wind. This informal, volunteer arrangement first took place when a pilot in distress buzzed town one night while a Chamber of Commerce meeting was in progress. This meeting broke up temporarily and everyone took his car to the airport to help guide the pilot to an uneventful landing.

We asked Mr. Peterson about the possibility of landing on many dry lakes in the area. "If the surface is snow-white, it will probably be very powdery or have water just under the surface and you'd wreck your airplane," he explained. "Extremely dark brown color indicates wet spots from recent rains. These dry lakes don't make good landing spots unless you're very familiar with them, and even then, you're usually a long walk from civilization when you land."

Assayer Gene Gates (AOPA 196821) has his Cessna 140 parked in his backyard at Mina and taxies it out to the flight strip. He uses the plane to pick up mineral samples from many nearby communities.

And handling Sue's Motel for a few days while the owners were on vacation were Mr. and Mrs. C. L. Cunningham, who develop mining properties. He recently sold his *Apache* and is looking for another light twin. Even in these small towns, it seems that you're never far from another pilot.

After takeoff from Mina, we headed for Death Valley. It was only 27 miles to the Coaldale omni and we could hear Tonopah's weather report "five-by-five." However, the remote receiver scheduled for Coaldale had not yet been installed and we had to climb over 11,000 feet to establish VHF communications. We filed a flight plan via Death Valley, Trona and Inyokern to close with Palmdale Radio by 6 p.m. This was flight insurance for the extremely lonesome stretch of high desert between Coaldale and Scotty's Castle at the north end of Death Valley.

When you fly over this dry, barren desert, cruising comfortably at 135 m.p.h. (bumps and all), you can't help but admire the raw courage of the pioneers who opened up these isolated mines, working with nothing but a prospector's pick, a burro or two and a meager grubstake. These were real men who established some 1,600 towns in this general area.

We passed over the few remaining buildings at Silverpeak, Lida and Gold Point before letting down over Death Valley Scotty's famed castle, surrounded this weekend by a swarm of tourists and campers.

We peered into the Ubehebe Crater, and it didn't seem very impressive when compared with the country we had recently traversed.

Then we headed for Furnace Creek, 211 feet below sea level. What has happened to this Park Service airport shouldn't have happened to a dog! The latest charts show 3,500 feet available, but more than half of the airport is X'd out and completely unusable because of deep ruts. It seems that a former scheduled airline operation frequently sank through the thin oiled surface, and repairs have never been made. The old-time airport, just east of the highway, is now a parking lot full of trailers and campers.

From Death Valley, we circle around Telescope Peak and let down to view the few adobe buildings that remain at Ballerat, a town that served as a general supply point for mines throughout the area in the early 1890's. Again we barely resisted the temptation to land on a road and hopped over the low Slate Range for a landing at the good gravel strip at Trona.

John and Carol Husted (AOPA 120159) live on the field at Trona in what was once a World War II radio shack; they've added a bath, kitchen and bedroom. The Husteds have 80/87 fuel available and offer transportation for visitors to the nearby American Potash and Chemical Corporation swimming pool and recreation center. Pilots landing at Trona are considered guests of the company.

If the Husteds happen to be away from the field in their venerable Stinson *Gullwing*, there's a phone booth right by the office. Mr. Husted advised that many local lightplane pilots explore nearby ghost towns with landings on roads or nearby dry lakes. A subsequent check with FAA safety inspectors indicated that they could care less if you made such landings—with two exceptions. One—if you bend up your airplane, you'll be charged with reckless flying. Two—if you are cited by the State Highway Patrol for a nonemergency highway landing, the FAA would be forced to follow up with a violation. One pilot we heard of made a highway landing near Mina and had the misfortune to nearly run a State Patrol car off the road. His license is still suspended.

The short flight from Trona back to Van Nuys and "civilization" was certainly an anticlimax both for us and the *Musketeer*.

There are some Western folks who build up their cities, scenery, climate and history in true Chamber of Commerce style. In contrast, the quiet "rock-hounds," geologists and miners consider the ghost towns as sacred monuments, comparable in their way with Plymouth Rock, Valley Forge and Gettysburg. These Western shrines were built with ingenuity, and plenty of sweat and blood. Many local inhabitants are reluctant to give out any information about them because of the "junkies" and visiting souvenir hunters. These pioneer towns of history are without benefit of the four walls of a museum to protect them. Though miles from nowhere, these towns and their aging contents are still someone's private property.

Some remaining pioneers have invented their own methods to take care of petty thievery from the tourist. When a "No Trespassing" sign is posted, believe it! There are various "gimmicks," all the way from a wired general alarm system to animal traps behind posted doors. And, did you ever hear of a load of rock salt in a shotgun barrel? To each his own code.

Next time you fly in the Far West, make a date to visit these "living" ghosts. It's a wonderful education in Americana. ◆

ABOVE *Twin Beech parks at Flying E Guest Ranch Airport, four miles southwest of Wickenburg, Ariz. The Flying E is classified as a "winter ranch" and hits its peak season from November to May*

BELOW *Lake Pleasant Guest Ranch, 34 miles north of Phoenix, Ariz., has excellent facilities for winter guests who come by private plane. Two strips (not seen in photo), 2,500 feet and 1,500 feet long, and parking space for 25 planes are available*

Western Guest Ranches

By LEE W. CRAGER | *AOPA 60840*

You merely fly over the ranch house, then go on to the airstrip and land. In a matter of minutes, the ranch station wagon roars up, spilling out its contents of gaily-attired people with huge grins and a friendly "Welcome, podner!" Then the fun on the ground begins.

That's guest ranching for more and more owners of private planes.

For the past nine years, I have been flying to guest ranches all over the West, both for pleasure and to learn the guest ranch business from all angles. Then, a year ago, I opened a special kind of travel bureau in Los Angeles — the Guest Ranch Reservation Center at 6000 Sunset Boulevard, making reservations at guest ranches exclusively. We now represent 49 of the finest, both winter and summer types, in 11 western states.

The difference between a summer and a winter guest ranch is mostly a difference of season, area, economics . . . and good navigation.

While on one of my flying trips visiting guest ranches, I was over Idaho when I recalled hearing about a ranch near Dubois. I took a new heading and flew miles out of my way to see if I could find it. Arriving over Dubois, I flew in ever-widening circles, but saw no ranch answering the description of the one I was looking for. I flew back to Dubois, landed at the little airport on the edge of town, and questioned the CAA operator on duty at the range station. He said, "Why, there's no ranch by that name around here. You probably want Dubois, Wyo., 150 miles east of here." How silly can you feel?

The winter ranch season is generally from the early part of November to the first of May when it begins to get uncomfortably warm. A large number of winter ranches are located in the Wickenburg and Tucson areas of Arizona, and some in other parts of the state. In southern California, the Palm Springs desert area has several.

Winter ranches are designed for "fun in the sun"-type guests. Activities center mostly around the swimming pool. Guests at these ranches are usually of the executive type who are taking a winter break to give their office ulcers a rest by just lolling around the pool under the desert sun. Or perhaps you may find them leisurely knocking a golf ball around a pitch and putt course.

The summer ranch season, on the other hand, runs from about the first of June to the latter part of September, depending on the area and elevation. Some ranches open earlier and stay open longer to take care of fishermen and hunters. These ranches are scattered all over the western states, particularly in Colorado, Wyoming and Montana.

Summer ranches are designed mostly for active, out-of-doors-type guests; however, you can be as lazy as you please and not feel guilty about it. They feature horseback riding, pack trips into the beautiful and seldom-seen backcountry, mountain climbing, rodeos, cookouts, barbecues, and roundups. More and more, the summer ranches are welcoming families with children during the summer vacation. Some have special activities planned for the kids while mom and dad are riding the trails through tall timber, or breaking in their new cowboy boots square dancing to a western hoedown. Small fry too, get their share of riding . . . daydreaming of Matt Dillon.

It was a beautiful September day at the Bar B Q Ranch in northern Idaho when I took Lloyd Jones, owner of the ranch, for his first plane ride. We were going out to check up on his waterfront airstrip. As Jones climbed rather gingerly into my plane he said something about getting sick even in an automobile.

The takeoff into a stiff breeze was easy. But from 50 feet altitude on up we hit rough air that tossed us up and down and sideways and shook my little Luscombe until our teeth rattled. For 15 minutes it was a fight to keep the plane flying, but we finally got above the roughness at 2,500 feet. Later, over a cup of coffee at the Coeur d'Alene Airport, Jones managed a grin and said, "Well, I've seen worse—on the back of a bucking bronc!"

I made a mental note then and there never to take a ranch owner up for his first plane ride just after a cold front has passed through.

The White Sun Ranch, 10 miles south of Palm Springs, Calif., is located right at the end of Palm Desert Airpark, which has two 3,000-foot grass runways. There is a tiedown area at the White Sun for about 20 planes. I know—I did most of the work of putting in the cables and cement anchors myself.

In the Tucson, Ariz., area, there is the Rancho Del Lago, approximately 18 miles southeast of the city. It has a 2,000-foot strip at 3,200 feet elevation. The Lake Pleasant Guest Ranch, 34 miles north of Phoenix, has two runways, 2,500 and 1,500 feet, and Unicom on 122.8. You can't miss this one—it's the only landing area near the lake, and the only lake in the area.

It isn't always quite that easy. One hot July afternoon, I took off from the Idaho Falls Airport with a full load of gas and all my gear, cameras, fishing tackle, coil of baling wire, and so forth. I headed for Teton Pass, elevation 8,431 feet. As I said, it was a hot afternoon over those rugged mountains. I figured it would be the better part of valor for me to have several thousand feet between the wheels of my sturdy little Luscombe and the rocky crags below.

But every time I whipped the 85 horses under the cowling up to 8,000 feet, a downdraft would wipe out a thousand. Clearly, this looked like a case where it was better to live to fly through Teton Pass another day, so I headed south and flew 35 miles to the little town of Afton, Wyo., to spend the night.

The Afton airport is owned by the Callair people who make the Callair plane used for mountain flying and agricultural work. Tiedown was "on the house" and they helped me to get motel accommodations. It was still early in the afternoon. I dropped into a cafe for a cup of coffee. The cafe owner said he had a saddle horse if I would like to kill some time riding back into the hills. He even drove me to his home across town, caught and saddled his horse, and I had a very large afternoon indeed. That canyon ride was out of this world.

That's another example of the kind of hospitality a pilot will find so much of while guest-ranching by air in the West.

So now, before you pull junior away from in front of the TV and his favorite "Gunsmoke" or "Have gun . . .," and pile the family into the air-going flivver, there is one thing that should be considered: the difference between guest ranches. One may be small, with spur-of-the-moment activities, while another may be large with many activities planned in advance. One may be new, spic-and-span, while down the road a piece there may be a ranch mellowed with the age of many seasons of fine guests. Picnics, barbecues, overnight pack trips, and rodeos may be frequent diversions at one, while another may cater especially to fishermen because of those rainbow trout in the stream close by. Still others are operating cattle or haying ranches where guests can help with the ranch work if they really feel energetic.

But, regardless of the type selected, there is one stock in trade common to all—friendliness! And somewhere in this great and glorious West there is the ranch just suited to you and your family. With some reliable advance information—and a confirmed reservation in your pocket—you will have the most wonderful vacation ever. ◆

The Cheyenne RODEO

An old-fashioned week-long rodeo and a modern, well-equipped

airport make Cheyenne an attractive destination

for a summertime cross-country

It's the "daddy of 'em all," folks out in Cheyenne, Wyo., will tell you of that City's Frontier Days rodeo.

They could well be right. The Cheyenne rodeo has been an annual celebration for almost 70 years, dating back to the 1890's when the city was a wide-open cow town, and the Cheyenne rodeo hasn't changed much since then. Man and beast are still battling it out today in the same bronc-riding, steer-roping and bull-dogging contests as they did when Wyoming was one big cattle range.

The City of Cheyenne is another story. Its AOPA-approved Municipal Airport has three paved runways, ranging from 5,000 feet to 9,300 feet in length. Operated around the clock, the Cheyenne Airport has Unicom, hangar and tiedown facilities, handles major and minor repairs. The new, modern-design airport terminal building has a pilots' lounge, as well as a bar and restaurant.

On each of the six days of the rodeo, events get underway with the "Grand Entry." This is a colorful parade of the contestants, members of the Ogalala Sioux Indian tribe, Miss Frontier and her court, and riders carrying the flags of the 50 states.

As the parade winds off the field, a loudspeaker blares a name and number over the roar of the crowd. The bronc-riding contest, usually the first of the day, is about to begin. A cowboy tugs again at his hatbrim and eases down into the chute. Beneath him waits 1,700 pounds of quivering fury, the rodeo bronc. Gripping the bucking horse's rope, the rider yells to the gateman, "Let 'er buck." The rodeo has begun.

In bronc-riding, the rider is required to keep one hand in the air at all times and the other on the rein (or in bare-back bronc-riding, on the surcingle or strap around the horse). If the cowboy is still on the horse when the 10-second timing gun goes off, he's faced with another problem: dismounting from the still-bucking horse. The pickup rider rides in close and, if he can, helps the rider off.

The most dangerous contest of the rodeo is steer-riding, which usually means Brahma bulls. An eight-second ride is the goal of this event, with dismounting even more dangerous than in bronc-riding. The Brahmas have vicious tempers and horns to match, so there is no pickup rider handy with a horse. The cowboy must slide off the bull and make a dash for the fence on his own. If a rider is thrown or falls, the rodeo clowns dash into the ring to distract the bull and draw him away from his victim.

In steer roping and calf roping, a great deal depends on the cowboy's trained roping horse. First the horse must be quick enough to follow the dodges and dashes of the calves or steers. Then when the lariat settles around the calf's neck or the steer's horns, the horse must keep the rope tight while the rider leaps off and runs to hogtie the animal.

A variation of steer roping is "bull-dogging." In this event, the contestant jumps from his running horse to catch a running steer by the horns. The object is to wrestle the steer to a stop, and down onto its side. Time is not called until the steer is lying flat with all four legs and head straight.

Chuckwagon racing is newest and one of the most popular events at the Cheyenne Frontier Days. Each wagon is pulled by four fast horses, harnessed as a stagecoach team. A driver or "cookie" sits on the box of the wagon while four outriders on saddle horses

follow the wagon. Out in the center of the field are barrels around which the wagons and outriders must race.

The last, and wildest, event of each day's rodeo is the wild horse race. Unbroken three-year-old mares are roped and brought into the arena, fighting and kicking. A team of three men rush to each mare to attempt to calm her down. When the gun goes off, the men try to saddle the horse. Then one of the men mounts the mare, grabs the halter rope, and tries to stay on the horse while circling a half-mile track to the finish line.

Pilots flying in to Cheyenne for the Frontier Days rodeo will find plenty of activities planned for the evenings. At night there's outdoor square dancing, band concerts, ballroom dancing, Indian dances and, if that's not enough, there's even a carnival in town.

◆

ABOVE *In bronco riding, it's as important for the performer to know how to fall as to ride*

FAR LEFT *A bulldogger throws a steer at the Cheyenne Frontier Days rodeo. The rider must leap for the steer while riding at full speed, then wrestle the animal to the ground*

BELOW *Riding a Brahma bull is a feat for the expert. When a rider falls or is thrown off, rodeo clowns try to draw the bull's attention away from the fallen rider*

Parents who shy away from family flights until 'the kids grow up' are missing a great deal of fun

ON VACATION – with

Mother Goose

By DON L. TAYLOR | AOPA 111238

"**I**f only we could get rid of the little monkeys for a week or two so we could go flying!"

Sound familiar to you parents of small children who thought you'd have to put off your vacation flights "until the kids grow up"?

Well, there's no need to hangar your plane in mothballs during the best years of your (and your family's) life. There's also no need to burden grandma with your hungry hooligans—even if your kids are still in diapers.

There's a simple (and very pleasurable) answer. Take the babies with you!

Then you won't have to worry how Johnny is doing back home with his cousins, or how your poor, defenseless relatives are coping with your brood. You'll also find that you're in for one of the happiest experiences of your life. Sure, it's a little more work, but your travels and sightseeing will be infinitely more fun with the whole family along. And the memories—including the snapshots—will be among your most priceless possessions.

My wife Carol and I love to fly. Much of our romance was possible because the 250 miles between us were easily bridged by my

Cessna. Shortly after we were married, we flew from our Milwaukee home for a honeymoon in Fort Lauderdale and Nassau. The next summer, although our daughter's birth was only four months away, we flew to Halifax and spent a week in Nova Scotia, with pleasant flights through New England and Ontario.

Our friends told us then that our flying days were over. But when summer came again, we refused to let our eight-month-old daughter tie us down. We simply put our baby's "car bed" in the back seat of our 172, packed a liberal supply of baby food and paper diapers, and took off for a trip to Santa Fe, the Grand Canyon, Los Angeles, Sacramento, and back over the mountains to Salt Lake City and home. We flew almost 40 hours. To add to the fun, at the time of the trip we were expecting our new son just four months later.

This past summer, son Scott was eight months, and daughter Wendy was 20 months. Our stay-at-home friends were sure that we were finally boxed in. But we came up with another trick to keep our heads in the clouds. We persuaded a good friend, who had just

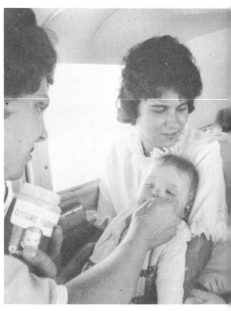

Mrs. Taylor feeds eight-month-old Scotty his in-flight dessert. Holding Scotty is Joan Clifford, a recent college graduate, who helped care for the children in exchange for room and board and the flight (her first)

graduated from Carroll College, to travel with us as a baby sitter. So our trip to Colorado included Miss Joan Clifford, as well as the four members of our family. We provided room and board, and Joan served without other pay. She was glad to have the fun of flying (for the first time, incidentally), and she enjoyed our week at a dude ranch almost as much as we did. It was a deal that made everybody happy.

Sound impossible? Well, let me tell you a little about our trip, and show you some of the photos.

AOPA furnished us with brochures which led to our selection of the Tumbling River Ranch, 9,000 feet high in the mountains west of Denver. The activities were what we wanted, and the price within reach. We made reservations in North Platte, Neb., for Saturday night, in Denver for Sunday, and at the ranch for the following week. With a careful eye on the weight limits of the plane, we shipped most of our clothes to Denver by Railway Express.

On Saturday, June 30, our wheels left the ground at mid-morning, with a half-dozen relatives on hand to see us off. The weather was excellent. We played tag with a few fleecy clouds at 8,500 feet on the way to Mason City, Iowa, for lunch. Scotty didn't seem to like the bed we had fixed on top of the baggage shelf, so he spent most of his time—including naps—in Joan's arms in the back seat. Wendy stayed in back, too, most of the time, but occasionally she wanted to be with Daddy or Mommy in the front. She got a little airsick once while we were landing. Damp, hot, and crying, she insisted on being in Daddy's lap while he came in on final approach.

The interior of the plane in flight looked like a flying nursery. There were plenty of baby blankets available for naptime. Jars of baby food were carefully packaged, along with plastic spoons wrapped in aluminum foil. Graham crackers were kept handy at all

times. Bottles of milk and water were refilled at every stop.

We were prepared and stocked with paper diapers, too. While at the ranch, we washed baby clothes several times, but we used the disposable diapers to reduce the size of the laundry pile.

Toys, crayons, books to read to Wendy, and other amusements were taken along in the plane to occupy the children on the longer flights. The sing-song noise of our engine was a lullaby, and the children slept much of the time.

The operator of the Rambler Motor Court picked us up at Lee Bird Field, North Platte, at the end of a happy day's journey. He loaned us his car to go to supper, and again for church the next morning. When he drove us back to our Cessna just before noon, he wouldn't accept any pay beyond the $14 for the two rooms. We departed with kind memories of him and his city.

We were in Denver in time for lunch where the plane was soon parked at Stapleton Field. We drove a rental car while sightseeing that afternoon and for shopping the next morning. Mrs. Meezie Keyes, from the Tumbling River Ranch, picked us up Monday afternoon and drove us into the mountains.

At the ranch we had two connecting rooms, each with bath and fireplace. Wendy slept in the bottom of a double-decker bunk, with Joan on top and Scotty in a crib alongside.

All of our meals were eaten together, and many of our excursions included the whole family. However, when we went horseback riding, or on a Jeep trip, or square dancing, Joan took charge of the little ones while Daddy and Mommy enjoyed themselves.

Wendy and Scotty made the trip much more fun, though. They each had a big felt cowboy hat, which, when the children wore them, seemed to change their personalities. We tried to fit Wendy into boots, too, but she couldn't get used to them. She would prance around in them so awkwardly that we

all doubled up with laughter.

Wendy loved the dogs and the pet goat at the ranch, and entertained us by the hour with her childish delights. And, of course, the swing and sandbox made a big hit.

After leaving the ranch, the family stayed in Denver for a couple of nights while Daddy was off on business. With Joan watching the children, Daddy and Mommy had time to see the Denver sights and ride in the paddle-boats at night.

Finally the day came to leave. The whole family got up early and made it to Stapleton Field in time for an 8 a.m. takeoff. We had to dodge thunderstorms all the way home, but we touched down at our home airport at Waukesha, Wis., shortly after six in the evening. What a pleasure it is, when you're traveling with children, to leave your vacation site in the morning and be home in your own beds at night! The same trip by auto would be a hard two-day grind—filled with constant hazard.

My friends, of course, chuckle when I mention the dangers of travel on the public highways. But on this trip, for instance, the only close call was when the left front wheel on the T-R's station wagon twisted outward and threw the car out of control. We were fortunate that the accident happened when we had slowed for a red light in Denver. Thirty minutes sooner, in the midst of the mountains. . . .

Our vacation was the most enjoyable we have ever experienced. This was due in large measure to the fact we took the children with us. What could ever match the memory of Scotty and Wendy in their cowboy togs at the ranch? Or the warm feeling of contentment as fond parents looked back at their two sleeping babies in the plane?

What will happen if our family continues to grow? Well, the problem isn't here yet and perhaps it will never come, but—there had better be a good used Cessna *Skywagon* available by the summer after next! ◆

Twenty-month-old Wendy takes time out from listening to Joan read nursery stories for a banana. The Taylors kept their flying nursery well stocked with snacks for the children, as well as toys, books, and, of course, disposable diapers

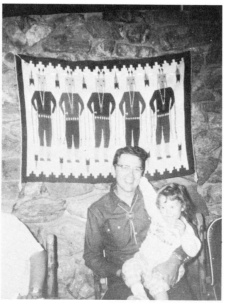

Planes have played a very personal role in the Taylor's family life; Don credits his successful 250-mile courtship of his wife to his old Cessna 140. He and Wendy are shown here at the western dude ranch where the family spent a week

THE AUTHOR

Don Taylor, author of "On Vacation—With Mother Goose," returns to The PILOT after almost a five-year absence since his Never Again! account of a 200-mile-an-hour spiral over Lake Michigan appeared in the magazine's first issue back in March 1958. Taylor was then an Army lieutenant who, while on furlough, had taken the near-miss plunge in his Cessna 140, named "Carol's Angel", "because of her unfailing habit to carry me gently and safely at every opportunity to my fiancee, Carol." Taylor is now married to Carol, has two children, and lives in Waukesha, Wis., where he is assistant vice president of the Waukesha State Bank. Since the "Angel's" mission had been accomplished, the family replaced her with a roomier Cessna 172.

Snow covers the slopes usually until mid-June, and in many cases

the pilot can land at or very near the ski resort of his choice

Springtime Skiing In Colorado

By ALAN ARNOLD | *AOPA 66034*

For the pilot-outdoorsman and his family, the slopes of the Colorado Rockies are a paradise in the springtime.

Some of the world's finest skiing is at the fingertips of the pilot who heads his plane toward Colorado, and, in many cases, he can land at or very near the ski area he plans to visit.

Snow covers the 14,000-foot Colorado Rockies usually until mid-June each year. Skiing, ice-skating and snowshoeing are rated as excellent until the white mantle begins fading under the summer sun.

But a word of warning if you have had no mountain flying experience and want to give the Colorado wonderland a try: Don't attempt to mix bad weather and the craggy mountain peaks. The mixture is fatal. Keep abreast of the en route weather via radio and, if there is any indication that there is marginal weather at your destination deep in the heart of the mountains, do a 180° and set down at Denver's Stapleton Airfield, located well east of the mountains.

Even if you have to set down short of your destination, ground transportation from Denver to the ski area you want to visit is excellent.

Notes about some of the more popular Colorado ski areas:

—*Arapahoe Basin*, located 66 miles from Denver on the western slope of Loveland Pass on U. S. Highway 6 in the Arapahoe National Forest. Skiing at Arapahoe is excellent until mid-June. The area features five miles of rolling open slopes and ski trails, half the area above timberline, affording Alpine skiing.

The nearest airport is Denver's Stapleton Airfield, but driving time from Denver is less than two hours.

The area has excellent overnight accommodations at varying prices.

—*Aspen Mountain*, Colorado's best-known ski facility, is located 169 miles northwest of Denver in the White River National Forest. Aspen has more than 50 miles of slopes and ski trails, and spring skiing is usually rated excellent.

An all-weather airport serves Aspen (check the latest navigation charts for up-to-date de-

tails). Aspen's Sardy Field (Denver Sectional) is located 3.5 miles northwest of Aspen, field elevation 7,900 feet. Longest runway is 6,500 feet, hard surface. Fuel, oil, light servicing and tiedown are available.

The pilot who doesn't want to tackle mountain flying can set down at Denver and take Aspen Airways, 38 minutes' flying time from Denver.

There are other ski and winter-spring sports facilities in the Aspen area, too. Aspen Highlands, located 1½ miles from town, features a five-mile ski run.

Buttermilk Mountain also is located at Aspen, and has some 30 miles of open ski slopes.

—*Berthoud Pass*, located 57 miles west of Denver where U. S. Highway 40 crosses the Continental Divide in the Arapahoe National Forest. Especially caters to amateurs and intermediate skiers. Features 14 runs. Nearest aviation facility is Denver.

—*Breckenridge Ski Area*, 86 miles from Denver in the Arapahoe National Forest. [The 1965 AOPA Airport Directory currently lists Breckenridge, Colo., as having a 4,000-foot gravel strip—Eugene E. Hanson Airport, located two miles north of the city and open to the public. The Directory carries the following caution about the Hanson field: "Approach from north only; wind-tee is fixed in one direction only. Entrance road reported very rough."—Ed.] Skiing is excellent into May and is open weekends much longer—usually into the summer.

Most of the ski runs are below timberline. There are, of course, excellent overnight accommodations.

—*Ski Broadmoor*, located on Cheyenne Mountain five miles south of Colorado Springs. The nearest aviation facility is Petersen Field (Denver Sectional) at Colorado Springs, an airport with all modern facilities which is heavily used by commercial airlines.

A special snow-making machine at Ski Broadmoor assures the sportsman of good snow regardless of normal snowfall.

—*Crested Butte*, a 30-minute drive from Gunnison, Colo., on the western slope of the Continental Divide. There are 23 miles of

ski trails and skiing is good until very late in the spring ski season.

Gunnison County Airport (Denver Sectional) is an all-weather airport with usual aviation facilities for a commercially used field.

—*Loveland Basin*, located 56 miles west of Denver, has good skiing into June. Nearest aviation facility is Denver.

Called Denver's most accessible ski area, Loveland is located in the Arapahoe National Forest and offers a variety of ski conditions.

—*Monarch Pass*, located 21 miles west of Salida, Colo., in the San Isabel National Forest.

Salida has two small airports open to light aircraft: Harriet Alexander Field, two miles west of Salida, with a 6,020-foot gravel strip, and Salida Airport, located four miles west of the city, with a 3,600-foot gravel runway. Both strips are on the Denver Sectional.

Monarch Pass features good skiing through May each year.

—*Steamboat Springs*, called "Ski Town U.S.A.," is 162 miles west of Denver in the Routt National Forest. Area also has world-known ski jump facilities.

Steamboat Springs Municipal, three miles northwest of Steamboat Springs, has a 3,600-foot blacktop runway, 80 fuel, weather information, tiedowns, charter services. It is not attended.

—*Vail Ski Area*, located in the White River National Forest some 110 miles west of Denver.

Spring skiing usually is excellent at Vail, and there are trails for beginners through the most advanced skier.

Nearest aviation facility is Denver.

—*Winter Park*, located 67 miles from Denver west on U. S. Highway 40. Spring skiing is excellent. Nearest airport is Denver.

But skiing is not the only winter-spring snow sport Colorado has to offer. Most of the major ski areas have ice-skating, sledding areas and sleigh rides. Many have heated outdoor swimming pools.

So if you want an unusual spring vacation—a trip you'll never forget when you see the snowcapped Rockies appear over the instrument panel—chart a Colorado course. ◆

BELOW *Fly-in skiers' equipment at the Aspen, Colo., airport. Aspen is Colorado's best known ski resort; its Sardy Field has 6,500-foot paved runway*

ABOVE *Taking a jump at Winter Park ski area, some 67 miles from Denver. Most of Colorado's major ski areas also have ice skating, sledding, sleigh rides, and some even have heated swimming pools*

BELOW *Taking a break from the ski slopes at Breckenridge ski area. There's unpaved, 4,000-foot strip two miles north of ski area at Breckenridge*

Western Massachusetts and southern Vermont
offer wealth of skiing and airport facilities

Skiing In The Berkshires
And Nearby Vermont

The Berkshires area of western Massachusetts offers the skier a wide choice of slopes, trails and accommodations. This mountain-range area also has a number of good airports that will accommodate the flying skier. For detailed information on skiing in the Berkshires, you can write the Massachusetts Department of Commerce, 150 Causeway Street, Boston 14.

Southern Vermont has a heavy concentration of ski resorts, and ample lightplane facilities are within reach of them.

Because of the large number of ski areas in southern Vermont, not all can be discussed in this article. For additional information on Vermont skiing you can write the Vermont Development Dept., Montpelier 99.

Middlebury College Snow Bowl, Middlebury, has three expert trails, two intermediate and one novice, and 26 acres of open slopes. There are two jumps, 15 and 50 meters. Tows are two Pomalifts. Other facilities include instruction, patrol, shelter, cafeteria and sundeck. The Annual Intercollegiate Winter Carnival will be held there next Feb. 26-28. (Middlebury Airport)

Pico Peak, nine miles east of Rutland, has nine trails for beginners, intermediates and experts; five slopes; a double chair lift, two T-bars and a J-bar. Other facilities include a ski school, patrol and cafeteria. There are lodges nearby. (Rutland Airport)

Killington Basin in Sherburne claims to have Vermont's highest skiing. Four trails for novice, intermediate and expert total 26 miles, and there is also a beginners' area. There are five double-chair lifts and five Pomalifts, one slow-moving especially for beginners and children. Among other facilities are warming shelters, base lodges, ski school, patrol, nearby nursery facilities, social program. (Rutland Airport, 14 mi S. of Sherburne)

Mt. Tom Ski Area, one mile north of Woodstock, has open slopes, one Pomalift and one slow-speed Babypoma for children and beginners. Other facilities include ski school, patrol, ski shop, warming hut and snack bar. (Lebanon Regional, 11 mi E of Woodstock)

Suicide Six, also near Woodstock, combines tickets with Mt. Tom Area. There are eight trails for intermediates and experts and 70 acres of open slopes. Tow is a Pomalift. Additional facilities are ski school, warming hut and snack bar. (Lebanon Regional)

Birdseye Mountain, Castleton, has an open slope, practice slope for slalom, separate children's area with tow, 40-meter jumping hill, disc lift serving open slope ski school with separate slope and tow. The area is operated weekends, holidays and school vacations. There is night skiing on Thursday, Friday and Saturday. (Rutland Airport, 13 mi from Castleton; Grandville Airport, 15 mi from Castleton)

Round Top Mountain, Plymouth Union, claims to have skiing from mid-November through April. It has six trails for intermediates and advanced intermediates, including three slalom trails and two practice areas. There are two chair lifts, a T-bar and a rope tow. Other facilities include ski school, base lodge and mountaintop inn. Tentative opening date for this new area was November, 1964. (Rutland Airport)

Okemo Mountain, Ludlow, has 11 trails and 20 acres of open slopes. There are six Pomalifts and a "baby" lift for beginners and young children. Other facilities include ski patrol, ski shop, nursery, restaurant and snack bars. (Rutland Airport, 15 mi NW of Ludlow; Hartness, 10 mi S of Ludlow)

Mount Ascutney, five miles west of Windsor, has 19 trails serviced by a double-chair lift and three T-bars, two open slopes, ski school, ski shop, nursery, and lodge with cafeteria. (Claremont Airport, 8 mi SE of Windsor, Miller, Hartness)

Big Bromley, seven miles east of Manchester, has nine intermediate trails and four expert ones; eight slopes for beginners, four for intermediates and one for experts; one double chair lift, five J-bars and one Poma. Among other facilities are ski patrol, school, shop, restaurant and lounge. (Bennington Municipal, 34 mi from Manchester)

Magic Mountain, Londonderry, has four open slopes, a separate ski school slope, a double chair lift, T-bar, ski shop, patrol, cafeterias, lounge, sundeck, a "village" of lodges, motels, chalets and restaurants near-

Ski practice at Mt. Snow, Vt. A ski-week package at Mt. Snow includes instructions, lifts, swimming, skating and entertainment

by. Additional luxury features include ski movies, dancing. (Hartness Airport, 17 mi from Londonderry)

Stratton Mountain (in Stratton Mountain) claims to have trails and slopes for the whole family. Tows are four double chair lifts and two T-bars. There's a ski school and a junior ski school. Other facilities include ski shop, restaurant, lounge, nursery and chalet village. (Bennington Municipal, 20 mi W of Stratton Mountain)

Mt. Snow (in Mt. Snow) has more than 40 trails and slopes for skiers of all abilities. Lifts are six chair trams, four double chair lifts and a two-passenger gondola. There is a ski school with classes daily. A ski-week package includes instructions, lifts, swimming, skating and entertainment. Other facilities include lodges, ski slopes, cafeterias, indoor ice skating, heated indoor pool, sun terrace and lounge. (Bennington Municipal)

Hogback, 15 miles west of Brattleboro, has three expert slopes, six intermediate and five novice. There are three T-bars, one Pomalift and one rope tow. Other facilities include ski school, patrol, shelters and food. (Dillant-Hopkins, 16 mi NE of Brattleboro)

Burrington Hill at Jacksonville-Whitingham has six novice and intermediate trails and an open slope for beginners and for practice. Other facilities include instruction, rentals, warming hut, skating pond and tobogganing. There's a ski lodge and a furnished chalet for groups of four to eight. (Bennington Municipal, 23 mi WNW of Jacksonville-Whitingham)

Pine Top at Vernon, nine miles south of Brattleboro and three miles north of East Northfield, Mass., has a "tiny tot" tow and slopes for small and older children. For adults, there are trails for expert, intermediate and novice, 25 acres of open slopes, and three tows. Other facilities include instruction, patrol, ski shop, shelter and food. (Dillant-Hopkins, 18 mi NE of Brattleboro; Turners Falls, 10 mi from Northfield, Mass.)

Here are some of the airport facilities for flying skiers:

Bennington Municipal (Albany Sectional), 3 mi W of Bennington. Runways: 2,350-foot bituminous, 2,000-foot sod. Services available: fuel, minor repairs, runway lights on request, weather info, Unicom, hangars, tiedowns, courtesy car. Hours attended: daylight.

Claremont (Albany Sectional), 1 mi W of Claremont, N. H. Runways: 2 bituminous-concrete, 2,400 and 2,750 feet. Services available: fuel, minor repairs, beacon and runway lights, weather info, Unicom, hangars, courtesy car. Hours attended: evenings and weekends; weekdays call 542-5151.

Dillant-Hopkins (Albany Sectional), 2 mi S of Keene, N. H. Runways: 2 bituminous, 5,500 and 4,000 feet. Services available: fuel, major and minor repairs, beacon and runway lights, weather info, Unicom, hangars, tiedowns, taxi. Hours attended: 8 a.m.-dark.

Granville (Albany Sectional), 1 mi N of Granville, N. Y. Runway: 2,068 feet, asphalt. Services available: fuel, major repairs, runway lights on request, weather info, Unicom, hangars, tiedowns, taxi. Hours attended: daylight.

Hartness (Albany Sectional), ½ mi NNE of North Springfield. Runways: 4,000 and 3,200 feet, hard. Services available: fuel, major repairs, beacon and runway lights, weather info, Unicom, hangars, tiedowns, taxi. Hours attended: 8 a.m.-6 p.m.

Middlebury (Albany Sectional), 4 mi SE of Middlebury. Runway: 2,200 feet, sand-turf. Services available: fuel, major repairs, Unicom. Hours attended: 24.

Miller (Albany Sectional), 3 mi S of Windsor. Runway: 1,500 feet, sod. Fuel available. Hours attended: none.

Rutland (Albany Sectional), 6 mi S of Rutland. Runways: 2 asphalt, 5,000 and 3,500 feet. Services available: fuel, major repairs, beacon and runway lights, weather info, Unicom, tiedowns, taxi, Hertz. Hours attended: daylight.

Turners Falls (Albany Sectional), 4 mi N of Turners Falls. Runway: 3,100-foot asphalt. Services available: fuel, major and minor repairs, hangars, tiedowns, courtesy car. Hours attended: 8 a.m.-7 p.m. ◆

PHOTOS (ABOVE, BELOW AND FAR LEFT) BY VERMONT DEVELOPMENT DEPARTMENT

TOP *Ski slope at Great Barrington in the Berkshires of western Massachusetts. A large number of ski resorts in the Berkshires are accessible from Great Barrington Airport*

CENTER *Skiing the lift line at Stratton Mountain, Vt. There's a nursery for children at Stratton Mountain and a junior ski school*

BELOW *Trail skiing at Killington Basin. This ski area in Sherburne, Vt., is 14 miles north of Rutland Airport*

OCEAN BEACHES

Flyers will find the very best in accommodations if

they take the seaside route in the summer

What better way to spend a summer vacation than to fly your own plane down the seaside route? Whether it be the rockbound coast of Maine or the semitropical sands of Texas' Gulf shores, there's little that can equal the ocean as an attraction for airborne tourists.

Lightplane pilots will find that many ocean resorts are well-equipped to handle aircraft, either maintaining their own landing strip, such as the Sea and Sky Portel on Long Island, N. Y., or located within a short distance of the local field, such as the Bahia Hotel, five miles from Lindbergh Field in San Diego, which provides a car to meet incoming pilots and their passengers.

Because the greatest attraction of some resort areas is their untouched, close-to-nature environment, such as Cape Hatteras in North Carolina, facilities for aircraft are the most basic you'll find, but this shouldn't discourage the flyer with a yen for adventure, who is willing to put up with a few inconveniences to enjoy the splendor of windswept sand dunes and uncrowded beaches.

Stepping out on the proverbial limb, the AOPA Flight and Travel Department along with The PILOT staff have pieced together a kind of "beach-hopping tour" for lightplane pilots, giving a representative sampling of ocean resorts with appeal for flyers around the coastal limits of the United States. No attempt was made to try to cover every resort with landing strip on the ocean, or every motel with ocean view within stone-throwing distance to the local airport—which would be, as anyone can see, an insurmountable task. However, those who find they've been left out should write AOPA about their facilities, for we're always glad to hear about new "places to fly."

Our "tour" starts with Bar Harbor, Me., and ends with Pacific City, Ore., covering 11 varied vacation resort areas on the Atlantic, Gulf of Mexico and Pacific coasts. You're guaranteed a wonderful time at any one of them.

Bar Harbor, Me.

A healthy contributor to the state's $272,000,000-a-year tourist industry, Bar Harbor has been a vacation mecca from the days that genteel Boston and New York society built summer homes along the rocky battlements around the town. Located on Mount Desert Island, Bar Harbor is the gateway to Acadia National Park. It offers perhaps the most varied natural environment, combining the beauties of sea, mountain, lake and forest —one of the more spectacular sights is watching the surf pound the bases of great cliffs, rising vertically from the ocean. Points of interest: Cadillac Mountain in Acadia Park, 1,530 feet and the highest point on the U. S. Atlantic coast; Sand Beach, formed by shell fragments, for swimming and surf fishing; Thunder Hole where waves rushing into a chasm produce thunder-like sounds; Abbe Museum of Archeology containing relics of stone-age Indian culture.

Bar Harbor Airport, located eight miles northwest of town, is attended 24 hours a day and has three paved runways, longest of which is 4,500 feet. Gas (80, 90, 100 octane) is available as well as major repairs. Airport Manager Tom Caruso lists several motels in the area which cater to incoming flyers, among them the Bar Harbor Motor Inn and Testa's Hotel, both in town but accessible from the airport by limousine service. Bar Harbor Motor Inn is on the shore near the municipal pier where deep-sea charter boats are available for fishing. The Inn offers golfing, badminton, swimming—either in French-man's Bay or their own heated swimming pool—playground and baby-sitter service for the children, restaurant specializing in New England fare. Rates (June and September) are $10-$15 European plan, $12-$22 in July; children free (up to two).

Testa's is in the heart of Bar Harbor, conveniently located to the shopping district and local sightseeing. Rooms are $8-$12 single, $12-$16 double, and their dining room is open 7 a.m. to 1 a.m. with continuous service.

Cape Cod, Mass,

Cape Cod needs little introduction to flyers, especially AOPAers. The PILOT Travel section, in the July 1958 issue, focused on Cape Cod, listing several suitable airports on the Cape available to flyers who want to make the trip in their own planes. Arbitrarily, for this round-robin tour, we've selected Barnstable Municipal Airport, Hyannis, because of its centralized location on the Cape, and nearby Green Harbor Village, run by Bill Munroe (AOPA 71295), because it caters especially to fly-in families.

Barnstable Airport, one mile south of Hyannis (Boston chart) has three runways, two 4,000 feet and one 5,000 feet long. Runway lights and rotating beacon are on at dusk, two-way radio is required (123.0 mc), and overnight storage and tiedowns are available. Services include gas (80, 100, 115 octane), major repairs, charter aircraft, restaurant, and limousine and taxi service. However, if you're staying at Green Harbor Village, just call Hyannis Unicom, ask them to call the resort at SP 5-0351 and a courtesy car will meet you at the ramp, just one mile away from the resort.

Green Harbor on the south shore of the Cape at West Yarmouth has 23 housekeeping units with full kitchens designed to sleep two to five persons with rates ranging from $85 to $170 per week during July and August (35% reduction in June and September),

Air view of Bahia Hotel on Mission Bay, San Diego, Calif.

which includes daily maid service. Green Harbor's private beach is on gentle Lewis Bay and is safe for children. If you're a sailor or would like to learn, the resort has a 12-foot sailboat you can rent at $5 a half-day, or, with instructor, $5 an hour. Restaurants, theatres, gift shops are all close by as well as the unlimited seashore amusements of Cape Cod.

Montauk, L. I., N. Y.

Montauk is Long Island's jump-off place into the Atlantic. Located 120 miles across the island from New York City, Montauk is a popular summer resort, particularly for New Yorkers who escape from the bustle and heat of the Great City in large numbers every year to enjoy fabulous fishing and true surf bathing along the miles of beaches at Montauk

Point. As of 1958, flyers gained an advantage over sea-bound tourists clogged on Long Island's busy highways with the completion of the Sea and Sky Portel. The Portel has its own 3,800-foot, oiled-surface airstrip and complete facilities for private aircraft including 80 and 100 octane gas, Unicom and tiedowns. It also has Montauk's only yacht marina, accommodating 24 boats. Besides swimming (4,000 feet from the tiedown area) and fishing (tuna, marlin and swordfish), visitors enjoy golfing on an 18-hole course, tennis and boating. For horse lovers there is Western riding over rolling countryside where ranch cattle graze as they did in the 1700's.

The Portel's accommodations are housekeeping cottages with equipped kitchenettes, but a new Flying Fish restaurant and cock-

tail lounge opened last year for those who prefer not to do it themselves. Sleeping rooms with baths are also available. Rates during the summer season (June 29-Sept. 11) for two persons are $130 weekly for efficiency apartments or $85 for sleeping rooms.

Cape Hatteras, N. C.

Cape Hatteras is a place for true lovers of the sea. Tourists find pleasure merely in standing at the Hatteras lighthouse point, watching the Gulf Stream and Labrador currents clashing together offshore with resulting 20-foot waves pounding the beach. Walking the beach searching for seashells, surf-bathing, deep-sea fishing are popular pastimes—if these do not sound very exciting, Cape Hatteras is not the place for you. Small vil-

King and Prince Hotel, St. Simons Island, Ga.

lages on the island exist as they did 200 years ago remote from mainland influence, and much is made of the fact that island people, mostly descendants of ship-wrecked sailors, have a way of speech peculiarly their own. All land on Hatteras Island as well as two other islands composing North Carolina's Outer Banks is owned by the U. S. National Park Service who established a recreational area there in the 30's, insuring that the islands would remain in their primitive state forevermore.

1960, the state built an airport on Hatteras Island between two towns, Buxton and Hatteras village, which have the closest accommodations for flyers. The airport, called Billy Mitchell Airport, was named for the late World War I ace who made the Hatteras offshore area his base of operations in 1926 to prove that surface craft were vulnerable to bombing attacks by aircraft. The paved runway is 2,400 feet long with unlimited approaches, running NE-SW with adequate tiedown space for several planes. The strip is unattended and has fuel only in the summer (91 octane), but if the pilot will circle Hatteras village, three miles west, an auto will pick him up at the field. It's best to make advance contact with Wheeler Ballance, owner-operator of Ballance Texaco Station in Hatteras, at Hatteras 2726. Ballance can help flyers find accommodations at one of several motels in town, as well as provide fuel from his bulk tanks. Incidentally, the fishing's fine on Hatteras, ranging from small inshore species to giant blue marlin in the Gulf Stream offshore. Charter boats for deep-sea fishing as well as "beach buggies" for driving along the sandy beaches can be rented in Hatteras.

St. Simons Island, Ga.

St. Simons Island and its luxurious King and Prince Hotel are as sophisticated a resort as Cape Hatteras is a primitive one. The island airport at Brunswick, McKinnon Field (Jacksonville Chart), has four paved runways, three of them over 4,000 feet long. Complete facilities include storage, adminis-

tration building, weather, major and minor repairs, 80, 91 and 100 octane gas and charter service, and taxi or rental car will get you to the King and Prince, only 1½ miles away.

The hotel is the last word in resort living with planned social activities including nightly entertainment and dancing. Facilities include private ocean beach and freshwater swimming pool, golf, private horse stables, fishing — both freshwater and surf casting. For fun, you can hire a car, bike or take a sightseeing tour around the island which has a romantic past of southern plantations long famous for the production of Sea Island cotton. Luxuriant vegetation—moss-draped live-oaks, oleander and palms—provide a tropical setting in a seaside atmosphere. The King and Prince is open all year, and rates, European plan, are $8-$16 single (per day), and $10-$22 double.

Florida Keys

Some time ago, Florida publicists began telling the world that Florida is a good place to go in the summertime, too, and our Sunshine State has been year-round resort country ever since. Perhaps the island keys which surround the peninsula have the greatest advantages for a summer vacation, for here is where sea breezes from the Atlantic and the Gulf of Mexico go first. Accommodations on the keys are as extensive and luxurious as those on the mainland with excellent boating, fishing and swimming facilities available. We've chosen two resorts with special appeal to flyers, one on Key Largo just 30 air miles south of Miami, and one on Longboat Key in the Gulf across the bay from Sarasota.

Key Largo's Ocean Reef Club has a 2,650-foot private airstrip, rolled rock-oil sealed with a sand finish. Accommodations consist of ocean-front rooms in the main inn, and individual "villas" with kitchenettes. Guests have a choice of swimming either in the man-made lagoon (fed by ocean tides) or fresh-water swimming pool, but the most striking feature is the layout of waterways and dock frontage for yachtsmen and fishermen. Dur-

ing the 1961 summer season, Ocean Reef offers a "golfer's two-day special" which includes lodging, meals and two-day golf privileges (green fees included) plus free use of the other attractive facilities at the resort, all for $24 per person in the inn or $27 in a villa.

Longboat Key. Though Far Horizons on Longboat Key does not have its own landing strip, it's just a 15-minute trip by rent car from Sarasota-Bradenton Airport with its three paved runways, two of which are 5,000 feet each. It's worth the trip. Far Horizons is ultra-modern in style and up-to-the-minute in its accommodations for tourists. Besides the usual seaside recreational facilities, after-dark entertainment this summer will be highlighted by three famous dance bands—those of Claude Thornehill, the Quintetto Allegro, and Charlie Spivak. Sarasota's proximity offers sightseeing opportunities with the Ringling Museums and the Circus Hall of Fame high on most visitors' lists. Far Horizons provides either hotel rooms, studio apartments or penthouse and beach level suites with daily rates from $10 to $50 (two persons).

Padre Beach-Port Isabel, Tex.

The twin communities of Port Isabel and Padre Beach located in Texas' Lower Rio Grande valley are good examples of the old and the new—an aspect which seems to characterize the state as a whole. Port Isabel's "history of the white man" goes back to 1519, and during the Mexican War, General Zachary Taylor used it as an operational base and hospital site during his victorious campaign. Since then, Port Isabel has thrived as a Gulf shipping port and resort city. Connected to Port Isabel by a causeway across the Laguna Madre is Padre Beach whose history began in 1954 when a real estate firm began its development. Already it has become a popular recreational and resort area on the Gulf of Mexico.

The twin communities' popularity comes not only from their excellent fishing and salt-water swimming but also from their proximity to Mexico as well as other Texas recreational areas in the Lower Rio Grande valley.

The area is of special interest to pilots now that an airport has been built one-half mile west of Port Isabel. Port Isabel-Cameron County airport has four paved runways. The longest is 8,000 feet, and there are two 5,000-foot runways and one 5,315 feet. Eighty and 100 fuel are available. Among other services offered are hangars and tiedowns, minor repairs, courtesy car, beacon and runway lights on request, weather information, and possibly Unicom 122.8 by now. The airport is attended during daylight seven days, and the operator is on call 24 hours a day. A phone booth on the field can put you in touch with numerous motels who will furnish transportation to and from the airport. Among them are Miramar Resort Motel owned by Joe Williamson (AOPA 167085), Sea Island Resort Motel and Sandy Retreat Hotel, all on the Gulf. All the above also furnish free limousine service to Brownsville International Airport, 21 miles away, which has complete facilities for private aircraft. Miramar has housekeeping units; Sandy Retreat and Sea Island have both housekeeping and hotel-type bedroom units. All have swimming pools as well as surf-bathing on the beach, and rates vary from $10 to $20 (two persons) per day during the summer season.

San Diego, Calif.

Located on one of the world's greatest natural harbors, San Diego's fame as a resort playground is widespread. Sightseeing attractions here include Balboa Park, site of the 1915-16 Panama-California Exposition and 1935-36 California-Pacific International Exposition; Old Globe Theatre, home of the San Diego Community Theatre and the annual San Diego National Shakespeare Festival; Old Town, with its excellent examples of Spanish architecture and the site of the original mission and settlement of 1769. Old Mexico with its colorful bazaars and year round horse and dog races, jai alai and bullfights is just a half-hour's drive away.

While accommodations in San Diego are unlimited, one of the best you'll find is the Bahia Hotel on Mission Bay. Land at Lindbergh Field and a Bahia car will meet you by advance arrangement. Bahia is a complete resort in itself with pool and surf swimming, golf, fishing, sailing, waterskiing all at the doorstep of your modern suite (all have private patios and some have private beach). For sailing enthusiasts, Bahia maintains a fleet of sailing dinghies for use by guests; supervised playground and pool for children, and two dining rooms serving excellent food are other inducements. Bedrooms and suites with or without kitchenette are available and rates are from $15 to $20 per day for two.

Monterey Peninsula, Calif.

The Monterey Peninsula stretches for 17 miles from Pacific Grove on the north to Carmel on the south, and a more attractive, interesting 17 miles would be difficult to find elsewhere. Terrain slopes from white sandy beaches to hillsides dotted with houseroofs to mountains beyond. The city of Monterey is a favorite with lovers of antiquity, having Colton Hall where the first Constitution of California was signed in 1849, and various other historic buildings which are now museums open to the public. Nearby is Pacific Grove with its picturesque three-mile long shoreline, and Carmel, established in 1904 as a retreat for artists and writers, which today displays the works of local artists in various galleries and exhibits throughout the village.

Monterey Peninsula Airport, located just two miles ESE of Monterey, has two paved runways—5,000 feet (EW), and 4,000 feet (SW-NE)—has ample storage and tiedown space and is lighted at night. All grades of fuel are available, as are major repair service and ground transportation into town. Monterey's Mark Thomas Inn, 1 mile from the airport, provides free limousine service for pilots. The inn has dining room, cocktail lounge, heated swimming pool and excellent adjoining golf course; rates for two run from $10 to $30 per day. In Carmel, both the Highlands Inn and La Playa Hotel have magnificent views of the ocean. The La Playa has direct limousine service for pilots from the airport at slight additional charge. Rates, modified American plan (including breakfast and dinner), run from $25-$39 for two at Highlands and $24-$34 at La Playa. Both have complete resort facilities.

Gold Beach, Ore.

Gold Beach, at the mouth of the Rogue River, is said to have received its name from the "gold" found in the sand of its extensive ocean beach area. Even now there is some mining of gold and platinum in streams nearby, but Gold Beach's real wealth lies in its excellent salmon and steelhead fishing in the Rogue River. A popular tourist activity, besides ocean bathing, is a scenic 32-mile boat trip up the Rogue which offers an awe-inspiring view of forest and water.

Gold Beach Municipal Airport has a 3,200-foot blacktop strip paralleling the Pacific Ocean. Operated in daylight hours, the strip has hangar and tiedown space and carries 80 and 100 octane fuel. Sunset Inn overlooks the north end of the airport as well as the ocean and the mouth of the Rogue River. It's ideally located near the center of town on five acres of landscaped grounds, and double rooms run $5.50-$7.50 a day.

Del Rogue Resort across the river from Gold Beach is just three miles from the airport and is run by Tom Matthews (AOPA 99403). Del Rogue has accommodations both with or without kitchenette with rates from $7 to $10.50 for two. A complete marina with boats and motors for rent is a special feature at Del Rogue. Both Sunset Inn and Del Rogue Resort furnish transportation for pilots, and a call on 122.8 mc before landing will bring a car.

Pacific City, Ore.

A state-owned airport in the heart of Pacific City now permits flyers to walk a short distance from plane to fishing, bathing, boating, stores, restaurants and motels in this lovely resort town. The strip, 1,850 feet long and paved (Portland Chart), stretches from within 50 feet of the Big Nestucca River to within 300 yards of Pacific City's sea-washed beach. Gas and repair service are available at all times. Most people go to Pacific City for the variety of fish—both ocean and freshwater types—which can be caught there. In the rivers are salmon, jack salmon, steelhead, trout and flounder; ocean dory fishing offers salmon, cod, red snapper, halibut, bass and tuna. Boats with or without power may be obtained at resorts in the area; accommodations are numerous, and Dean Reddekopp, manager of the Pacific City Airport, can refer you to the better ones. ◆

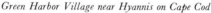

Green Harbor Village near Hyannis on Cape Cod

PHOTO BY CRAIG STUDIO

PENNSYLVANIA'S
Poconos

Doors never close at year round mountain resorts. Activity is as varied now as it will be in spring and summer

The Pocono mountains of Pennsylvania are neither high—terrain doesn't rise above 2,500 feet—nor very extensive —about 1,200 square miles in all. Yet the area is probably one of the most popular resort sections in the Northeast.

One reason undoubtedly is because of its proximity to both New York and Philadelphia. By lightplane, the trip is a matter of minutes instead of hours, from either city. But the salient facts are that the Poconos contain beautiful wooded hills and rolling valleys, are dotted with numerous resorts— many open the year round—and sports facilities that run the seasonal gamut from skiing to golf.

Midway to all points in the Poconos is the Mount Pocono Airport whose 4,000-foot paved strip has often taken planes as large as the Convair and Fairchild F-27. The shorter runway is 2,700 feet and is also hard surfaced. Unicom (122.8) is available 8 a.m. to 8 p.m.,

and the field has 80 and 100 octane fuel, tiedowns, telephone and rotating beacon.

Typical of Pocono resorts and just a mile from the airport is High Point Inn, a rambling 75-room hotel. It is owned and managed by George Colovos (AOPA 69624), longtime pilot and airplane owner, who on request will send a courtesy car out to the airport to meet incoming pilots. "Whether a pilot wants to fly in for an overnight stay or just for a meal, he will always be welcome," says Colovos.

The atmosphere at High Point is informal with emphasis on sports. Guests swim even in February in the heated indoor pool (there's one outdoors, too). Skiing, tobogganing and skating facilities are on Inn grounds with equipment available at the Inn itself. In the spring there's hiking, riding, bowling, golf, boating and fishing in mountain lakes and stocked streams. Abundance of game brings hunters for miles around in the fall—the first

two days of deer season this past year netted a kill of seven buck.

For evening entertainment, there's dancing in the Inn's gaily painted Parisian Cafe. A new transient dining room is being added this winter for guests who come for the food alone (the Inn's reputation as a good eating place is well known). Colovos says the Inn has played host to many breakfast flights, and last fall, a conference of the Northeast Region of FAA was held there.

A point to consider when planning your stay is that High Point Inn's rates are American plan, three meals a day; they run from $14.50 to $17.50 per person per day (double).

This winter, with the combined efforts of the Inn staff and those of neighboring resorts, an attempt will be made to keep runways of Mount Pocono Airport free of snow. "However," says Colovos, "I would suggest that pilots call the hotel or check Notams for the condition of the field." ◆

Mount Pocono Airport with three "heavyweights" on the ramp: (left to right) Fairchild F-27, Convair and Beech Queen Air (Army version)

Rambling High Point Inn is open year round, provides courtesy car for pilots landing at Mount Pocono Airport